RACISM AND CRIMINOLOGY

RACISM AND CRIMINOLOGY

edited by

Dee Cook and Barbara Hudson

SAGE Publications
London · Thousand Oaks · New Delhi

SAGE Publications Ltd
6 Bonhill Street
London EC2A 4PU

SAGE Publications Inc
2455 Teller Road
Thousand Oaks, California 91320

SAGE Publications India Pvt Ltd
32, M-Block Market
Greater Kailash – I
New Delhi 110 048

British Library Cataloguing in Publication Data

A catalogue record for this book is available from the
British Library.

ISBN 0–8039–8762–5
ISBN 0–8039–8763–3 (pbk)

Library of Congress catalog card number 93–085706

Typeset by Type Study, Scarborough
Printed and bound in Great Britain by
Biddles Ltd, Guildford and King's Lynn

Contents

Notes on Contributors   vi
Preface   viii
Acknowledgements   xvi

1 Racism and Criminology: Concepts and Controversies   1
  Barbara Hudson

2 Research, Policy and Racial Justice   28
  Navnit Dholakia and Maggie Sumner

3 'Racism': Establishing the Phenomenon   45
  Marian FitzGerald

4 Race Issues in Research on Psychiatry and Criminology   64
  Deryck Browne

5 Approaching the Topic of Racism: Transferable Research
  Strategies?   77
  Loraine Gelsthorpe

6 Theoreotyping: Anti-racism, Criminology and Black
  Young People   96
  John Pitts

7 Constructions of Black Criminality: Racialisation and
  Criminalisation in Perspective   118
  John Solomos

8 Racism, Critizenship and Exclusion   136
  Dee Cook

References   158
Index   173

Notes on Contributors

Deryck Browne is Policy Development Officer (Mental Health) at the National Association for the Care and Resettlement of Offenders (NACRO).

Dee Cook is Lecturer at the Centre for Criminology, Keele University. She has worked as an executive officer in the DHSS and as a tax officer in the Inland Revenue. Publications include *Rich Law, Poor Law* (1989) and *Paying for Crime* (1989, co-edited with Pat Carlen). Current research interests include aspects of citizenship and exclusion, and environmental crime.

Navnit Dholakia is Principal Officer at the Commission for Racial Equality and a magistrate; he was a member of the Carlisle Committee on the Parole System, and is currently a member of the Ethnic Minorities Advisory Committee of the Judicial Studies Board and Chair of the Race Issues Advisory Committee of NACRO.

Marian FitzGerald is currently Principal Research Officer at the Home Office Research and Planning Unit where she has special responsibility for work on race relations/race equality issues generally and for related criminal justice research. She previously worked as a freelance researcher. Her publications have covered race and politics, race relations policies in local government and racial harassment, as well as race and criminal justice issues.

Loraine Gelsthorpe is Lecturer at the Institute of Criminology, University of Cambridge. Her books include *Women and Crime* (1981, co-edited with Allison Morris). *Gender Issues in Juvenile Justice* (1985), *Sexism and the Female Offender* (1989) and *Feminist Perspectives in Criminology* (1990, co-edited with Allison Morris). Current research interests include inter-agency aspects of crime prevention, race and gender issues in pre-sentence reports and community penalties, juvenile justice issues since 1945, and the social and political context of criminological theories since the early 1970s.

She also works with voluntary organisations on juvenile justice issues and is involved in moves to encourage prisoners' creative writing.

Barbara Hudson is Lecturer in the Department of Social Work and Social Policy and Director of the Centre for Criminal Justice Studies at the University of Northumbria at Newcastle. Publications include *Justice through Punishment* (1987) and *Penal Policy and Social Justice* (1993) as well as several articles on race and criminal justice. Current research interests include theoretical and practical limits to criminalisation and penalisation, and responses to crimes which do not fit easily into a proportionate punishment policy.

John Pitts is Reader in Applied Social Science at the West London Institute, a college of Brunel University. He has worked as a secondary school teacher, a youth worker and an Intermediate Treatment Development officer. He is author of *The Politics of Juvenile Crime* (1988), *Working with Young Offenders* (1990), and co-editor (with J. Dennington) of *Developing Services for Young People in Crisis* (1991). He has a particular interest in the victimisation of children and young people and is currently coordinating the 'bullying' strand of a 'repeat victimisation' action research project, and undertaking a comparative study of the role of social workers in the French and English child protection systems.

John Solomos is Reader in Public Policy at Birkbeck College, University of London. He has written widely on questions of race and racism in contemporary Britain, urban unrest and related issues. Among his books are *Black Youth, Racism and the State* (1988) and *Race and Racism in Contemporary Britain* (1989).

Maggie Sumner is Principal Research Officer at the National Association for the Care and Resettlement of Offenders (NACRO).

Preface

This book is for people concerned with the problems of racial injustice in state systems of control and regulation.

Students and teachers of criminology, sociology and law, policy makers and criminal justice professionals are, in the main, persuaded that minority ethnic groups suffer substantial injustices. While it is recognised that more research needs to be specifically directed at race issues, and that *all* criminological research should encompass dimensions of racial differentiation as well as gender differentiation, actually doing this can be difficult and painful. This book acknowledges the pain and the problems, and aims to help students and others engaged in research on race issues by opening up methodological debates and by presenting a range of theoretical options.

Difficulties have in part centred on the fragmented and contentious nature of available literature. A student or researcher sitting at a library computer trying to locate work on 'racism and criminology' would have difficulty compiling an intellectually coherent set of references. S/he would be led into different disciplines – sociology, cultural studies, criminology, history, politics, social policy – just for starters. In many of these disciplines the presence of racism and the sorts of problems which need explanation are, at least, agreed, so that theoretical disputes can be progressive and fruitful. When it comes to racism and criminology, the student will find more attention given to definitions of the problem than to productive theorising.

Major theorists argue about whether or not there is a problem of 'black crime' or of black criminalisation, while policy researchers argue about whether there is or is not discrimination by the criminal justice system. Theoretical analyses are criticised for offering speculation unworried by empirical data, whereas policy research is questioned on the grounds that it endlessly seeks data which are ultimately fruitless in the absence of theorised speculation.

Although criminological understanding of racism seems not to have progressed beyond the rather polarised debates of the 1980s, the volume of literature – theoretical, policy-orientated and campaigning – has certainly increased. This book therefore attempts something of a stock-taking exercise, seeking to document what is available, both in terms of empirical and analytical work, which can advance understanding with a view both to reducing racial injustice and to enriching criminological theory.

The volume of available work demonstrates two worrying features, both of which derive from the relationship between data and theory. First, the contradictory and inconclusive nature of research data allowed theorists to construct elaborate intellectual edifices without testing their often shaky empirical foundations. Even more, it allowed them to advance their claims without conceding anything to 'the other side': if data were unnecessary for theory construction, they were certainly insufficient for theory demolition. Secondly, policy research, while assiduously setting about the task of collecting data on discrimination, felt itself able to proceed unhampered by an conceptual baggage, especially concepts around the nature of discrimination itself.

Recently, there have been significant advances in the official acknowledgement of racism in the criminal justice system. Section 95 of the Criminal Justice Act 1991 requires the Home Secretary to publish information annually in order to 'avoid discrimination' on grounds which include race and gender. In order to compile these data the Home Office in turn requires all agencies within the criminal justice and penal systems to collect data relating to their own organisations. This should mean that not only will data be available on minority ethnic groups as victims, offenders, suspects and workers in the criminal justice and penal systems, but that a national aggregate picture will be possible. And the information gathered will be more standardised as well as more readily available.

In the past, researchers have not only had to produce data, but have also had to validate and defend it. The resistance of the system to acknowledging the problem of racial injustice had led to the demand, not only for hard data, but also for the highest levels of statistical significance in order to demonstrate the problem as irrefutable. The Criminal Justice Act 1991 has come into effect at a time when public confidence in the criminal justice system has been undermined by a series of dramatic events: recognition of miscarriages of justice such as that involving the Birmingham Six and Tottenham Three, disbanding of the West Midlands Serious Crimes Squad and concerns over the injuries and deaths of black suspects in custody. These events have created a climate of opinion in which greater recognition of the injustices perpetrated by the system is now possible.

This combination of greater availability of, and greater willingness to accept, evidence of racial injustice should mean that independent researchers are freed from the task of generating and defending basic data, and can concentrate their attention on providing explanation and theory. What is on offer for them? Like the empirical literature, the theoretical literature has been stalled, at the point of rival claims about what is or is not 'the problem', but now appears in a position to move forward. The enlargement of the literature allows for increased specialisation and this should lead to greater depth of analysis because a less highly charged atmosphere, with entrenched conflicts diffused, offers scope for proper weighing of competing claims.

This is somewhat reminiscent of the development of criminology's engagement with gender: only when issues concerning the absence of women from the criminological literature and the establishing of 'numbers' for comparison with male counterparts had been faced and left behind could imaginative and differentiated theorising proceed.

If the difficulties of confronting race issues, mentioned earlier, are diminishing, the pain remains. Conscious of the need not to neglect race issues, more criminologists, white as well as black, are becoming involved. This raises questions about what kind of understanding can be achieved by people as criminologists and as white and black subjects. In approaching this work we were aware of ourselves as white academics who could not subjectively understand the experiences of black people. We are involved with, and are members of, powerful institutions and so have been led to seek understanding of racial oppression not in terms of subjective experience, but in terms of the workings of state institutions. We therefore sought contributions from researchers and theorists who have investigated the policy and practices of those institutions.

Organisation of the Book

The book brings together a number of accounts of doing research on race issues and a range of criminological perspectives within which race, crime and criminalisation have been discussed. We invited contributors to share methodological issues which they had found to be difficult and to outline and explore theoretical approaches which they had found to be useful. Therefore, within this volume, a range of perspectives is presented: no one particular theory is advanced and no one particular research strategy is recommended. In addition to 'stock-taking', our aim is to encourage theoretical and methodological debate, thereby opening up possibilities for further advances in both research and theory.

The first two chapters together give an overview of existing achievements in criminological work on race issues. In Chapter 1

Barbara Hudson looks at the contributions of administrative criminology, radical realism and critical criminology. She highlights
administrative criminology's preoccupation with criminal justice
processes and relative neglect of racially just outcomes; radical
realism's contribution to understanding the relationship between
social inequality (of which race is an important dimension) and
crime; and critical criminology's insight into processes of criminalisation. She argues that administrative criminology must turn to the
other perspectives for explanations, and that choice between radical
realist and critical paradigms must depend primarily on the questions
being asked.

Navnit Dholakia and Maggie Sumner concentrate on policy-
orientated research and they too share the hope that more systematic
and more easily available criminal justice data will enable researchers
to concentrate on providing insights and explanations of the 'how'
and 'why' of race discrimination rather than being enmeshed in the
'whether'. Like Barbara Hudson, they emphasise the importance of
encompassing indirect as well as direct discrimination, and the
importance of seeing the criminal justice and penal systems as a
whole, rather than abstracting particular stages and processes. They
conclude that the contribution of research to policy making and to the
delivery of racial justice has so far been fairly limited.

The next three chapters are by experienced researchers who have
encountered in different contexts the problems of definitions,
classifications and institutional politics. Marian FitzGerald gives
three case studies which deal with issues of what is racial and what is
not, what are the proper uses as well as the limitations of quantitative
research, and how to develop classifications which, while large
enough to generate sufficient data, do not lose diversity of experience
in catch-all categories. Her conclusions on quantitative research are
original: she argues that instead of using quantitative research to
establish the existence of a problem and then qualitative research to
describe its form, the reverse might often be the case. Qualitative
research can, she argues, often give more convincing evidence of
discrimination, and quantitative monitoring can then come into play
to measure change following policy intervention. She argues for the
dichotomy 'racial/non-racial' to be dissolved in favour of an appreciation that, racist behaviour (such as abuse accompanying street
attacks) is frequently an additional element in crime and injustice
suffered by black people, and she points out the distortions to
understanding that can arise by subsuming people who tend to be in
different socioeconomic circumstances under over-general racial
headings.

Deryck Brown in Chapter 4, looks at the integration of the criminal justice system not just in terms of its component parts, but with other social sub-systems, in this case the psychiatric services. He gives a summary of research on black people and mental health, concentrating particularly on compulsory detention and differential diagnosis, and then moves on to describe his own approach to a study of psychiatric remands made by courts. The problems of non-availability of data are manifest here, as Deryck Browne describes how he was forced to spend a major part of a project with limited funding on compensating for the lack of ethnic data in the records of both the courts and the psychiatric services. In his discussion of dilemmas of classification he offers encouragement to those of us who find ourselves in difficulties about which categories are currently acceptable by telling us not to let our concerns about political correctness lead us to give up on the issues altogether.

These dilemmas are further explored by Loraine Gelsthorpe, who recounts how she was faced with three different classification systems in the three probation services which were the focus of her research. She also makes the point that while, ideally, recorded ethnic category should both correspond to the subject's (offender/victim etc.) self-perception and suit the purposes of the research, in practice one may well have no option but to use the system of the agency being researched. In this case, reflection on the categorisation system itself may be of value, and she argues that how people are classified reveals much about the form of racism at any one time.

Loraine Gelsthorpe engages with the problem of being a white researcher. She describes the deskilling impact of coming to see herself as a white researcher rather than as an experienced re-searcher, wondering what kind of understanding of racism, if any, she can achieve. She draws on arguments about whether men can ever understand sexism and whether feminist research should be 'by, with and for women', and concludes that the epistemology of standpoints developed in recent feminist research provides guidance as to the kinds of approaches to 'knowing racism' that are possible.

The following three chapters move from issues which are predominantly methodological to issues of theory. In Chapter 6 John Pitts describes criminology's rediscovery of class analysis. Without this, he argues, it cannot understand problems of crime and criminalisation, and therefore cannot advance understanding of *black* crime and criminalisation. If racism is extracted from a broader context of social disadvantage, not only do we lose sense of the material reality of discrimination and injustice, but we also lose any sense of black people as real occupants of disadvantaged social roles. He focuses our attention on this question by asking 'who' and 'what' are we talking about when we talk about 'black crime', arguing for research which is socially and historically specific, appreciating the importance not only of class location of black communities but also of the cultural–political context in which the response to crime occurs. John Pitts argues that the anti-racism that has been adopted by criminal justice and welfare agencies fits with the managerialism of contemporary approaches to law and order and penal policy and also with the concerns of administrative criminology.

In Chapter 7 John Solomos traces the transformation of political discourse on race issues over the past two decades, arguing that issues of policing black crime emerge as a constant theme. Initially centred on issues of 'street crime' they have, since the urban disturbances of the 1980s focused on the issue of social order. Black youth, in particular, has increasingly been constituted as a potential threat to social order and as 'the enemy within', and the formulation of social policy responses to the problem has been conceived within a racialised law and order discourse. Through analysis of texts relating to politics and to policing, he illustrates the nature of the processes whereby the emphasis of policing of the black community has shifted from crime control to order maintenance, within a highly charged political climate. Particularly since the 1980s strategies of control have developed to police those localities perceived not only as crime prone but as potential 'trouble spots'.

In the final chapter Dee Cook examines the utility of the concept of citizenship in understanding the conditions (material and ideological) under which black people are criminalised. She distinguishes between legal and subjective citizenship in terms of the promise of 'rights' which citizenship offers, and the exclusions from full citizenship which black people subjectively experience. Analysis of postwar immigration and social policy reveals the ways in which black people are by definition regarded as 'other' than British citizens. For black people, citizenship is at best partial and contingent; they are not once-and-for-all full citizens, but must constantly re-prove their entitlements in a series of day-to-day encounters with a variety of state officials – benefits officers, immigration officers, health officials – as well as with police. For all these agencies, black people are questionable and 'suspect'. Dee Cook demonstrates that criminalisation is a powerful component of this discourse of exclusion.

One omission from this volume is any account of research particularly addressing the treatment of black women by criminal justice and allied agencies, or any theorisation which tries to focus on gendered racism. Several of our contributors make clear that their work did address gender issues, while others have tried to include some reflection on the implications of the perceptive from which they write for black women. There are, of course, some works which address these issues, but their preoccupations are generally the absence of criminological concern, with the subsuming of black women's experiences under the general concepts 'race' or 'gender', or documentation of the ways in which black women are the subjects of state oppression. This area is still, however, at the stage of demonstrating and lamenting rather than theorising, but we would hope that the contributions which have been made to date to bring the problems faced by black women to criminological attention, will lead to the development of theory. We would hope to be able to include such a contribution in any future edition of this volume.

Future Directions

Debates about crime, law and order and race seem currently to be undergoing yet another transformation. During the 1980s the threat of political dissent became a more dominant theme than that of crime as such, and thus the moral panics around black crime exemplified by the 'mugging' phenomenon of the 1970s gave way to the law and order crusades, with the growth of paramilitary policing, that were such a pronounced feature of the 1980s.

In the 1990s, crime has again become the dominant theme. In particular, panics about the crimes of young people are leading the way in, for example, calls to alter the Criminal Justice Act 1991 to give greater powers to imprison persistent offenders, children as well as adults. The moral panics of the summers of 1991 and 1992 were not about race, but about car crime, and the crime of 'ram-raiding' was invented. Disturbances in Tyneside's Meadow Well, Blackbird Leys in Oxford, in Cardiff and elsewhere were blamed on the infiltration of those areas by hardened, criminal ringleaders, and on the general lawlessness of youth. These were predominantly white areas, and so mainstream political rhetoric has become focused on youth crime rather than on black disorder.

We remain, however, an intensely racist society, and so the 'new racism' integral to the law and order discourse of the 1980s has not disappeared, but has been displaced into another discourse – that of citizenship. John Major's vision of a 'classless society' is intimately connected with the promise of equality through citizenship. The Citizen's Charter, a central plank of Major's programme, stresses the importance of the responsibilities and duties of citizenship as well as its entitlements. In policy terms this means that parents are in effect responsible for the crimes of their children, and householders are responsible for protecting their property. To qualify for the entitle-ments of full citizenship, the responsibility now lies with individuals to be dutiful, active and independent, that is, not dependent upon the welfare state. The poor, the unemployed and the criminal are by definition beyond the bounds of full citizenship and the political, civic and social rights with which it is endowed. Black people are vulnerable to exclusion from full citizenship through the experiences of poverty and criminalisation, which they share with their white counterparts. Not only are black people more likely to be poor and to be criminalised, but they are never fully accorded citizenship in its subjective sense: even if they pass the tests posed by ever tightening legal criteria, they may fail the subjective tests of 'membership' which they face daily in a racist society.

What are the implications of this discursive shift for theory and research around issues of racism and criminology? The most obvious implication is that criminology must be 'transgressed' (Cain, 1989) if it is to contribute anything to understanding of this latest transformation of contemporary British racism. Just as 'taking crime seriously' in the 1980s involved the re-articulation of criminology within a wider sociology of class and inequality, so 'taking racism seriously' in the 1990s must involve re-articulating criminology within the wider field of social control.

Dee Cook
Barbara Hudson

1

Racism and Criminology: Concepts and Controversies

Barbara Hudson

My aim in this chapter is to present an overview of the principal approaches that have been taken to the study of race issues by criminologists, highlighting the most important concepts that have been generated and the most valuable insights that have been produced. Some of the major controversies and unresolved contradictions that have arisen within and between different criminological perspectives will be discussed, and some closures in the various perspectives will be suggested.

It is not my intention to try to provide an exhaustive summary of research undertaken on race and racism in crime and criminal justice. Any such review would inevitably fail to be properly comprehensive, and it would be out of date by the time it appeared in print. My purpose is, rather to focus on the theoretical allegiances and assumptions that underpin criminological engagement with race issues, with a view to assisting readers in finding their way through a growing and often disputatious body of literature, helping them in making their own theoretical choices and in developing appropriate frameworks for investigating their own key questions.

Race issues which have been addressed by criminological research can generally be fitted under one of three main headings:

1 Race and criminality.
2 Race, racism and criminal justice.
3 Racism and criminalisation.

I shall look at how these clusters of issues have been dealt with by the major orientations to criminology, following the descriptions of criminological paradigms used in reviews of the development of British criminology (Rock, 1988). Although, therefore, organising my consideration of work within British styles of doing criminology, I shall also make reference to North American and European data and research.

Engagement with race issues in criminology can be found princi-
pally within:

1 Administrative criminology, which is orientated primarily to issues
   of criminal justice policy.
2 Radical criminology, with its aim of illuminating the true nature of
   the crime problem.
3 Critical criminology, with its aim of analysing the true nature of the
   state, and in particular, the exercise of state power.

There is, of course, feminist work on crime and criminal justice, and a
strong case could be made for delimiting a distinctive feminist
problematic. Most of the feminist work can, however, reasonably be
located within the radical and critical approaches, and it is more
helpful to think in terms of feminist perspectives within the appropriate paradigm than to put forward a separate feminist paradigm. My
preference for a 'feminist perspectives' approach is to indicate the
diversity of feminist criminology, and also to indicate my belief that
criminological paradigms cannot realise their potential contributions
without incorporation of feminist perspectives.

A Note about Mainstream Criminology

'Mainstream criminology' is a term generally applied to criminology
that was not or is not influenced by the paradigm shift away from
positivist criminology developed by the labelling theorists and
interactionists in the 1960s and 1970s, and then by the Marxist
criminologies which came to intellectual prominence in the 1970s and
1980s (Young, 1988). As Young and other commentators have
pointed out, mainstream criminology is not mainstream in that it is
necessarily most numerous or most intellectually dominant, but in
that it has not departed from the mainstream positivist–empiricist
orientation of applied social science. Indeed, the notion of paradigm
shift used by Young (1988), Rock (1988) and Reiner (1988), in their
analyses of developments within criminology, implies a change in
academic orthodoxy, with 'radical criminology' coming in from the
margins to occupy the commanding heights of theoretical criminology, at least in sociology departments. The chief challenger to
radical criminology now is the 'administrative criminology' practised
or sponsored by the Home Office Research and Planning Unit.
Administrative criminology, moreover, is as far removed as radical
criminology from the individualistic, deterministic approach that
characterised criminology before the intervention of Becker,
Lemert, Matza and the other 'new deviancy' theorists and before the

publication of watershed texts such as *The New Criminology* (Taylor et al., 1977).

Mainstream criminology may itself now be on the theoretical margins, but it continues. It can be identified primarily by an absence of concern with the role of the state in producing crime, an absence of concern with the part played by social reactions in producing criminal identities, an absence of any appreciation of crime and criminal justice as contingent outcomes of social–political configurations. In mainstream criminology there is no deconstruction of definitions of crime and no fundamental challenge to state punishment strategies or practices: its concern is to assist state correctional policies by providing information about criminals which will facilitate fine-tuning of penal practices.

Because of its lack of concern with structural factors, one would not expect mainstream criminology to have contributed anything to the understanding of racism. Its interventions on race issues have been entirely addressed to the race/criminality question: what, if any, are the differences between black and white criminals; what are the predictors of criminality among black and other minority ethnic groups? Mainstream criminology poses its questions and therefore produces its explanations at individual and cultural levels of analysis but not at structural levels (Reiner, 1989, 1992): it uses established definitions of crimes, and proceeds by established methods and theories.

Individualist explanations of criminal behaviour are not at all prominent among British criminologists (Reiner, 1989), but residues of biological and psychological positivist perspectives on race and on crime remain in popular consciousness to give content to the stereotypes that fuel the mythologies of black criminality (Gilroy, 1987b). Some work in the social–psychological tradition of examining race-correlated personality differences continues to appear, however; for example, in the mid-1980s the *British Journal of Criminology* carried a study comparing 'acceptance of self' in white and black delinquents confined in a youth custody institution (Emms et al., 1986).

One of the hallmarks of mainstream criminology is its uncritical acceptance of official criminal justice and law enforcement statistics as accurate indicators of participation in crime. Rather than investigating the social processes which go into the production of statistics (decision-making of law enforcement and criminal justice personnel, activities of legislators in criminalising behaviour), mainstream criminologists take the outcomes of these processes as their starting point for the construction of explanations about crime rates among sections of the population: prisoners with oddly shaped heads, or

with extra male chromosomes; residents of young offenders institutions with disorganised or differently organised families etc.

Much research on race, crime and criminal justice has started from
supposed facts and figures of black and minority presence in penal
populations. The racial composition of penal and arrest populations
is derived from prison statistics, where ethnic information is recorded
in the annual census, and the Metropolitan Police who record the
ethnic origin of all those arrested, cautioned or referred for
prosecution. Less regularly and systematically, information is also
available through the British Crime Survey (Skogan, 1990), through
information sometimes recorded by other police forces, and by
research studies. Under Section 95 of the Criminal Justice Act 1991
the Home Secretary is required to: 'in each year publish such
information as he [sic] considers expedient for the purpose of
enabling persons engaged in the administration of criminal justice
. . . to avoid discrimination against any persons on the ground of race
or sex or any other improper ground.' The first Section 95 bulletin
reports that the various sources show arrest rates to be proportionately higher for Afro-Caribbeans than for whites and Asians; and
that minority ethnic offenders are charged with different offences
from whites and from each other (Home Office, 1992a: 14). Minority
ethnic groups currently make up about 5 per cent of the total
population of Britain, and about 1 per cent of the general population
is Afro-Caribbean. Yet in 1990 Afro-Carribbeans made up around 11
per cent of the population of male sentenced prisoners and 24 per
cent of female sentenced prisoners (Home Office, 1992a: 15–16).

These differences in black and white presence in arrest and penal
populations are also found in the USA, where blacks and hispanics
are imprisoned and arrested in proportionately higher numbers than
whites and other minorities; and in Europe, where minority ethnic
groups are generally listed as foreigners, rather than classified by
ethnic origin. In France it is North Africans; in Germany, The
Netherlands and other northern European countries it is people
originating from former colonies (as in England and France) and also
migrant workers who feature so prominently in law enforcement and
criminal justice statistics (Hudson, 1993; Junger, 1988).

Official statistics have, not surprisingly, been used by mainstream
criminologists as a starting point for the investigation of biological/
psychological/cultural reasons for high black crime rates. New Right
and mainstream criminologists find explanations for high black crime
rates in elements of the culture of members of the so-called
underclass or ghetto poor. In these accounts, criminal behaviour is a
conscious choice of members of social groups who are hostile to or
disrespectful of authority in general and the police in particular, who

have no strong adherence to the work ethic, who lack law-abiding parental role models, and who are involved with drugs and prostitution as suppliers and users (Wilson and Herrnstein, 1985).

While the New Right criminologists stress the element of choice in the criminality of black ghettos, broader sociological accounts describe the culture of dependency resulting from reliance on welfare benefits, and the effect of affirmative action policies in enabling the 'brightest and best' of black community members to leave the ghetto (Auletta, 1982). These versions of underclass theory are reminiscent of the earlier Chicago School criminologies which described inner-city areas as *zones of transition* characterised by family disorganisation and weak informal social controls. Similar explanations have been put forward for crime among the migrant workers and colonial immigrants of Europe (Junger, 1989). The essential ingredients are that criminogenic elements of black and migrant cultures are taken as given, and it is their role in black criminality which is being uncovered, rather than the causes of these (presumed) cultural aspects themselves.

Where there is some explanation undertaken for hostility to police, or lack of zeal in finding work, the New Right blames those social policies which were designed to help improve the chances of ghetto residents finding work or avoiding extreme poverty (affirmative action, generous welfare benefits) rather than the structural unemployment and racism which necessitated the adoption of such policies in the first place (Glazer, 1975; Murray, 1984). The emergence of a black middle class is taken as evidence that racism is not a significant factor in the production of crime-prone black and minority sub-cultures (Inniss and Feagin, 1989). While this underclass theory was developed primarily to explain the black and hispanic ghettos in the 'rust-belt' cities of northern and mid-west USA rather than England, the term 'underclass' became commonplace in Britain during the 1980s, and is used by European sociologists in explaining crime and unrest in the north African communities of ghettoised suburbs of cities such as Paris and Lyons, and the Moluccan suburbs of Amsterdam and Haarlem.

Administrative Criminology and the Search for 'Pure' Discrimination in Criminal Justice

'Administrative criminology' is a term which came into common criminological currency during the 1980s. It describes the work of criminologists engaged in applied research aimed primarily at assisting criminal justice and penal system professionals in policy development and decision-making. Its objectives are effectiveness and efficiency, and the closer match of practice to policy, rather than any grand theorising. The intended consumers of administrative criminology are government departments, those who staff the courts, criminal justice and penal system agencies, rather than students or fellow researchers. Much administrative criminology is commissioned directly or indirectly by the Home Office, or else by well-established non-governmental agencies such as the National Association for the Care and Resettlement of Offenders (NACRO); it therefore arises from practice and policy concerns rather than the concerns of scholarly curiosity or theoretical debate.

Although administrative criminology encompasses both crime and criminal justice, it has, as Cohen (1981) predicted, largely concentrated on criminal justice, an exclusive concern with the operation of the system, rather than the causes of people's coming to involvement with the system as victims, suspects or defendants. Much of administrative criminology's interest in race issues has been focused on whether or not criminal justice and penal system agencies and processes discriminate against people on account of their skin colour or ethnic affiliation.

Unlike mainstream criminology, administrative criminology appreciates that criminal justice records and decisions are the outcome of social processes. Its concern is with the processes themselves: it does not concern itself so much with the rights or wrongs of the outcomes, but whether the outcomes can be justified by proper adherence to processes and procedures. The efforts of administrative criminology have been directed to the production of predictive instruments to aid decision-making, and monitoring instruments to curb discretion.

As Chapter 2 describes, such research has been almost exclusively concerned with 'direct discrimination', defined by the Race Relations Act 1976 as a person being treated less favourably on racial grounds than someone else in the same circumstances. In research terms, this means testing whether or not a 'race effect' can be shown when all other variables are accounted for. Studies of police stops, decisions to caution or prosecute, court sentencing, remand decisions and parole decision-making have been undertaken to try to demonstrate whether or not this race effect exists.

Findings have inevitably been contradictory and inconclusive. English studies appear to show discrimination by police in stops, and in cautioning and prosecution (Reiner, 1989), but until recently had not been able to demonstrate a direct race effect in sentencing (Crow and Cove, 1984; McConville and Baldwin, 1982). Conventional wisdom was that police racism might well be responsible for black people appearing in court in disproportionate numbers, but that once there, they were treated equally (McConville and Baldwin, 1982: 658).

Elsewhere, evidence has tended to suggest the opposite, that there is less discrimination at the 'front end' (i.e. police stops) than at subsequent points in the criminal justice system, such as sentencing and parole decisions. Marianne Junger, for instance, in arguing for the validity of arrest data as an indicator of actual participation in crime, cites studies in the USA, Canada, Switzerland and Germany which suggest that racial discrimination does not bias arrest data but does influence later stages in criminal justice (Junger, 1990). Junger agrees that decisions to caution or prosecute in England are influenced by race, but her reading of studies on stops is at odds with the more usual contention that Afro-Caribbeans are more likely to be stopped by police than whites even when factors such as age and employment status are allowed for (Skogan, 1990).

The English studies of court decision-making cited above fail to prove discrimination, even though there are generally findings of higher proportions of Afro-Caribbeans going into custody than white or Asian defendants. This differential imprisonment rate is variously ascribed to discrimination at earlier stages (implied by McConville and Baldwin, 1982), to association with other social–personal variables such as unemployment, or to other criminal justice variables. Moxon (1988) in his study of crown court decision-making, says that sentencing is overwhelmingly linked to offence type, but allows for the significance of factors such as whether or not a probation report is presented; other studies accord significance to the greater proportion of Afro-Caribbean defendants who elect for trial by jury rather than adjudication by magistrates (Hood, 1992; Walker, 1989).

Some American and European studies have claimed not merely to fail to find lack of excess severity in the sentencing of black defendants, but to find comparative leniency. Evidence from English studies suggests that this might be connected again to discrimination at the charging and prosecution stage; for example, Crow and Cove (1984) find that the proportion of black defendants charged with assault when no actual injury has been sustained by the victim is higher than with white defendants, a finding consistent with that in some of the arrest studies (Stevens and Willis, 1979). It has been suggested not only that crimes are more likely to result in arrest and prosecution if suspects are black than if they are white when there is no injury or very little property involved, but also that people are more likely to report a crime, or recognise themselves as victims of crime, if they are white and the perpetrators are black (Bottomley and Pease, 1986: 28; Carr-Hill and Drew, 1988: 33; Shah and Pease, 1992).

One facet of indirect discrimination that has been recognised in the

English literature is the effect of greater proportions of black defendants pleading not guilty to offences. Indirect discrimination arises when rules that are supposed to apply to everyone consistently seem to favour some groups and disadvantage others. In this case, contesting guilt rather than race *per se* affects criminal justice decision-making, but the contesting of guilt is itself racially correlated. Admission of guilt affects decisions at all stages of the criminal justice system: cautions can only be given to people who admit guilt; pre-sentence reports are only prepared by probation officers on defendants who plead guilty; there is an informal 'discount' in sentencing for those who plead guilty. Black people have been shown to be less likely to be cautioned than their white counterparts, less likely to have a probation report presented on their behalf; less likely to receive a probation order (Hudson, 1989a; Moxon, 1988); insisting on trial by jury means that a higher proportion of black defendants are tried at crown court, with a greater likelihood of a custodial sentence (Moxon, 1988; Walker, 1989), and sentences are longer if the guilty plea discount is not applicable (Hood, 1992). Even the 'not guilty' plea differential has been contested. One study, that also finds proportionately more black than white defendants committed for trial at the crown court, suggests that this was because of recommendations by the Crown Prosecution Service rather than not guilty pleading (Brown and Hullin, 1992).

These attempts to establish or refute discrimination in criminal justice processes – especially in the courts – have been fraught with methodological difficulties. The large samples needed to control the numerous legal and non-legal variables and to ensure an adequate number of black defendants; the fact that courts do not routinely record the race of defendants; the difficulty of generalising from studies of one court, or one judicial division, have made the studies vulnerable to criticism, and as Reiner (1992) has argued, this statistical approach is bound to remain bogged down in fruitless methodological wrangling about whether all the relevant variables are included, whether the sample is sufficiently large or sufficiently representative: 'It is inconceivable that this approach could ever conclusively establish racial discrimination' (Reiner, 1992: 10).

Attempts to establish and quantify direct discrimination in criminal justice continue, however, and continue to produce contradictory results. Often, it has been claimed that small sample sizes mean that research is unable to deal with the number of variables involved, and that in any case, because of single-court samples, findings cannot be generalised to other situations. Two studies of sentencing which have had large samples and have covered several courts are an American study of 11,553 cases in California (Klein et al., 1990) and an English study of 6,000 cases in the West Midlands (Hood, 1992). Both studies considered rates of custodial sentences and also lengths of custodial terms given. The Californian study concluded that, except in drugs cases, race appeared to be a factor in neither decision, whereas Hood claimed to find a direct race effect in the courts in one of the towns included in his study (this research is discussed in more detail in Chapter 2).

The fact that researchers continue to produce different findings, and that differences are found between courts in the same study, means that any discrimination is attributed to the exercise of discretion. Racial prejudice on the part of individual judges, police officers or prison administrators is put forward as the explanation and the target of intervention, rather than structural factors, whether social structural factors in the sense of the social position of minority ethnic groups, or the way that criminal justice itself is structured. If a prima facie case of discrimination can be sustained against the criminal justice system (Harris, 1992: 116), it is a case against individual practitioners which has been conceded, not against the system as a whole, still less the social role of criminal justice and criminalisation.

Influential studies, such as the report of the Policy Studies Institute (1983) report by Lord Scarman (1981) have thus confirmed the existence of prejudice and stereotyping among the police, but have concentrated on racism among beat officers. (Indeed, Scarman expressed confidence that racist attitudes would not be found among the higher ranks of the police, a confidence which has been proved misplaced by the public pronouncements of some chief constables as well as by Reiner's (1991) research on them.) An interactionist framework is employed to suggest that decisions to stop, and the conduct of police during stops, interviews, taking into custody etc. which use racist language, attitudes and stereotypes, provoke and reinforce hostility, on the part of Afro-Caribbean youth, occasioning the kind of aggressive and uncooperative demeanour which, according to interactionist 'conventional wisdom', is believed to influence decision-making in favour of arrest and prosecution rather than no action or caution (Piliavin and Briar, 1964).

Police officers have been subject to more observational research than any other law enforcement and criminal justice professionals. Research on other agencies has usually had to content itself with looking at the products rather than the personnel themselves. Most research on probation has concentrated on social inquiry reports (termed pre-sentence reports since the Criminal Justice Act, 1991), comparing the likelihood of black and white defendants being referred for reports, comparing recommendations for probation and other non-custodial sentences for black and white offenders, or rates of acceptance of recommendations by sentencers (Mair, 1986). One of the undisputed facts about race and criminal justice is that black offenders are less likely than their white counterparts to be made the subject of probation orders (Hudson, 1989a; Moxon, 1988).

More qualitative studies have looked at references to race in reports and analysed the frames of reference within which these occur. A much quoted study of social inquiry reports by probation officers (Whitehouse, 1983) found black defendants being discussed in ways which investigations of social inquiry reports on juvenile offenders had established as making custodial sentences more rather than less probable. Depictions of family pathology, of rootlessness and traumas resulting from upheaval, while they might be intended to provide mitigation, can have the effect of making the defendant's prognosis seem so hopeless that the magistrate or judge feels that the risk of re-offending is too high to justify a community penalty. Reports on black defendants were found to contain references to migration, to cultural traditions of child-rearing outside marriage, of black parents having children with several partners, in short, depicting family patterns that are far from the ideals of the largely white, middle-aged, middle-class magistracy and judiciary.

Subsequent studies have looked more closely at the depiction of black and white defendants *as offenders*, obviously important as the emphasis of probation work has shifted from presenting comprehensive accounts of offenders' personalities and circumstances to concentrating on their attitudes to offending, compliance with previous sentences etc. One study (Waters, 1988) classified reports according to whether the defendant's race was marginal as a theme in explaining the offending; whether the defendant was depicted in terms of culture conflict; or as being 'alien', in the sense of being very much 'other' to the report writer. Another study (Pinder, 1984a), which looked at explanations of offending offered in reports, found oppositional stances in black defendants and inadequacy in white defendants; my own study of reports found black offenders being viewed as hostile and aggressive, and not being credited with the same attempts to change to non-criminal lifestyles that were put forward in the case of white defendants (Hudson, 1988).

These studies of policing and probation work have all focused on the behaviour of professionals. Even when they have been concerned to illuminate general trends in the way criminal justice personnel deal with black offenders, they have been concerned with the exercise of discretion, rather than with deeper structures of criminal justice. Some studies have gone beyond the normal liberal assumptions of the agencies which they are investigating (Pinder, for example, asks the question 'What if blacks really are different?'), but in the main they do not go beyond the remit of the assumptions and attitudes drawn on in the routine practices of practitioners. The policy implications are usually anti-racist training and/or the restriction of discretion through the introduction of gatekeeping, guidelines, standards and such-like: procedures to restrict discretion, and training to educate discretion.

Administrative criminology's role of assisting in producing compliance with policies and directives means that there is little concern with the actual outcomes in terms of black people being sent to custody, or otherwise excessively penalised. If the goal is policy compliance and the reduction of discretion, then the fact that people are being imprisoned, prosecuted or whatever *in accordance with the guidelines* comes to be seen as satisfactory. This policy compliance goal must necessarily engender preoccupation with direct discrimination and neglect of the importance of indirect discrimination. The success of administrative criminology in assisting the development of guidelines, predictive instruments etc. may well contribute to increasing rather than decreasing indirect discrimination.

The sentencing guidelines, mandatory sentencing laws, parole guidelines, risk of re-offending scores, risk of custody scores and the other predictive and regulatory instruments which have been produced in Britain, in the USA and elsewhere to formalise decision-making have had two sources: either incorporation of existing practices in more standardised ways (determinate sentencing laws based on average existing lengths of prison sentences) or research to reveal factors associated with high crime rates or high imprisonment rates. Such factors are then built into decision-making criteria, and compliance with them becomes the sign that there has not been discrimination in decision-making, even though such factors might be highly racially correlated (Hudson, 1992; Sabol, 1989). Factors such as community ties, employment record, age of first conviction, juvenile justice record, drug involvement are built into bail information schemes, targeting for non-custodial sentences, parole guidelines, proposals for preventive sentences etc. Furthermore, each stage in the criminal justice/penal system pays no regard to direct and indirect discrimination in previous stages, so that previous arrests, for instance, are likely to figure in predictions of the risk of re-offending in spite of what is known about police discriminatory decision-making.

Such considerations may well explain why the American research quoted earlier can conclude that there is no significant race effect in sentencing in California, in spite of the fact that The Sentencing Project has found that, while for the total US population the incarceration rate is 426 per 100,000 residents, for black American men the rate is 3,109 per 100,000 (*Social Justice*, 1992: 3). Similarly, in England and Wales, despite the widespread introduction of monitoring, gatekeeping, anti-racist training and the use of various instruments to regulate decision-making (although there has as yet been no systematic ethnic monitoring or restriction of discretion imposed on the magistracy or judiciary) the proportion black prisoners continues to rise, and the rate of participation of black offenders in community penalties does not seem to be increasing significantly (Vass, 1990).

Administrative criminology has, then, focused too much on discretion and on individual processes or agencies rather than seeing criminal justice and the penal system as a whole. It has produced statistical enquiries which, even as they have become more methodologically sophisticated, continue to produce findings which contradict each other, and contradict lived experience, particularly black experience. Administrative criminology has contributed much to the better management of the various agencies and processes, but it has contributed little to racial justice or to criminological understanding. It has, as one influential legal theorists has described: 'reached a high level of technical competence and generous coverage of most stages of decision-making, but without similar advances in theoretical frameworks which can be applied specifically to the problems of the criminal process' (Ashworth, 1988: 247).

Radical Criminology and the Understanding of Black Crime

If administrative criminology has been influential with policy makers and practitioners, it is 'radical criminology' which has been most influential with academic criminologists. The central claim of radical criminology is that crime and state reaction to crime can only be understood in the context of a fully sociological framework: the nature, extent and location of crime and the nature, extent and location of control can only be explained with reference to the material and ideological relationships that exist within a social formation. To be more precise, crime in a capitalist society can only be understood in the context of the class relationships generated by capitalism. Radical criminology is:

> that part of the discipline which sees the causes of crime as being at core the class and patriarchal relations endemic to our social order and which sees fundamental changes as necessary to reduce criminality. It is politically at base socialist, libertarian/anarchist, socialist or radical feminist. It quarrels amongst itself – as such a radical mix has throughout history – but it is quite distinct from those parts of the discipline which see

crime as a marginal phenomenon solvable with technical adjustments by control agencies which are, in essence, all right and in need of no fundamental change. (Young, 1988: 160)

Radical criminology sees a high incidence of crime as inevitable in a society characterised by gross inequalities in wealth and opportunity. It merges together the basics of Merton's (1964) version of anomie theory and Cloward and Ohlin's (1960) opportunity theory – that if material goals are stressed in a society, but opportunities to achieve these legitimately are not equally distributed, significant numbers of those without legitimate opportunities will have recourse to illegitimate means of acquiring the things they want – with the insights of control theory, and theories such as Matza's, which show that crime and delinquency are likely when people feel no compulsion to conform to social rules. Radical criminology also sees, however, that class relationships do not merely affect the probability of various forms of criminal behaviour, but that the definitions of crime, the policing of crime and the punishment of crime will also be contingent on the class and patriarchal relationships of society.

Contemporary formulations of radical criminology have theorised relative deprivation and marginalisation as the prime cause of the massive crime rates of Britain, the USA and similar societies today. Not only are there large discrepancies between the material circumstances of the haves and the have-nots, but the have-nots are well aware of the lives of the haves. This consciousness of relative poverty is more likely to lead to weakening of adherence to social rules when the poor feel that society does not care about them and the circumstances in which they struggle to survive. Whether through neglect of the fabric of the inner cities, lack of jobs, lack of youth facilities, withdrawal or real cuts in welfare benefits, or political statements that unemployment is a 'price worth paying' for the control of inflation, people become marginalised in the sense that they feel themselves rejected by the conscience of society, as well as being marginalised in the sense that participation in society is organised around work and consumerism.

With their understanding of the political economy of crime and penalisation, radical criminologists expect there to be bias in the processes of law enforcement, criminal justice and penality and therefore view statistics of black participation in crime, law enforcement and criminal justice with scepticism, but also expect them to reflect some real and significant black criminality. If crime is linked to economic deprivation and marginalisation, then it is black unemployed youth who suffer most from these conditions. Black unemployment rates, black residence in areas of urban decay, black exclusion from the political and cultural milieu would all lead to an expectation of high black crime rates. Radical criminologists, then, do not ask whether race/crime statistics are derived from black crime *or* from racist law enforcement and criminal justice, but expect them to reflect *both*.

This analysis of the race/crime problem was stated vividly and succinctly in the book *What is to be Done about Law and Order?*, which appeared in 1984 and has been much discussed since (Lea and Young, 1984). The authors argued that there was a genuine social problem in that street crime, perpetrated by disaffected, unemployed youth, had reached levels in working-class communities such that communal life was becoming unacceptably hazardous and unpleasant. Since black youths featured prominently in the populations of the unemployed and disaffected, they – not surprisingly – featured prominently among populations of these street criminals. The problem was compounded by policing which although it may have been oppressive, non-accountable and infused with race stereotyping and hostility to blacks, nevertheless proceeded from the prevalence of street crime rather than from repression of black communities for its own sake:

> young blacks in the inner cities were not, in the main, being hounded by the Special Branch and anti-terrorist squads or charged under the Prevention of Terrorism Act, but being subjected to intensive stop and search operations, arrested under the vagrancy or 'sus' legislation and by various means associated with certain types of street crime such as robbery and violent theft. (Lea, 1986: 158)

The split that has appeared within radical criminology between the so-called left realists and the critical criminologists (or left idealists as the realists style them) has centred largely on whether or not there is a 'real' problem of increased street crime (and especially black street crime), or whether the real – and only? – problem is state repression and criminalisation of the deprived and disaffected. Although both realists and critical criminologists would agree that there is excessive repression of inner-city populations, the difference is whether or not it is conceded that there is a real crime crisis which provides the impetus and occasion for repression. The radical realists might disagree with police tactics for dealing with the street crime crisis, but they agree that there is indeed a crisis to be tackled (Cashmore and McLauglin, 1991: 3). Radical realists depict an amplification spiral whereby economic and political marginalisation engenders high crime rates, and these high crime rates create and reinforce stereotypes of the marginalised as highly criminal. Law enforcement becomes coercive as police start to think of whole communities as criminal or tolerant of crime.

Black crime, on this account, needs no additional explanatory factor such as cultures derived from the situation of enslavement, unstable families etc.: black crime is prompted by the same economic and political deprivation as is white crime; if there are higher crime rates among black communities this is because there are higher rates of unemployment and associated deprivations. Few radical criminologists have dealt specifically with black crime, seeing sufficient explanation in the class position of black and migrant communities. As John Pitts points out in Chapter 6, black middle-class crime is no more a social problem than white middle-class crime.

In so far as there has been attention to the specific characteristics of black crime, this has been in the direction of pointing out that there is in fact *less* of a sub-cultural tradition of crime spreading over several generations than there is in indigenous white working-class communities. Pitts, in his study of juvenile crime among Afro-Caribbeans, repeats the widely held view that crime among immigrant groups is generally less than among established economically disadvantaged groups, but that if material conditions deteriorate, crime levels among migrant groups will rise to match those of the established groups (Pitts, 1986). This is because immigration is usually encouraged at times of labour shortage, so that there is little economic necessity for the new arrivals to turn to crime for material survival. If employment levels decline, however, future generations of those communities will not find work and welcome, but unemployment and hostility, and so will have recourse to so-called crimes of poverty to survive. Such crime will be, Pitts tells us, localised, opportunistic and instrumental, as indeed most crime is intra-class and intra-racial. Black youth crime is frequently a break with rather than a carrying on of family or community traditions; black juvenile offenders are:

> not in the main drawn from families who have previously been a cause of concern to welfare agencies. Observations of young black people in penal establishments tend to support this in that they have a broader spread of academic abilities and tend in many ways to be more socially and academically able than their white counterparts. They are also much more likely to be drawn from 'respectable' rather than 'disrespectable' families.
>
> What we are not seeing here is the apparently inexorable unfolding of a criminal and institutional career which may be traced back, sometimes over generations, but rather a rupture, a departure, from a previously conventional mode of existence by a group of young people, many of whom had until shortly before their first court appearance been successful conforming schoolgirls and schoolboys. (Pitts, 1986: 130)

In short, black and migrant young people have no special tendency to criminality until they enter the labour market and are rejected by it. If they do resort to crime, insensitive and coercive policing, with the use of sweeps and stops to clamp down on crimes of poverty, will lead to young black offenders being rapidly drawn into and propelled upwards through the penal system, and will also provoke further crimes such as resisting arrest, assault on police and various public order offences.

Similar explanations are put forward by radical criminology for urban disorder as well as for urban crime. Benyon and Solomos (1987: 181) put forward five conditions which they say are characteristic of areas in which rioting occurred in the 1980s: high unemployment; manifest racial discrimination and disadvantages; political exclusion and powerlessness; and common mistrust of, and hostility to, the police. Although the presence of these conditions means that riots and disturbances may occur, Benyon and Solomos argue that there needs to be some trigger event actually to spark off the riot, and this is nearly always a confrontation between police and black people.

Apart from racial discrimination, these conditions are suffered by white lower-class youth as well as black, but it is argued that higher proportions of black suffer them, and so may turn to crime and violence in higher proportions (Brake, 1985). Racial discrimination is an additional burden on this account, the basic one always being unemployment and associated marginalisation. This analysis, therefore, fits situations such as The Meadow Well riots in Newcastle in 1991, where a police operation against car crime in a deprived white area provoked rioting.

Radical criminology similarly sees social control as overdetermined by class relationships and labour market conditions. Policing is related not just to crime, but to the perceived expectation of the ruling elite that marginalised populations will turn to crime or violent disorder out of disaffection with their conditions of existence. This power-threat hypothesis has been used to explain why regional or state expenditure on law enforcement correlates not with crime rates or with proportions of black residents, but with the potential for violent or illegal forms of dissent that are attributed to the deprived sections of populations (Box, 1987; Hawkins and Hardy, 1989).

Penalisation generally, and imprisonment in particular, are seen by radical criminologists primarily as a means of controlling surplus labour. Pitts, for example, in his study of young black offenders quoted above, draws on Mathiesen's (1974) analysis of prison as a means of dealing with categories of people who are surplus to economic requirements by 'expelling' them to total institutions (1986: 142). If they are further damaged by the institution this is of no matter, since the state is not wanting to reclaim them for the labour force. Imprisonment impinges on blacks and other minorities because they figure so prominently in the surplus populations. This casting of penal systems, particularly in their use of imprisonment, as regulators of the labour supply is well established in criminology (for example, Melossi and Pavarini, 1981; Quinney, 1977) and has been readily adapted to explanations of why blacks are thus excessively imprisoned. The primary correlation is seen as that between imprisonment and unemployment, and disadvantaged minority ethnic groups are imprisoned because of high unemployment rates rather than because of racism directly (Adamson, 1984; Box and Hale, 1982).

Historical investigations of policing and the use of imprisonment in the USA have enriched this analysis by including the patterns of control that developed in slave and post-slave societies. It is argued that after the abolition of slavery, convict-licence became an important source of free or cheap labour. Control tactics were therefore developed to keep blacks from stepping outside their allotted social and economic roles (Hawkins and Thomas, 1991) and to provide a supply of convict labour from among freed slaves (Hawkins, 1986). Like their European counterparts, such as Box (1983, 1987), Jankovic (1977) and Laffargue and Godefroy (1989), these North American Marxist criminologists argue that the penal system is primarily labour driven: changes in labour supply needs and labour–capital relations best explain changes in prison populations, including changes in black–white imprisonment ratios. Changes in the need for labour are said to be more important for changes in the social–demographic composition of prison populations than changes in crime rates, changes in penal policy or changing attitudes towards race issues generally (Hawkins, 1986).

The literature on female crime tends to put together questions of criminality and questions of penalisation, but it is generally held that most female crimes are crimes of poverty and powerlessness (Carlen, 1988, *inter alia*). As with the analysis of male crime, it is implied that if black women do have higher crime rates than white women (although writers on female crime have largely – and wisely – eschewed the 'how much black crime' arguments) it is because higher proportions of them than white women are in poverty. The proportion of female prisoners coming from minority ethnic groups doubled from 12 per cent in 1986 to 24 per cent in 1990 (Home Office, 1992a: 16). This is attributed by the Home Office primarily to an increase in the number of women serving sentences for drug smuggling, many of whom are women from Africa and South America. Such women provide clear if dramatic examples of poverty crime, in almost every case motivated by economic desperation rather than criminal inclination or greed.

Women criminals, and especially women prisoners, are acknowledged as frequently suffering forms of oppression specific to patriarchy, especially sexual or physical abuse, in a society which does little to protect women and children from male violence. While patriarchy and class are given so much importance as root causes of crime in contemporary societies, patriarchy itself is generally untheorised in (predominantly male) radical criminology. In particular, how patriarchy impinges on women from different class or race groups is unexplored (Rice, 1990). Racism is something which is added-on, again in an undifferentiated, untheorised way.

The literature on women and criminal justice has shown that the women who are disadvantaged are those who do not meet the dominant stereotypes of conventional femininity, good motherhood or demure and rational behaviour. What is known about women, crime and justice includes:

1 That women's crimes are predominantly the crimes of the powerless.
2 That disproportionate numbers of women from ethnic minority groups are imprisoned.
3 That typifications of conventional femininity play a major role in the decision whether or not to imprison women.
4 That the majority of women appear to be law-abiding and when in trouble are much more likely to be in receipt of medical, psychiatric or welfare regulation than caught up in the machinery of criminal justice. (Carlen, 1992: 65)

Black women are powerless in relation to white women, and to white and black men; they are often unemployed, single parents, and with lifestyles that do not conform to middle-class expectation. They come into contact with law enforcement agencies as suspects, as mothers of suspects, as suspected illegal immigrants, and as mentally disturbed (Chigwada, 1991: 137). They suffer from what has been called a criminal justice 'double-bind', as vulnerable to both institutional sexism and institutional racism (Richey Mann, 1989). For radical criminology, these oppressions are mediations of class disadvantage, and will be lived as pressures towards committing crime and as vulnerabilities to penalisation.

Jefferson has urged the gain which could be made by combining radical criminology's concern with outcomes with administrative criminology's attention to processes (1990: 59). Certainly, radical criminology can provide explanatory frameworks for some of administrative criminology's findings, and can throw some light on apparently contradictory findings. Discrepancies in English and

European studies of police stops, for example, can be understood if one looks at the differences in units of analysis. If comparisons are being made across whole cities, then the findings will be complicated by the fact that black youths may be concentrated in the more deprived areas, whereas white youths will be more evenly distributed across the city. Many of the European studies concentrate on stops of youths in the same residential area, as does a study in an English provincial city, which showed that although black youths were stopped more frequently than white youths if population comparisons were of the whole city, black youths were not stopped more than white youths in the same residential area (Jefferson et al., 1990). These findings open up the possibility that the differences in police behaviour, reported by often-quoted studies such as the PSI survey and some earlier Home Office sponsored studies, reveal variations in policing tactics in separate areas, either different tactics for working-class and middle-class areas, or differences between London and the rest of the country, rather than reflecting the operation of a ubiquitous race prejudice (Smith, 1983; Stevens and Willis, 1979; Tuck and Southgate, 1981).

Similarly, research which goes beyond a simple search for racist attitudes among police can provide some explanation of how it arises, and is sustained. Studies of police attitudes from the 1960s through to the 1990s have consistently found racist attitudes held by officers, and it has convincingly been argued that this 'canteen culture' (Brown and Willis, 1985; Fielding, 1988; Holdaway, 1983) carries over from joking with fellow officers to encounters with the public. It is held that racist police culture arises because recruits share the racist culture of the group from which the majority is drawn – the macho, authoritarian, prejudiced working class – and that such attitudes are reinforced not only by socialisation processes once they have entered the force, but also by the confrontational situations in which many encounters between police and black citizens occur (Colman and Gorman, 1982; Jefferson, 1988; Reiner, 1985).

Critical Criminology, the State and Criminalisation

Radical criminology is, as Young (1987) describes, a broad grouping of left/libertarian perspectives, and contains many factions and spawns many disputes. The most significant of recent disputes, where race issues and criminology are concerned, is that between the left realists and the critical criminologists. In developing their project of 'taking crime seriously' (Young, 1987), the left realists have differentiated themselves from those they describe as 'left idealists', whom they say are too paralysingly persuaded of the impossibility of reforming crime control in humane and progressive directions without wholesale transformations of society to have any influence on policy developments, and from the critical criminologists who have denied that there is any real crisis of rising rates of urban crime, and particularly black urban crime.

The dispute between the radical realists and the critical theorists began with the publication of *Policing the Crisis* (Hall et al., 1987), which drew on Marxist critiques of ideology (especially Gramsci's writings on hegemony) to provide a more structured analysis of some of the insights generated by labelling theory and interactionism, especially 'folk devils and moral panics' (Cohen, 1972). Hall and his co-authors examined the phenomenon of 'mugging', tracing its development from the use of the term in a newspaper report of a particular incident of robbery to a full-blown hue and cry over some sinister new forms of street crime which was supposedly sweeping the country. While these writers and those who have utilised the same framework might not deny that events such as street robberies occur, and while the radical realists might not deny that black youths are too easily seen as suspects by police, that newspapers include the race of the perpetrator when this is black but seldom say 'a white youth', and so forth – the point of dispute was whether the reaction of the state to mugging and similar forms of crime has been *out of all proportion* to the scale of the problem itself (Reiner, 1988).

As well as policing and penalisation, the opposing sides of the argument have taken different stances on fear of crime, the radical realists maintaining that fear of crime has a rational core and that to disregard it is to disregard the troubles of the powerless, while the critical criminologists maintain that fear of crime, and especially fear of black crime, has been whipped up by the establishment for its own purposes. The rift between realist and critical criminologists deepened with the publication of *The Empire Strikes Back* (Centre for Contemporary Cultural Studies, 1982) which continued the project of analysing the ideological promotion of black criminality as an important element of contemporary racism.

Radical realists and critical sociologists share the conviction that crime and penalisation can only be understood within the framework of a fully sociological understanding of material and social relationships in capitalist society; both place at the centre of their enterprise the gap between the real state of affairs and the state of affairs that is made to appear to be the case – the gap which is created and filled by ideology. But while the radical realists strive to replace ideological understandings with real understandings, critical theorists strive to provide understandings of the ideologies themselves. In other words, radical realists wish to establish the real causes of crime in place of the ideological motivated stereotypes on which policy so often seems to be based; critical criminology wishes to expose the ideologically motivated stereotypes and demonstrate how and why they have formed the basis of policy.

The investigation of racism undertaken in *The Empire Strikes Back*, and the theorisation of the rise of a moral panic in *Policing the Crisis*, have been important contributions to critical sociology's wider engagement with the idea of a crisis of legitimacy which has confronted capitalist societies as they have moved into recession. In essence, the argument is that as economic downturns mean that compliance with social rules can no longer be assured through the expectation of the rewards of jobs, money and status if people go to school, obey the law and so on, then compliance will have to be imposed through repression. Assent – legitimation – to increased repression must be obtained by inducing the majority to blame the minority who do actively dissent, for social ills, rather than blaming the system itself and/or its elite. Thus, workers are encouraged to blame strikers for redundancies and closures; householders are encouraged to blame irresponsible procreation for homelessness and, above all, the law-abiding are expected to blame criminals for urban decay and we are all induced to identify crime as the most urgent social problem.

The project of critical criminology/critical sociology is to demonstrate the precise ideological constructs deployed at particular historical moments, and the investigation of ideological shifts in contemporary Britain and the USA has focused on the 'drift to law and order' in the Thatcher–Reagan era (Hall, 1980). Moving from securing compliance by rewards to imposing compliance by repression involves the criminalisation of various sub-groups of the disadvantaged, and their marginalisation by legal regulation as well as by economic privation. We can see this in the division of the unemployed into scroungers and genuine claimants, the restriction of rights to housing benefits, the campaigns against New Age travellers, squatters etc. Black people are, therefore, not the only group to be stigmatised as 'the enemy within' in the ideological drive to blame sub-sections of the powerless for their own predicament. There is, moreover, nothing new about either moral panics about law and order or about casting sub-sections of the poor as dangerous and/or undeserving (Gilroy and Sim, 1985).

What is specific to the criminalisation and exclusion of black people is that these dividing practices are not employed: all black people are harassed at ports and airports under suspicion of illegal entry; black communities are seen as 'no-go' areas where all residents are expected to be hostile to police; comments such as Norman

Tebbit's 'cricket test' show that we suspect all Afro-Caribbeans and Asians, whether young or old, middle-class or working-class, employed or unemployed, to be fundamentally disloyal to Britain. Critical sociology's discussion of black criminalisation, then, combines a study of the general trend to criminalisation of (potentially) disaffected sub-groups of the powerless with a study of the character and dynamics of what has been termed 'New Racism'.

It is argued first of all that 'race' is a common element, a concept which joins together the various elements of the presentation of the crisis facing society as a crisis caused by its victims (Solomos et al., 1982: 27). Race is easily depicted as the common denominator of the full range of social pressures: too many immigrants, high birthrates in black communities mean too many people chasing too few jobs; they mean pressure on schools and health services; unstable black family patterns mean excess demand for housing and welfare services; black culture and personality traits mean excess crime. Secondly, Gilroy, Gordon and others have demonstrated that the centrality of black crime to this is that it allows characterisation of blacks as the destroyers of British culture from within as well as the imposers of pressure of numbers from without (e.g. Gilroy, 1982, 1987a; Gordon, 1988); it is crucial in the shift from understanding the crisis as being about resources and lack of capital investment in the inner cities, to seeing it as being about the invasion of an alien, lawless culture.

Again, critical criminologists do not argue that there is anything new about this, or that it is inevitably directed at blacks. There is a historically well-established tendency to find groups of 'aliens' who can be blamed for society's ills, and different groups have at various times been singled out as the social scapegoat. Pearson's description of the stereotyping of the Irish 'hooligans' a century ago makes the point by its familiarity: ' "Hooliganism" was invariably portrayed as a totally alien presence, but here we see Hooligans acting in concert with their neighbours, reflecting the fact that in many working-class neighbourhoods hostility towards the police was a remarkably cohesive force' (Pearson, 1983: 86).

Two transformative moments have been highlighted by critical criminology in the criminalisation of black people. The first was the shift in police attitudes towards black communities: from recognising them as characterised by generally low crime rates, with the police task being (as in white communities) to assist generally law-abiding neighbourhoods to catch and control the small percentage of lawless members, to identifying whole areas as black 'criminal sub-cultures'. The new perception was expressed in John Brown's report *Shades of Grey*: 'the couple of hundred "hard-core" Dreadlocks who now form a criminalised sub-culture in the area live in squats. Almost all are unemployed. And apart from the specific crimes for which they are responsible, they constantly threaten the peace of individual citizens' (Brown, 1977, quoted by Gilroy, 1982: 160).

The second transformative moment was the 'racialisation' of the urban disorder that took place in British cities in 1981, and then in subsequent years during the 1980s (Solomos and Rackett, 1991). As young black people came to be seen as a group posing threats to social order through their criminal activities during the 1970s, any outbreak of disorder could readily be fitted into a framework which vindicated construction of young black people *en masse* as trouble, rather than individual miscreants being seen as an untypical minority. Minor disorders during the early 1970s, and the eruption of violence at the Notting Hill Carnival in 1976 (see Chapter 7) had added the idea of anti-police violence and disorderly political protest to the imagery of black trouble, so that black crime and black protest were conflated into the single issue of black threats to law and order.

More serious disorders in British cities in 1981 vindicated police and right-wing politicians' warnings of the black threat to social stability and security of persons and property, and the police recast their role in relation to black communities. Instead of detecting crime and apprehending the few black criminals, they now saw their duty as the maintenance of law and order, if necessary abandoning concern with minor crime in pursuance of this – as they saw it – more pressing task. With the change in the definition of their task came a change in styles of policing, and critical criminologists have devoted considerable attention to the growth of 'paramilitary policing' (Cashmore and McLauglin, 1991; Jefferson, 1990).

Police methods in areas with a high proportion of black residents were adaptations of policing in particularly troublesome colonies; and, under the leadership of Sir Kenneth Newman in the mid-1980s, they were the methods deployed in Northern Ireland. Newman had been head of the Royal Ulster Constabulary before he became Commissioner of the Metropolitan Police, and took upon himself the task he had pursued in Belfast: the reclamation of 'symbolic locations', more popularly known as no-go areas, to police control (Cashmore and McLaughlin, 1991: 34).

Critical criminologists have been concerned with policing to keep order, whereas administrative and radical criminologists have been more concerned with the response to crime. Thus, critical criminologists have looked at issues such as the use of the Special Patrol Group to police actual and expected outbreaks of disorder, and have examined changes in policing tactics more than they have examined arrest rates. Campaigns like the SWAMP 81 exercise in Brixton, the escalation of paramilitarism during and after the Broadwater Farm riots in 1985 have been described, and the point that emerges is that black communities are policed in the same manner as industrial and political disputes, rather than in the Dixon of Dock Green style of community policing or in the technocratic mode of contemporary crime detection.

Radical criminologists also make the distinction between 'consensus' and 'coercive' styles of policing (Lea and Young, 1984). What is different is that for radical realists, consensus policing is a *response* to a crisis of crime in neighbourhoods where police can expect minimum levels of public cooperation, whereas for critical criminologists coercive or paramilitary policing marks the *abandonment* of concern with crime in favour of containment of disorder. While radical realists argue for recognition of the roots of crime in deprivation and marginalisation, critical criminologists show how perception that certain groups are marginalised and excluded is used as evidence that containment tactics are necessary; while radical criminologists argue for more realistic policy responses to the crisis of crime and disorder, critical criminologists show how widespread belief in and fear of crisis has been used to justify increased police resourcing and increased violence of police methods.

As well as increased coerciveness of policing methods in relation to crime and disorder, the race/crime/alien culture imagery has been incorporated into debates about immigration, and critical criminologists have pointed out that oppressive legislation and oppressive policing to control migration have also been on the increase (Gilroy and Sim, 1985). Hostility towards immigrants and migrant workers is currently manifest throughout western Europe; a constant refrain in neo-fascist justifications about their attacks on north Africans and eastern Europeans (particularly gypsies in the incidents in mainland Europe during 1992) is that they are 'criminals'.

In policy debates over migration in western Europe, we see the conflation of the idea of 'immigrant' and even 'refugee' with ideas of crime, especially drug trafficking, robbery and prostitution. The 'problem-centred' view of black people and other dispossessed minorities is dominant in debates on immigration and asylum, whilst racism and neo-fascism, though duly deplored, are accepted as inevitable if numbers are not restricted. Rather than seeing racism as a problem for all the citizens of Europe, we are locked in to seeing minorities and migrants as a problem for Europe (cf. Bowling, 1990: 491).

Like radical criminology, critical criminology can offer insights into some of the contradictory evidence produced by administrative criminology, and explain some of the apparently inexplicable. The contradictory findings on race and sentencing, for example, with some studies even reporting comparative leniency, can be understood if we appreciate that the criminalisation of black people is so entrenched that there is considerable resistance to seeing them as victims. An explanation which has been put forward for the American studies which show comparative leniency to black defendants is linked to the fact that most crime is intra-racial. It has been suggested that a crucial difference in decisions at all stages of the criminal justice process, and especially at the sentencing stage, derives from the race of the victim, with the victimisation of black people being taken less seriously than that of whites (Petersilia, 1985). Since most victims of black crime will be black, this means that they will not be taken as seriously as crimes with white perpetrators and white victims. The most notorious instance of this differential response to black-on-white and white-on-black crime concerns not the no-injury assault cases that appear in the English research data, but homicide cases in the USA (Radelet and Pierce, 1985). Even reviews of research which claim to find no discrimination, or even comparative leniency, in the sentencing of black offenders, accept that in homicide and rape cases, race of both defendant and victim is influential (Kleck, 1985).

The English studies referred to in the section on administrative criminology do not, in the main, contain information about the race of victims, but the force of the argument can be seen if we compare the ease with which 'mugging' and the black crime phenomenon were accepted with the resistance to accepting the existence and volume of racial assaults. There has been no moral panic about racial assaults and abuse!

While radical realists advocate non-custodial penalties that are more appropriate and feasible for black offenders, young offenders, female offenders and addicted offenders (Carlen, 1989, 1990; Matthews, 1989; Pitts, 1990; Vass, 1990), critical criminologists have been more ready to argue that the role and structure of criminal justice and the penal system as a whole mean that it should be dismantled in favour of a more restorative system of justice (De Haan, 1990). Reform of the prison or the development of more or tougher community penalties is thought unlikely to lead to a change in the socioeconomic and racial composition of penalised populations (Mathiesen, 1974, 1990).

Most critical writers on penology would subscribe to the 'homogenisation thesis' which shows that from a heterogeneity of wrongdoings perpetrated by a heterogeneity of actors, the criminal justice system filters some out and some in at each successive stage: by legislating that some forms of wrongdoing will be dealt with by criminal law and some by administrative regulation; by dealing with some by cautioning or informal justice processes; by punishing some by community penalties and some by imprisonment. At the apex of the penal system, the prison, the population is much more homogeneous in terms of age, sex, type of wrongdoing, educational and economic status, and of course, race (Headley, 1989; Hudson, 1993).

Critical theorists have also been wary of administrative criminologists' (and some radical realists') faith in due process, just deserts and proportionate punishment, since their appreciation of criminal justice as a homogenising filter has lead to incorporation of the critical legal theorists' (and especially legal theorists') challenge to law as a system which treats all fairly. They see law as resting on assumptions such as procedural equality, free will and general protection of rights which express white, male, middle-class standpoints (Fitzpatrick, 1987; Hudson, 1992, 1993; Kerruish, 1991). Again, the critical sociological approach to law and punishment is that of decoding ideologies, rather than searching for 'real' remedies.

Conclusions

From this description of the contributions to our understanding of issues of race/racism, crime/criminal justice, policing and punishment that have stemmed from administrative, radical realist and critical criminology, it will be apparent that choice of framework depends primarily on the topic to be addressed or the question to be explained. Administrative criminology has raised questions and more than anything else represents the state's willingness to take issues of racism and criminal justice seriously. Its findings remain contradictory and controversial, and for explanations it must call upon one of the other paradigms. It is bounded by its limiting concern with process: use of discretion, adherence to policy and process, targeting of resources may be important in the administration of criminal justice, but they cannot be the only issues of concern to criminology.

The debate between radical realists and critical criminologists was extremely heated during the 1980s. Controversy centred on whether there was or was not a crisis in street crime and the potential for crime and disorder among dispossessed and disaffected youth. Titles given to the various position statements reveal the stances of the protagonists: *What is to be Done about Law and Order?* assumes that there is a problem which needs to have something done about it, while *The Myth of Black Criminality* makes it clear that there is no distinct or disproportionate problem of black crime. Another difference has been the centrality given to notions of race and class. Radical realism subsumes race under the more general division of class, whereas critical criminology points out the power of 'race' in ideologies of division and of blame of the 'enemy within', and also highlights the specific forms of oppression experienced by black people as black people, rather than as working-class, unemployed, criminal or even female black people.

The work of individual authors illustrates this relation of concepts to questions. Tony Jefferson, for example, one of the authors of *Policing the Crisis* and a leading writer on paramilitary policing, uses a class analysis in his work on crime and the policing of crime rather than public order (Jefferson, 1991; Jefferson et al., 1990). Similarly, John Solomos in his work with Benyon on the causes of urban unrest shares the radical realist emphasis on relative deprivation, but elsewhere shares critical criminology's preoccupation with processes of criminalisation, and the constitution of black people as a problem for (white) society (see Chapters 7 and 8). The article by Ruth Chigwada (1991) quoted in the section on radical criminology, could have appeared under both headings. She points out that black women are policed not only on grounds of crime (as suspects and as mothers of suspects), but also in connection with immigration and mental health. My reference to her work in the section on radical realist criminology was because her discussion of specific forms of contact between police and black women is prefaced by the remark that 'many black women are unemployed, single parents and their lifestyle does not match middle-class expectations. *Therefore*, they are vulnerable to being picked upon and harshly treated by the police' (1991: 141, emphasis added). In other words she is giving primacy to the class position rather than the race of these women.

Both of these perspectives have much to commend them. As Pitts points out (Chapter 6), a black chartered accountant is unlikely to commit much crime, but a black chartered accountant is far more likely than a white chartered accountant to be questioned by immigration officials or asked to produce documents to show that the car he is driving is really his own. Choice of explanatory framework, then, depends first and foremost on whether one is concerned with crime or with crimalisation. Critical criminology has little to say about the causes of crime, because that is not its focus; radical criminology, on the other hand, because of its understanding of the causes of crime will conclude that social policy and economic regeneration will have more impact on crime rates than penal policy, but it needs to turn to critical criminology for an explanation of why policy choices have been in favour of criminal justice rather than social investment.

2

Research, Policy and Racial Justice

Navnit Dholakia and Maggie Sumner

The purpose of this chapter is to consider the contribution of research to the development of policy on race and criminal justice and the extent to which it meets the concerns of black people[1] and others involved in the promotion of racial equality in the criminal justice system. It is now well established that people from racial minorities are more likely than whites to be arrested, charged, convicted and imprisoned and there are widespread concerns about remand conditions, bail conditions, stop and search, the police response to racial harassment complaints, deaths in custody, and police tactics, particularly in relation to drugs raids. The need to tackle these problems and the related issue of the declining confidence of black people in the criminal justice system has been recognised in a series of policy initiatives over the past 10 years. While much has been achieved in relation to some aspects of the operation of the criminal justice system, there has been less progress on certain key matters. The development of policies and strategies to have real impact on the disproportionate number of black people in prison has proved difficult. The aim of this chapter is not to present a comprehensive review of policy development (see, for example, NACRO, 1989 for a review of what has been done by the main agencies) or of the available research. It is rather to outline our main concerns about race and criminal justice and, in the second part of the chapter, to suggest some reasons why more progress has not been made. A different approach is needed to understand the processes which propel so many black people into the prison system.

Policy Development

Undoubtedly a great deal has been achieved in terms of policy development on race issues over the past 10 years or so. The main government departments concerned, the relevant agencies, organisations and professional groups have all formulated equal opportunities policies, have given attention to the recruitment of black people to their staff (NACRO, 1992a), to training on race issues (NACRO,

1993) and to improving the quality of service they offer to black people. This is not to say that there is not a lot still to be done to ensure that policies are implemented and that working practices change at every level, so that the effects are felt on a day-to-day basis in every court, every prison, every probation office and so on. Translating policy into concrete action has proved a very difficult process (NACRO, 1992b) and there is a long way to go before provision of equal opportunities is embedded in the structures of the criminal justice process.

Crucially, these many welcome changes have had little impact on one of the most startling and worrying features of racial difference in criminal justice, namely the marked disproportion of black people in prison relative to their presence in the population at large. Black people currently constitute about 5 per cent of the population of Great Britain, but make up 18 per cent of the prison population (Home Office, 1992a). The disproportion is particularly marked for Afro-Caribbean people who constitute about 1 per cent of the general population but just over 11 per cent of the prison population. Black people are more over-represented in the remand than the sentenced groups in the prison population (19 per cent of adult males on remand as against 16 per cent of adult males under sentence in 1990). The over-representation is remarkably high for women of Afro-Caribbean origin who in 1990 made up virtually one-quarter of the female prison population, although part of the high proportion of black women in prison is accounted for by the presence of foreign nationals convicted of drugs trafficking offences (Maden et al., 1992). This disproportionate number of black, particularly Afro-Caribbean, people must be a matter of great concern for those involved with race issues and criminal justice policy and practice.

Change in respect of race policies can be hard to achieve. It can be difficult to persuade those involved of the need for change without hard evidence that racial discrimination occurs. As the Chairman of the Ethnic Minorities Advisory Committee of the Judicial Studies Board has written, commenting upon the high proportion of ethnic minorities in prison:

> Much more research is needed before the causes of this phenomenon are properly understood, but in the meantime allegations of bias and racism co-exist unhappily with a judiciary and a magistracy which maintain that they are doing everything possible to be fair and to deal evenly with all who come before the criminal courts. There is confusion about the use of terminology on both sides of the divide which makes a complicated situation even more difficult to unravel. (Judicial Studies Board, 1992: 1)

One of the difficulties is the concept of racial discrimination itself. To many people this concept implies direct discrimination, whereby people are treated less favourably because of their race, skin colour or ethnic origin. However, discrimination can also occur when a rule which ostensibly applies to everyone has detrimental effects in practice on particular racial groups. Indirect discrimination of this kind, like the direct form, is prohibited by the Race Relations Act of 1976, although criminal justice does not come within the terms of that legislation. Indirect discrimination can be much harder to challenge precisely because it is indirect rather than overt. Moreover, some of the rules which can disadvantage racial minorities embody deeply held norms and beliefs about how systems should work. It can be very hard for people working to administer justice to accept that what they do may be discriminatory even though they themselves strive to avoid direct discrimination.

Evidence of discrimination is one contribution for which policy makers and those concerned to influence them have looked to researchers. Another equally important role for research is the provision of an analytical understanding of the processes and points in the system where changes are most needed and might be most effective. In both of these respects, the role of research on race and criminal justice over the past 10 years has been valuable but limited. This is partly because of the rather piecemeal way in which research has been carried out but, more fundamentally, it reflects a wider compartmentalisation of the criminal justice system, a tendency to see criminal justice as somehow separate from the rest of society and a rather narrow understanding of what discrimination means.

Racial Disparities and the Criminal Justice System

Ten years ago there was a dearth of information about racial differences in all aspects of the criminal justice system. Through the activities of researchers and the monitoring of some, though far from all, of the routine operations of the agencies concerned, much more is now known. This must be regarded as an achievement, despite some remarkable gaps: the ethnic origin of those appearing before the courts is still not routinely recorded, for example. The information gathered over the past 10 years suggests four main areas of concern.

Black People as Criminal Justice Workers
The criminal justice system is largely run and administered by white people. As noted already, racial minorities currently make up about 5 per cent of the total population. About 1 per cent of the police force, 2 per cent of solicitors, 6 per cent of barristers, 7 per cent of the Crown Prosecution Service, 2 per cent of the magistracy and less than 1 per cent of the judiciary are black: there are no reliable figures

available for either the probation or prison service, but it is thought that the proportion of black people is about 1 per cent for prisons and about 2 per cent for probation. Even in those professions where the percentages of black people appear favourable, it should be noted that black staff tend to be concentrated in junior grades and in particular specialisms. For example, the Bar Council has taken a number of active steps to address racial discrimination including the commissioning of a survey published in 1989, which showed that black barristers were concentrated in a few sets of chambers, often newer and smaller sets without the library and other supports which would enable them to expand the scope of their work (Bar Council, 1989). While the enormous social value of the criminal defence work carried out by these black chambers cannot be denied, prestige and prospects for promotion in this branch of the legal profession had traditionally attached to civil rather than criminal work. The Bar Council has done a great deal to redress the situation shown in the 1989 survey and in this respect has a record which compares very well with other relevant agencies and organisations (NACRO, 1992a). The point to be made is that even in a profession in which black people are not under-represented and which has given a high priority to race issues, black people still suffer disadvantage. The link between the ability to recruit more black staff and the quality of service provided (Holdaway, 1991) makes this an important area for policy development and changes in practice for all the relevant agencies.

Crimes against Black People

Black people are disproportionately likely to suffer from crime. The 1988 British Crime Survey (Mayhew et al., 1989) estimated that 30 per cent of whites, 33 per cent of Afro-Caribbeans and 36 per cent of Asians had been victims of household crimes such as burglary, vandalism and vehicle crime. Ten per cent of whites, 16 per cent of Afro-Caribbeans and 15 per cent of Asians were victims of personal crime, including assaults, threats and robbery. A Home Office study of rapes recorded by the police in two London boroughs between 1984 and 1986 showed that Afro-Caribbean women were twice as likely to have been victims as would be expected from their presence in the relevant local populations.

The extent to which crimes against black people are racially motivated is not clear. Racial violence is a term which is often used broadly to refer to a range of incidents and behaviour, including personal abuse, threatening behaviour, graffiti, damage to property, physical attacks and murder. It is, of course, difficult to prove racial motivation in such incidents, and consequently estimates of the extent of racially motivated crime often depend on the assessments and perceptions of the victims. Moreover, it is now well recognised that a substantial proportion of incidents of racial attack is never reported. In 1981, the Home Office estimated that about 7,000 incidents would be reported to the police in England and Wales but recognised that this was probably an underestimate (Home Office, 1981). Research has shown that this is indeed the case. A Policy Studies Institute (1983) study estimated that the real figure could be as high as ten times the Home Office 1981 estimate, and other locally based studies have confirmed that racial attacks are widespread and that there is a reluctance to report them to the police (Gordon, 1986). For example, a survey of local residents in North Plaistow, London in 1990 showed racial harassment to be a serious problem:

> Between one in five and one in six Afro-Caribbean and Asian men and women said that they had suffered what they felt to have been a racially motivated incident in an 18 month period. Racist insults, verbal abuse, threats and property damage were predominant but stone throwing, serious assault and arson were also mentioned. (Bowling and Saulsbury, 1992: 35)

As well as formal research (Bowling and Saulsbury, 1992), action projects such as Radio 1 helpline set up to support the Race Through the 90s campaign, have shown that racial attacks are widespread. The helpline received over a thousand calls in a week, about a quarter of which concerned racial attacks and harassment most of which had never been reported (*Caribbean Times*, 14 July 1992). This is mentioned as a very public and well-publicised indication of the level of concern among black communities. The experience of many ethnic minority groups and individuals is that racial violence is on the increase and that it is not treated as seriously as it should be (CRE, 1991b).

Racial harassment and attacks represent the most invidious aspect of racial hostility and their impact extends far beyond the immediate offences. The need to deal with racial violence has been addressed at a high level, for example by the Home Affairs Committee (1986) and in the report of an interdepartmental group on racial attacks (Racial Attacks Group, 1989). The general approach which has been preferred in these major policy initiatives has been to promote multi-agency cooperation and coordination, as well as improving the responses of individual agencies, to give greater reassurance to ethnic minority communities. Research on multi-agency initiatives has shown how difficult it is for statutory agencies with specific and defined responsibilities and powers to work together (Bowling and Saulsbury, 1992; FitzGerald, 1989; Sampson et al., 1988). There is a risk that such initiatives become an end in themselves in the sense that bureaucratic effort is increased without any real impact on the actual problem of racial harassment (Gordon, 1986). Moreover, such initiatives have been criticised for failing to involve black community groups to a sufficient degree: even projects which claim some success in other respects have made less progress in this (Neyroud, 1992). There is little evidence that the local inter-agency approach to dealing with racial harassment has yet been able to deliver effective protection or redress to black people.

Demands from ethnic minority organisations for a better response to racial violence have included the introduction of a new specific criminal offence. Among the arguments in favour of this proposal are that it would be an unambiguous expression of public policy in this area, that it would encourage the reporting of these types of crime and that it would enable the relevant agencies, including the courts, to deal more effectively with racially motivated crime. In assessing these arguments, it would be useful to know more about how a racial element in an offence does or does not impinge upon decisions taken by the Crown Prosecution Service, the presentation of such cases in the courts or what impact it has on sentencing. Racial violence and the inadequate response to it remain a major source of concern.

Black People as Suspects, Defendants and Offenders
Evidence that Afro-Caribbean people are much more likely to be stopped by the police was built up during the 1980s. The 1988 British Crime Survey found that 14 per cent of Asians, 15 per cent of whites and 20 per cent of Afro-Caribbeans reported being stopped by the police over a 14-month period (Skogan, 1990), a pattern similar to that found in previous research (Smith, 1983). Although significant differences in the frequency of multiple stops were not found in the British Crime Survey, higher proportions of Afro-Caribbeans than of whites or Asians reported being searched. These differences were found even after controlling for other factors. Racial differences in this context have clear consequences. As the British Crime Survey study concluded:

> There was some evidence that both police and public initiated contacts with the police had racially divisive consequences. Afro-Caribbeans were the most frequently and repeatedly stopped, they were more often searched and they were the most dissatisfied with how politely they were treated. They were also less satisfied than whites with how their cases were handled when they contacted the police. Asians were not disproportionately stopped but they were also more likely than whites to indicate that they were not treated politely, and they were less satisfied with how their cases were handled when they contacted the police. (Skogan, 1990: 51)

Black people also appear to be arrested disproportionately: for example, a study carried out by the Policy Studies Institute (1983) found that Afro-Caribbeans made up about 5 per cent of the population in London but 17 per cent of people arrested. The finding of disproportionate arrest rates has been found in subsequent studies in London (Walker, 1988, 1989). There is evidence that Afro-Caribbean juveniles are less likely than whites to be cautioned: a white juvenile with previous convictions may be more than four times more likely to receive a caution than a black juvenile in similar circumstances (Landau and Nathan, 1983). Ethnic minorities are charged with different offences from whites and from each other (Home Office Statistical Bulletin, 1989a,b). Afro-Caribbean people are more likely than whites or Asians to be remanded in custody before trial. A Home Office Statistical Bulletin in March 1989, for example, showed that in Greater London 9 per cent of black male defendants were remanded in custody compared with 8 per cent of Asians and 5 per cent of whites (Home Office Statistical Bulletin, 1989b). Black people are more likely to be tried at crown court – more than twice as likely according to one study of London courts (Walker, 1988) – but more likely to be acquitted after trial, although this latter point may not hold true for Asian defendants. As already noted, Afro-Caribbeans in particular are very heavily over-represented in the prison population. The first published comprehensive information about the ethnic origins of people in prison was the Home Office Statistical Bulletin (1986). This showed that black prisoners had fewer previous convictions than whites sentenced for similar offences. Overall, 62 per cent of white men aged 21 and over were known to have six or more previous convictions, compared with 50 per cent of those of Chinese, Arab or mixed origin, 48 per cent of Afro-Caribbean prisoners and only 20 per cent of those from the Indian sub-continent. However, black people in prison tend to be serving longer sentences and to be held in disproportionate numbers in closed conditions: about 16 per cent of Afro-Caribbean adults under sentence were held in Category B closed training prisons in 1990 compared with 11 per cent of the adult sentenced population as a whole.

There is therefore a substantial amount of evidence that black people are dealt with as suspects, defendants and offenders to a disproportionate degree. Moreover, the prima facie evidence is that black people are treated more harshly at each stage of the criminal justice process.

Confidence in Criminal Justice

The concerns which have been outlined are bound to raise some fundamental questions about the nature of British justice for black people. The picture described so far in this chapter is of a system which is staffed primarily by white people, appears to take racial crimes against black people less seriously than it should but treats black people more harshly as suspected or convicted offenders. It is not surprising that many black people lack confidence in the institutions of criminal justice.

There is evidence that a substantial proportion of the public believes that the criminal justice system is discriminatory, and that these beliefs are especially prevalent among racial minority communities. Reference has already been made to the findings of the British Crime Survey in relation to the police. It is worth adding that the problem of racial differences in confidence in the police seems to be getting worse. The 1988 sweep found that only 16 per cent of Afro-Caribbeans or Asians considered that the police did 'a very good job' compared to 27 per cent and 36 per cent respectively in 1982. The confidence of white people in the police has also declined (the equivalent proportions being 44 per cent in 1982 and 26 per cent in 1988) but remains higher than among blacks. A race issues opinion survey carried out in June 1991 by National Opinion Polls for the *Independent on Sunday* newspaper and the Runnymede Trust found, for example, that 75 per cent of Afro-Caribbean, 48 per cent of Asian and 45 per cent of white people interviewed believed that black people are treated more harshly by the police. Similar beliefs in respect of the courts were expressed by 57 per cent of Afro-Caribbean, 24 per cent of white and 19 per cent of Asian respondents (Shallice and Gordon, 1990). A smaller qualitative study of all stages of the criminal justice system found a similar pattern of a high proportion of black people believing that the system is discriminatory and that this view was shared by a substantial minority of white people (NACRO, 1991).

This lack of confidence in justice for black people cannot be ignored for it has very profound social consequences. In itself it is an important issue for policy makers to tackle, but it cannot be effectively tackled separately from the question of whether the criminal justice system does in fact discriminate against black people. This is a crucial but thorny question which research has found difficult to answer in a definitive way. As Shallice and Gordon have put it:

> there is an absolute discrepancy between the findings of researchers that there is no evidence of differential sentencing on racial grounds in the courts and the large numbers of people who readily assert the opposite, largely (though not unimportantly) on the basis of anecdotal, personal and collective experience. (Shallice and Gordon, 1990: 30)

Facts such as the over-representation of black people in the criminal justice system are now beyond dispute: what is at issue is how much of this is due to discrimination on the part of the courts or other criminal justice agencies and how far it might be explained in some other way, for example the unproved assertion that black people commit more crime or more serious crime. The processes which lead to so many black people being in prison are still one of the least well understood aspects of the operation of the criminal justice system.

The Contribution of Research

Reiner (1989: 12) has observed that, taken overall, the volume and quality of research evidence on the treatment of black people is 'such as to render any doubts about discrimination fanciful rather than reasonable'. However, in so far as policy makers have looked to research for conclusive evidence, the results have been rather disappointing.

One reason why research has been inconclusive clearly relates to the small scale and local nature of many of the available studies. Honesty requires that such studies should be tentative about the conclusions that can be drawn. The numbers may be too small to make possible meaningful comparisons of sentencing decisions about black and white offenders, even more so if any attempt is made to look at differences between racial minority groups or to compare, say, the treatment of black and white women.

A second problem is that there has been little consistency between the various studies in the methods they have employed, the sampling framework and the variables included for analysis. It has not always been possible for researchers to collect information about previous conviction, for example, resulting in incomplete data (Shallice and Gordon, 1990). In consequence, it has been difficult to use the findings of the various studies as a body, especially since the conclusions drawn have not all pointed in the same direction. With regard to sentencing, a number of studies could be cited to show some evidence of discrimination (Hudson, 1989a; Voakes and Fowler, 1989; Walker, 1988) and a number of others could be quoted as counter to this (Crow and Cove, 1984; McConville and Baldwin, 1982; Moxon, 1988).

Without much larger scale studies, such as that recently completed by Roger Hood for the CRE (CRE, 1992b; Hood, 1992), such limitations are perhaps an inevitability. Hood's research provides a very detailed examination of the sentencing of 2,884 men and 433 women dealt with in five crown courts in the West Midlands during 1989. The sample, the largest sample of crown court cases ever studied in this country, was specifically drawn with a view to examining race differences and to allow the treatment of women to be looked at separately. The framework of the research also allowed sentencing to be set in the context of the particular sentencing traditions of individual courts: the courts chosen had custody rates ranging between 61 and 46 percent. A wide range of information was collected on each case, including depositions of evidence, social inquiry and other reports, previous convictions and sentences and the police statement of antecedents. The size and scope of this study, which overcomes many of the methodological limitations of previous work, mean that it is of particular importance and much significance was attached to it by policy makers and others even before the findings of the research were known.

Hood's research provides the clearest evidence to date that race has in some circumstances an effect on sentencing independent of other factors. The raw figures on the use of custody for Hood's sample showed that for every 100 white men sentenced to prison there were 117 blacks and 82 Asians. A detailed comparison, centred on 15 variables, suggested that, all other things being equal. Afro-Caribbean offenders had a 5 per cent greater probability of being sent to prison than whites and Asians a lower probability of about 4 per cent. If race did not operate independently then it would be expected that for every 100 white men sentenced to custody there would be about 105 Afro-Caribbean and 96 Asians. Looking at this another way, the study suggested that about 80 per cent of the over-representation of black men in prison could be explained by the disproportionate numbers appearing at crown court and the serious-ness of their cases and about 20 per cent could only be explained by differential treatment by the courts. However, most of this 'race effect' on the prison population would result from the longer prison sentences imposed on the higher proportion of black offenders who pleaded not guilty and thus lost the discount which a guilty plea normally attracts.

While providing important evidence that race *per se* has an impact on the use of custodial sentences, the study did not at all bear out claims of blanket discrimination in sentencing. The differences between Afro-Caribbean, Asian and white people which could not be explained except by reference to a 'race effect' were found among men but not for women, for adults but not for those under 21; the effect was different for Afro-Caribbeans and for Asians (who were less likely to receive a prison sentence but those who did were likely to get a longer term). 'Whether or not black offenders were dealt with differently depended on a number of factors: the seriousness of the case, age, employment status, how they pleaded, and above all, the court where they stood trial and the judge who sentenced them'

(CRE, 1992b: 34). Quite why the differences should be sharper in some courts than others and for some judges more than others is not clear, but as the Commission for Racial Equality note in their published commentary on Hood's findings, the methodological rigour of the analysis and the range of factors taken into account makes it difficult to imagine what other legally relevant variable there could be which could explain the fact that for every 100 black men sentenced to prison in Birmingham there should 129 in Dudley and even more in other courts. The question must be raised whether there are not different racial stereotypes at work in the minds of some judges or in the sentencing cultures of certain courts. Clearly, action is needed to deal with this possibility and to prevent the occurrence of discrimination in sentencing. This should be given urgent attention by the Lord Chancellor's Department, which would be greatly aided in the task by more research on judicial perceptions of and attitudes to the black offenders on whom they are required to pass sentence. The absence of research on judicial attitudes to date can be attributed to judicial reticence rather than reluctance on the part of researchers, but there must now be a strong case for this research to be carried out.

The degree of difference in the use of custody for black and white offenders attributable to the 'race effect' may not be large but it is important to bear in mind its impact. A greater probability of 5 per cent in the likelihood of a black person going to prison may not sound a large figure but it becomes much more alarming when translated into actual numbers of people. As Hood has pointed out, if no 'race effect' had been operating on his sample, then 479 blacks would have been sent to prison in 1989 rather than 503. If this is multiplied throughout the country, then many people's lives are being severely damaged and their future prospects impaired for no reason other than that they are black. This is apart from wider considerations of the overall actual and perceived fairness of the criminal justice system as a whole. Policy makers must take this very seriously indeed.

But evidence that there is some racial discrimination in sentencing in certain circumstances, in some courts or in some types of cases should not be regarded as the solution to the wide range of policy questions which need to be addressed to promote racial justice. It is very important to have a well-based estimate that 20 per cent of the over-representation of black people in prison seems to be due to an unexplained 'race effect' and to do something to change that situation. But it is equally important that the less obviously problematic 80 per cent of the disproportion is not complacently accepted. An entirely appropriate concern about more direct forms of discrimination occurring in certain circumstances should not mean that the possibility of indirect discrimination on a more routine basis is overlooked. The whole process which leads to so many black people being in prison needs to be examined. Sentencing is a significant social event which has profound effects on people's lives but it is also only the end point of a very complex process. The possibility that discrimination can be indirect and cumulative is one which has been signposted by previous research, and quite clearly in the study by Hood discussed above, even when evidence of direct discrimination in the courts has not been found. But, generally, the signposts have not been followed up. In this sense research has raised as many questions as it has answered.

Cumulative and Indirect Discrimination

The difficulty of disentangling the role played by the defendant's race from a whole host of other factors, such as the vagaries of individual courts and the various other factors which shape the exercise of sentencers' discretion, has been an obstacle to identifying discrimination. Implicitly race has been treated as a residual variable in analysing sentencing decisions. Racial differences which cannot be explained as a consequence of some other factor are assumed to be due to discrimination and, conversely, where racial disparities appear to be explained by another factor, it is assumed that discrimination is not in play. But there are also several important questions about the extent to which those other factors themselves bear the marks of discrimination at a different stage of the criminal justice process or in the wider society. The conclusions reached by researchers such as Crow and Cove (1984), McConville and Baldwin (1982) and Moxon (1988) that there is no evidence of discrimination at the sentencing stage should not blind us to what happens earlier. The fact that 'defendants are treated equally once they attain the status of convicted defendants' (McConville and Baldwin, 1982: 658) cannot be taken in isolation from the host of decisions which result in people achieving this status.

Some examples may serve to make the point. First, we know that black people are over-represented in the prison population. Clearly the fact that black people are more likely to receive a prison sentence and one of longer duration does not of itself imply that sentencers are acting in a discriminatory way, either consciously or unconsciously. Black people may be more likely to be convicted of the kinds of offences which more readily attract a custodial sentence (Hood, 1992; Hudson, 1989a; Walker, 1988). This should direct attention to the processes which occur between the commission of an offence and the charge which is dealt with in the courts. Research hints at the potential importance of these processes, but there has been little follow up. Crow and Cove, for example, while finding that sentencing outcomes were similar for black and white defendants convicted of the same offences, noted some differences between the details and actual circumstances of offences which were charged in the same offence category. Thus the victim had suffered no actual injury in more cases involving Afro-Caribbean defendants than was the case for whites (Crow and Cove, 1984). It is not just a matter of more or less serious examples of offences of their kind – stealing a milk bottle and stealing a performance car are both theft (Shallice and Gordon, 1990: 51) – but also the shadowy boundaries between different categories of assault, for example. The conclusion that sentencing outcomes might not appear discriminatory, and indeed may not be in themselves, does not eliminate the possibility that they are still part of a process which does not treat black and white defendants equally at an earlier stage.

Another example of the difficulty of seeing sentencing decisions in isolation is the suggestion that the higher use of imprisonment for black people is related to the greater likelihood that they will be sentenced at crown courts without a report from the probation service being available (Hood, 1992; Moxon, 1988). Such reports are generally not available where a not guilty plea is entered, reflecting probation service policy. Social inquiry reports have been super-seded since the Criminal Justice Act 1991 by pre-sentence reports which have a rather different function in that they will not contain a recommendation to the court about the penalty to be imposed but will give information about the possibilities for community sentence provision. Depending upon how the provisions of the Act are applied, it is still possible that Afro-Caribbeans will be sentenced without a report to a greater extent than other racial groups since higher proportions are dealt with for offences triable only on indictment. In these cases, judges will have discretion about whether to sentence without report. It will be important to monitor the use made of this judicial discretion.

Those convicted at crown courts are more likely to receive a sentence of imprisonment than those dealt with at magistrates courts (Moxon, 1988). Sentences imposed after trial tend to be longer because they do not attract the 'discount' which goes with a guilty plea. Any defendant electing trial at crown court would be affected by these general rules. In themselves they are not discriminatory. However, black people are more likely to plead not guilty and to elect trial at crown court and are thus more likely to end up in the position of being at a high risk of a (longer) custodial sentence. Again, there are interesting questions to which research suggests some avenues for further study. Why are black people more likely to be dealt with in crown courts? Is it because magistrates are more likely to commit them for trial? Is it because they are more likely to elect trial (Shallice and Gordon, 1990)? Why should black people be more likely to elect trial: is it to do with the legal advice that they get or is it because they believe that they will get a fairer hearing (Riley and Vennard, 1988)? If the latter, is this belief borne out or not? Walker's study of London courts showed that black people were more likely to have their cases dismissed by the judge on grounds of insufficiency of evidence and more likely to be acquitted after trial. While it is possible that this reflects a greater reluctance to convict black defendants, a more likely explanation is that black defendants are brought to court on the basis of rather weaker evidence. In protesting their innocence, black people may be inadvertently presenting themselves in ways which are understood by those operating and administering the system to be associated with more serious types of offending. A review of the policy of offering a discount to offenders who plead guilty on the grounds that the policy may be indirectly discriminatory is one of the key recommendations drawn by the Commission for Racial Equality from the results of Hood's research (CRE, 1992b).

In the context of the tendency for black people to plead not guilty, it is interesting that young people from racial minorities, especially Afro-Caribbeans, are more likely to be referred for prosecution rather than cautioned (Cain and Sadigh, 1982; CRE, 1992a; Landau and Nathan, 1983). Various explanations might be offered for this. For example, if cautions are more readily given to young people who live with both parents and whose parents are in employment (Landau and Nathan, 1983), then it is less likely that Afro-Caribbean young people will be dealt with in this way. About 47 per cent of households whose members are categorised as 'West Indian' are headed by lone parents, compared with 17 per cent of white households, and unemployment rates for all the main racial minorities are higher than they are for whites. A different explanation is suggested by police monitoring statistics which showed that only half as many young Afro-Caribbeans as whites admitted the offence of which they were accused (CRE, 1992a) (a caution cannot be given unless the offence is admitted). The reasons for this are not entirely clear, but it would seem reasonable to suggest that black young people are being treated as suspects for offences which they did not commit.

This, of course, raises questions about policing. It is known that Afro-Caribbeans are significantly more likely to be stopped by the police (Skogan, 1990) and that arrest rates are higher. Whether this reflects racist attitudes among the police or the unproved assertion that black people commit more crime or whether it reflects the nature of the policing task as it is commonly understood remains a matter of contention (see Reiner, 1989). The policy implications for tackling this would be different depending on the nature of the explanation accepted, but the point here is not a discussion of the relative merits or demerits of these perspectives. It is rather to stress the need to look at the criminal justice system as a whole.

Research has tended to focus only on specific decision-making points rather than examining the relationships between them. The various stages needed to be related to each other in order to begin to see how some racial groups seem to be propelled through the system at a much faster rate than others. At present there is a general picture of what happens to black people in the criminal justice system. Research has provided some pieces of the jigsaw and suggested what other pieces might look like. Further progress really requires comprehensive and systematic monitoring of all stages of the process as a whole. In the absence of this it is difficult to pinpoint where and to what extent discrimination, especially in its less direct forms, may occur so that action can be taken to eliminate it.

The Need for Monitoring

Section 95 of the Criminal Justice Act 1991 provides a constructive opportunity for comprehensive ethnic monitoring to be introduced. Section 95 places upon the Secretary of State a duty to publish information which will, *inter alia*, enable those who work in the criminal justice system to fulfil their duty to avoid discrimination on improper grounds. The incorporation of racial monitoring data into all recording procedures, from the earliest point possible, will be of enormous value to the individual agencies concerned. Each will then be able to review its own policies and procedures. For example, the police will be able to evaluate and review decision-making areas for which they have responsibility. But, very importantly, a comprehensive monitoring system will allow assessments to be made of the cumulative effects of decisions by several agencies. Rates of acquittals, for instance, can be compared with those concerning charges and prosecutions, or remands in custody with decisions to allow or deny police bail.

Monitoring is not a substitute for research: of itself it explains nothing. But equally the role of research is not to substitute for proper monitoring procedures; the skills of researchers should not be wasted on unearthing basic information which ought to be routinely and publicly available.

Comprehensive monitoring will give a better idea of where inequality is occurring in the system as a whole, indicating where research efforts can best be used to provide a better understanding of the processes involved. This will provide a much stronger foundation for assessing where change is needed, what the changes should be and for assessing results.

It is necessary to monitor every point, from arrest and charge right through to parole decisions, including the operation of youth courts and the impact on young offenders. It is important also that the routine information is made publicly available: a system of justice should be transparent and accountable. It is particularly important when, as noted earlier, there are so many people who perceive criminal justice as racially unjust.

Racial Equality and Racial Justice

It would be somewhat surprising if the criminal justice system were entirely free of racial injustice. Criminal justice does not operate in isolation from the wider society and there is a great deal of evidence that black people suffer discrimination and disadvantage in many areas of social life, including access to housing, to employment, to health care and so on (Brown, 1984; Home Office, 1991). All of these factors impinge upon the level and nature of the contact which black people have with the criminal justice system and in all of these respects black people are more likely to be disadvantaged.

On one level it can be said that there is no evidence of racial discrimination if, for example, unemployed black people are sentenced in the same way as unemployed white people or that black people are treated no differently from white people who live in inner-city areas. To tell black people that they are refused bail not because they are black but because, being unemployed and without secure housing, they are 'bad risks' or that they are victims of crime because they live in inner-city areas is to fail to recognise the reality of the experience of being black in Britain today. A narrow definition of discrimination and an expectation that it will be manifest directly at a particular point in the criminal justice process are of limited value in the enterprise of ensuring that black people are treated fairly in a system in which they have confidence. To achieve this requires the continued development of policies to increase the recruitment of black people to criminal justice agencies, to ensure that people from ethnic minorities are treated with sensitivity and understanding and that all criminal justice staff have appropriate training, and it requires thorough monitoring.

Note

1 We use the term 'black' to refer to anyone who, whatever their nationality or culture, suffers from discrimination based on skin colour and is not accepted as 'white'. This definition does not imply that there is homogeneity in the experiences of black people: in particular, the experiences which Asian and Afro-Caribbean people have of criminal justice are known to differ in important respects. Where reference is made to the experience of a particular group this is specifically stated in the text.

3

'Racism': Establishing the Phenomenon

Marian FitzGerald

> the currently dominant approach to investigating ethnicity and criminalization centred on attempting to uncover by ever more sophisticated techniques the purely 'racial' dimension is a bit like sieving flour with ever finer meshes: eventually there is too little getting through to enable anything to be made . . . or . . . to construct a very meaningful account.
>
> (Jefferson, 'The racism of criminalization')

This chapter takes as given that 'racism' exists in British society. That is, certain groups suffer prejudice, discrimination and disadvantage on the basis of characteristics ascribed to them because of what others perceive as the racial group to which they belong (irrespective of whether they share that perception). The central concern of the chapter, however, is to explore some of the problems of establishing the phenomenon of racism in the field of criminology, both in terms of the concepts and the methods which tend currently to be used. It begins by looking critically at the convention of striving clearly to demarcate what is 'racial' from what is not; and it goes on to question the convention which strongly favours quantitative over qualitative research methods in this field.

Approaches which strive to distinguish the 'racial' from the non-racial have clear parallels in other social policy fields, both at the conceptual level and in terms of policy and practice. They have probably had their highest profile in policy areas associated with local authorities. They have created problems which are common to all fields but which manifest themselves differently in each.

The origins of this dichotomised approach lie primarily in 'progressive' reaction to a prevailing conservative position which was perceived as inimical to the interests of ethnic minorities. Superficially, however, there is an ironic contrast in the *direction* of this reaction depending on its social policy context. In the context of policy areas traditionally associated with local authorities (such as housing and education), the conservative position was to play down, and even, to refuse to discuss material differences between racialised groups, thus effectively avoiding the policy implications of racial disadvantage and the possibility of discrimination on the part of the authorities themselves. Thus Young and Connelly's key study identified the prevailing orthodoxy at the end of the 1970s as 'colour blindness' (Young and Connelly, 1981). The 'progressives', however, forced these issues onto local political agendas often insisting on 'a form of racial explicitness which is also racially exclusive' (Nanton and FitzGerald, 1990). In the field of crime, on the other hand, the conservatives have highlighted racial differences, implicitly (and, at times, explicitly) using statistics to stereotype certain racialised minorities as criminals, while the 'progressive' response to this has often been to try to explain away these apparently racial differences in non-racial terms (see, for example, Ramsay, 1982).

Attempts to claim that a wide range of actions and an even wider range of effects of policy and practice are demonstrably racist rely heavily on this stark 'either/or' approach. However, this quest for the Holy Grail of 'pure racism' (Reiner, 1992) is not simply a manifestation of political orthodoxy. It also derives from a persistent failure to grasp the concept of indirect discrimination. The ways in which non-racial criteria themselves may systematically – albeit unintentionally – work to the disadvantage of ethnic minorities were poorly understood in the authorities studied by Young and Connelly (1981) over a decade ago, and there is little sign that this has changed.[1] Yet indirect discrimination, which (as the following discussion illustrates) often provides the most convincing explanations for apparent racial differences, *de facto* precludes the conventional 'either/or' approach.

This chapter looks at three examples of issues where the question 'Is it racial or isn't it?' has been posed variously to practitioners, policy makers and researchers. The meaning – not to say the validity – of the term 'racial' has been the subject of extensive debate which is usefully summarised by Susan Smith in *The Politics of 'Race' and Residence* (Smith 1989, ch. 1). For present purposes, it is employed loosely to reflect the very diverse and imprecise ways in which it is applied in the British context to a range of non-white ethnic minorities. The chapter explores the approaches which have been taken in each of the three examples and the confusion which has often resulted. From this, it goes on to draw some broad lessons about the reasons for this and to suggest ways in which prevailing approaches – both conceptual and methodological – may need to be adapted.

The first example, which links the local authority experience with more obviously criminological concerns, is the case of racial harrassment in local authority housing. This draws largely on material from a research project for the Department of the Environment (DoE) which I worked on between 1986 and 1988.[2] The second – the question of apparent ethnic differences in rates of general victimisation –

draws on material from the 1988 British Crime Survey. And the third is the analysis of crime statistics by ethnic origin. The subsequent discussion aims to draw out the main issues raised by these three examples both at the conceptual level and in terms of methodology.

Racial Harassment

At the time of the DoE research, key features of the prevailing orthodoxy on which local authorities based their racial harassment policies were: racial harassment was a discrete phenomenon which could clearly be identified as such; its perpetrators were assumed to be white; and its victims were non-white ethnic minorities. Any ambiguity about whether an incident was racial or not was conventionally resolved by adopting a 'victim-centred' approach. That is, it was to be treated as racial harassment if that was how the victim saw it.

A preliminary trawl of relevant local authority documents had begun to suggest that policy makers were not infrequently faced with requests from practitioners for further clarification of the definition of 'racial harassment'. And subsequent in-depth studies of individual authorities shed light on the reasons for this. The orthodox view was valid at the level of broad generalisation. Certainly the great majority of victims were non-white and those responsible (where they were identified) tended mainly to be white. However, it did not fully reflect the day-to-day experience of those responsible for carrying out the policy; nor did it provide them with sufficient guidance to deal with a significant number of cases which the orthodox view appeared not to encompass.

The general conceptual problems of this approach have been rehearsed elsewhere (FitzGerald, 1989; FitzGerald and Ellis, 1991; Nanton and FitzGerald, 1990). Two are of particular relevance here. The first is that the study showed that racial harassment was *not* always discrete: on occasion it was an additional, exacerbating element to an issue which was not necessarily racial in its origins.[3] At its most complex, it might arise in circumstances where the aggrieved party retaliated in a form which constituted racial harassment thereby (according to the policy) becoming the offender.

Secondly, despite the emphasis on the victim-centred approach, there was, at best, confusion when the ethnicity of the parties involved did not conform to the orthodox view. There were cases of white victims who were Jewish or who were being harassed because they had non-white partners or mixed race children. But such cases were recognised, if at all, only belatedly and with reluctance, lest they open up the possibility of whites more generally claiming racial victimisation. Certainly, there was enormous sensitivity where the perpetrators were themselves of minority ethnic origin. One housing officer I interviewed was in despair at her inability to help an Asian family. Although they were under siege in their flat, their tormentors were not white and she was told they were not, therefore, eligible for priority transfer on grounds of racial harassment.

The scope for refining policy to deal more effectively with the problem was further limited by the available data. There were several ways in which monitoring returns could be seriously misleading as a basis for reviewing policy. Already the picture they provided was distorted inasmuch as the categories they used and the variables they covered were limited by the prevailing orthodoxy. But they also posed difficulties in identifying the areas within the authority where the problem was most acute. In part this was because the areas where housing staff were least aware of and concerned about the problem were likely to produce low returns, reflecting both a lack of confidence among victims in reporting and a lack of official diligence in recording. In part also, it betrayed extreme crudeness in interpreting the figures: the areas with the highest numbers of incidents were often *de facto* assumed to be those where the problem was greatest, irrespective of whether the ethnic minority population of the area was 5 per cent or 50 per cent.

Victim Surveys

In 1988 the British Crime Survey (BCS) for the first time included an over-sample of respondents of Afro-Caribbean and Indian subcontinent origin and found that these minorities were very significantly more likely than whites to be victims of crime (Mayhew et al., 1989). It, therefore, appeared unsurprising that both groups perceived an element of racial motivation, particularly in the case of vandalism, assaults and threats.

However, by applying multivariate analyses to the figures for victimisation rates, the differences in victimisation between whites and Afro-Caribbeans became statistically insignificant; and, for Asians, only a small residue remained unexplained. That is, the greater victimisation of ethnic minorities appeared primarily – if not entirely – to be attributable to non-racial factors, such as area, age, tenure, employment and marital status.

This, of course, raised the further and somewhat sensitive question of why – if statistically it could be proved that race was not a factor – ethnic minority victims so often believed that it was. But the BCS also asked the *reasons* why some ethnic minority victims perceived racial motivation. Of these, the most common was that the incident had, in fact, been accompanied by racial abuse. The BCS authors concluded that Afro-Caribbeans in particular would not necessarily be 'less at risk of crime than similarly-placed whites if racially motivated offences were not counted' but acknowledged that 'it may be that in some incidents a racial element is an unfortunate, additional causal factor' (Mayhew et al., 1989: 49).

However, police and local government officers whom I had found most resistant to the notion of racial harassment typically rejected the possibility that incidents which could have happened to 'similarly-placed whites' might also be racially motivated. The more unsympathetic (and less guarded) had told me squarely that ethnic minorities 'had a chip on their shoulders' and 'thought everything that happened to them was because they were black'. As already noted, they were reinforced in these attitudes by recording guidelines which were themselves based on assumptions that incidents could be divided into those which were racial and those which were not. The wider implications (including the relevance of alternative approaches) are drawn out in the discussion which follows. But it is also worth considering some further, methodological issues highlighted by the BCS data set and its analysis which are relevant to that discussion.

Mayhew et al. (1989) presented the results for three main groups – whites, Afro-Caribbeans and Asians – because for most purposes the sample sizes of more disaggregated minority groups were too small to allow meaningful statistical analysis. Nevertheless, further analysis did succeed in identifying some statistically significant differences between sub-groups of Asians. This group is very heterogeneous. At one extreme, it comprises Indians who in socioeconomic terms, are not dissimilar to whites; and, at the other, it includes Pakistanis and Bangladeshis who occupy a still more disadvantaged position than Afro-Caribbeans. We found some evidence (contrary to our original hypothesis, FitzGerald and May, forthcoming) that it was the Indians who suffered higher rates of crime; but the Pakistanis and Bangladeshis were more likely to say that crime against them was racially motivated. This suggests, although it does nothing to explain, a pattern which is distinctive from that for whites, but one in which the most important distinction is that between ethnic minorities themselves.

There was, however, no scope for testing two further hypotheses. The survey did not ask whites whether they thought their own victimisation was racially motivated. So the results did not cover harassment of whites who were victimised because of their own ethnicity or that of people they associated with. Non-whites' perceptions of racial motivation, therefore, were presented in absolute rather than in relative terms. Further, a national sample survey of this type precludes refined comparisons between areas.[4] Yet other studies[5] suggest that local variations may have specific implications for ethnic minorities and, in particular, that those living in areas with sizeable populations of the same ethnic origin may have very different experiences – and, indeed, attitudes – from those who are more isolated.

Crime Statistics

The only national crime statistics that have an ethnic breakdown are those that (in their present form) have been collected on the prison population since 1985. Tables based on these are published in the annual prison statistics; but the only official commentary appeared in 1986 in a Home Office Statistical Bulletin. Since 1977, however, the Metropolitan Police has been collecting information on the ethnic origin of those it arrests and prosecutes. These figures have been used in the work of Home Office and academic researchers (Demuth 1978; Walker 1988, 1989; Willis, 1983) and have also been the subject of several Home Office Statistical Bulletins (1989a,b). But they were publicised most controversially in 1982 as the result of a press release from New Scotland Yard which highlighted the rise in reported offences of robbery and other violent theft between 1980 and 1981 and provided figures (based on victims' perception) apparently showing a dramatic over-involvement of Afro-Caribbeans in this type of crime.

The prison statistics and the Metropolitan Police data use slightly different forms of ethnic classification and neither is directly comparable with figures for the population at large, since the two main sources of this information up to the present (the 1981 census and the Labour Force Survey) also employ different ethnic categories. More reliable benchmark data on ethnic origin will soon be available from the 1991 census, although this uses categories which are different again.[6]

Notwithstanding these mismatches, the broad picture which emerges is very similar: Afro-Caribbeans are very significantly over-represented both in the Metropolitan Police figures and in the prison statistics relative to their presence in the population at large. Further, in the prison statistics, the over-representation is still greater for Afro-Caribbean women. The proportion of Asians in both data sets, however, appears to be broadly in line with their presence in the general population.

While some (including sections of the popular press) have readily taken the figures as proof of Afro-Caribbean 'criminality', others have taken them to indicate discrimination in the criminal justice system; and, indeed, have referred to 'double discrimination' against Afro-Caribbean women (Chigwada, 1989). Most serious commentators have looked at possible 'structural' explanations for these differences; that is (like the British Crime Survey reports) they have focused on demographic and socioeconomic factors which, when adequately taken into account, might suggest that the differences are *not* racial after all; or that their racial component is much lower than it at first appears. And several have speculated about a combination of such 'explanations' and the likely balance within it (FitzGerald, 1991; Jefferson, 1988; Reiner, 1989).

The data pose important and disturbing questions: most obviously why such a high proportion of Britain's Afro-Caribbean population is currently resident in its penal institutions; but they hardly begin to provide the answers. This is due to problems of interpreting the data which are partly conceptual and partly methodological. More specifically, these problems derive from:

1 the categories used;
2 the lack of information on variables which may be highly relevant; and
3 the fact that the variables which are covered are open to different interpretations.

There are three main problems with the categories used. The aggregation in the prison statistics of the 'West Indian, Guyanese and African' categories explains much of the apparently greater over-representation of Afro-Caribbean women. A relatively high proportion of the female prison population has been sentenced for drugs offences[7] and, of these – although precise figures are not available – a relatively high proportion appears to comprise foreign nationals who are due for deportation at the end of their sentence. The effect of the large number of African nationals in this group may be to inflate the figures for women of 'West Indian' origin to such an extent that they are not strictly comparable with those for men.

The second problem with the categories used relates to the 'Asian' group, which comprises 'Indians, Pakistanis and Bangladeshis'. Taken at this broad level of aggregation, the prison statistics suggest that, relative to their presence in the population at large, 'Asians' are not over-represented in criminal activity. This has lent itself not only to complacency about 'Asians' but has, thereby, tended to reinforce assumptions about culturally based Afro-Caribbean 'criminality'. (The implicit argument is that, if the figures reflected racial discrimination and/or racial disadvantage one would expect to find high crime rates amongst Asians also.) However, the figures mask the strong possibility of significant over-representation of Pakistanis and

Bangladeshis. The socioeconomic characteristics of this group are those which are highly correlated with offending; yet, as has already been noted, this is in marked contrast to the Indian group who greatly outnumber them in the population at large.[8]

Thirdly, the figures, as published, consign prisoners of 'mixed' origin to a miscellaneous 'other' category. Yet the experience of this group is potentially of considerable interest, not to say concern. Although still relatively small numerically, it is growing fast. In recent years it has become highly over-represented in the peak age group for offending and this trend looks set not only to continue but to escalate indefinitely. By 1988, for example, the Labour Force Survey showed that children of 'mixed' origins under the age of 15 already outnumbered Afro-Caribbeans; and in the under five age group, the ratio of 'mixed race' to Afro-Caribbean children was nearly 3:2. Moreover, these figures are known to underestimate the 'mixed' group (Shaw, 1986).

The lack of information on other relevant variables is fully acknowledged in the various Home Office Statistical Bulletins and the work of other authors such as Walker. The bulletin on the ethnic origin of prisoners, for example, includes an elaborate 'health warning', thus:

> It is important to appreciate the limited explanatory value of these statistics in providing conclusive evidence, both as regards the involvement of particular ethnic groups in crime and in relation to the practices of the courts. There are many stages between the commission of an offence and receipt into custody . . . and at every stage offenders may be diverted from custody . . . It is likely, therefore, that the breakdown by ethnic origin of persons received into custody may show a different pattern from that which would be seen at other stages in the system if similar breakdowns were available . . . There are a whole range of possible explanatory factors for disparities between different groups at the stage of reception to prison, but this study could only take account of the readily available data . . . Other possible explanatory factors on which no data are available centrally include socio-economic variables such as social class, education, employment status, social deprivation or disadvantage.
> (Home Office Statistical Bulletin, 1986: para 2)

Despite these limitations, relatively sophisticated statistical analyses are conducted using the variables for which information is available. In the instance cited, these may be described broadly as social (age, sex and area) and as legal (previous convictions and offence type). Further 'legal' variables (in particular court of trial and plea) are taken into account in other analyses (including those based on the Metropolitan Police figures). The effect of statistical techniques which take these into account is usually to reduce the apparently racial differences revealed by simple cross-tabulations and, often, to eliminate them completely.

Yet the significance of these 'legal' variables themselves is by no means unambiguous. Some, such as the use of cautioning, offence category, as well as type of disposal, are known to vary considerably from area to area. They overlap with others which may be strongly influenced by 'social' factors, including, again, cautioning practices and the decision to remand defendants in custody. And many, in turn, have a knock-on effect at subsequent stages in the criminal justice process. Thus, for example, if 'social' factors or local criminal justice cultures have disproportionately precluded certain first offenders from being cautioned, they may subsequently appear before the courts with disproportionately more previous convictions; and if they are more likely to be remanded in custody or to be charged with indictable-only offences this will increase their likelihood of a custodial disposal if they are found guilty.

The implications of this will be drawn out more fully in the discussion. For the present, however, it should be noted that the relevance of the 'social' and 'legal' factors referred to will vary for different groups for two main reasons. The first is simply that in important respects, including both their socioeconomic and their geographical distribution, the broad profile of ethnic minorities differs from that of whites. And the other is that the wide variations in criminal justice practice (both between areas and between individuals) derives from the considerable scope for discretion within the system. This provides commensurate scope for discrimination, whether benevolent (for example in the exercise of lenience and recognition of mitigating factors) or punitive (deciding instead to 'throw the book' at someone).

Discussion

Taken together, the problems highlighted by the three examples presented raise two broad sets of issues which are relevant to understanding questions of race and crime more widely. That is, their implications are both conceptual and methodological.

At the conceptual level, the examples appear to challenge a number of prevalent notions in political and academic discourse about what is racial. On the one hand, they show that the more other relevant factors are taken into account, the more one can whittle apparently racial differences into insignificance. On the other, they suggest that real world perceptions (and, indeed, experiences) of what is racial do not always fit comfortably into standardised boxes which are convenient for policy makers, practitioners and researchers.

This is not to suggest that attempts to establish the phenomenon should be abandoned. Rather, it is to argue strongly for a revision of the notion that there is a clear distinction between what is racial and what is not. The examples suggest that we need to expand our notion of what is racial, while recognising more explicitly that phenomena which are communal are not *de facto* exclusive. That is, what is racial, however generously defined, must be seen in a broader context.

It is important to begin by re-emphasising the fact that everyday usage of the term 'race' is very loose. The concept here is socially defined (Van den Berghe, 1984). It reflects the particular historical, political and economic circumstances which effectively 'racialise' particular groups by attaching racial labels to them, usually to their disadvantage. That is, racial differences are real primarily inasmuch as the perceived differences between groups result in differences in their experiences within particular societies; and these experiences, in turn, may result in differences in the groups' social, political and economic relationships with the society at large and with particular groups and institutions within it. They reflect the environments of the groups to which they are applied rather than qualities which are primordially and universally inherent in group members.

The term 'race' is loose also inasmuch as it is applied to a diverse range of ethnic groups, most commonly and pejoratively on the basis of their being non-white. Yet, even at this crude level of physical appearance, the groups already differ markedly from each other. Further, their cultural origins and histories are distinctive; and there are wide differences in both their current economic and geographical distribution. Most important of all is the fact that many of these differences are also socially recognised, not only between the minorities but also by the white majority.[9] That is, at everyday level, the primary (social) use of the term – which assumes a commonality of treatment and of self-perception based simply on the fact of not being 'white' – is of very limited value. It needs at least to distinguish between people of West Indian and of Indian subcontinental origin and, ideally, between a multiplicity of subdivisions within these.

Thus the examples given here demonstrate the need to recognise that what is conceived of as 'racial' may vary according to its external determinants. Local differences – for example, in political traditions (Husbands, 1983), in ethnic make-up, and even (in the context of our particular concerns) in charging and sentencing practices – suggest that there will be variations in the experience of racism from one area to another. In particular, it is important to recognise that changes *over time* in the context (that is, in social, political and economic circumstances) will inevitably also be reflected in changing manifestations of what is racial.

The effect of these variations in the context that determines what is racial is, in turn, compounded by variations among the groups to which racial labels are applied. The geographical distributions and socioeconomic characteristics of minority ethnic groups differ from those of whites; but they also differ from each other to the extent that some are more similar to whites than they are to other minority ethnic groups. And they are further stratified internally along the same lines as whites (such as class, gender and age), and in some instances by other divisions which are more ethnically specific (such as language and religion). The range of these cross-cutting and overlapping divisions – along with some of their implications – merits fuller discussion than is possible here; but they have been well rehearsed elsewhere, for example in Yinger (1986) and Wallman (1986).

But the variations between and within the range of 'racialised' minority ethnic groups cannot adequately be captured at a single historical moment. Just as the context which defines them changes over time, so too do the groups themselves. In ignoring this, much current thinking lends itself dangerously to reification. Again, there is insufficient space for a full discussion of the concept, which is developed more fully by Nanton (1989). Simply stated, by giving the concept of ethnicity concrete properties, this leads to an assumption that variations based on ethnicity can be captured in fixed and measurable units. In fact, ethnicity should not be conceived of as a *thing*, but rather as a dynamic *process*. Of its very nature, this implies changes over time both in the groups' adaptations to social, political, economic and cultural circumstances and in the relationships between them. One of the most striking illustrations of such changes is the fact that a 'mixed' group is now displacing the 'Afro-Caribbeans'. These may also experience discrimination; but it is likely that the precise forms and consequences of this discrimination may be as different again as they have been for other minorities.

These considerations suggest that the concept of what is 'racial' should retain the notion of what is exclusive to racialised minorities (that is, the direct consequence of discrimination) but must *also* comprise the following:

1 An understanding of racial disadvantage in its widest sense: one which is capable of drawing out the links with other groups who are not primarily conceived of in terms of their ethnicity but who share some of the same disadvantages.

2 A recognition of the different levels and forms of disadvantage experienced by different ethnic groups and by sub-groups within these.
3 A generous definition of which groups are vulnerable to racism: one which is sufficiently flexible not only to accommodate variations between areas and within sub-groups but also to pick up new groups as they emerge.
4 An understanding of indirect discrimination, especially of the ways in which disadvantages which are generic may be disproportionately experienced by ethnic minorities and, therefore, disproportionately affect their experience of crime and of the criminal justice process.

The conceptual implications of the examples presented are, in turn, strongly related to their practical implications for research methods in the field of criminology. Again, there is insufficient space to rehearse them fully; but they are explored here in outline within two broad themes. The first concerns the type of research which is best suited to capturing the phenomenon, to understanding the processes which generate it and to developing (and evaluating) appropriate interventions to correct unjustified bias in the criminal justice process. The second concerns more technical questions about the tools which are most appropriate, in particular to gathering and interpreting statistical data for this purpose.

If we are serious about capturing the phenomenon, understanding how it occurs and developing and evaluating appropriate interventions, we must start by looking sceptically at the privileged status currently given to quantitative research. For once we try to reduce the issue to a set of discrete, measurable components we have already lost its essence. What is racial (in the broad sense used here) is not only multifaceted, it arises and manifests itself differently in different places at different times for different groups (and, indeed, sub-groups of these groups). It is not a 'thing' of itself but is produced variously by a wide range of interactions between combinations of factors from within a very large set. The full range of factors will never come into play together; and what produces a racial result for one group in one situation at one time may comprise none of the elements which produce a racial result for another group in a different situation at another time or in a different place. In short, what is racial is much more than the sum of its component parts: it is the product of their various and complex interactions. This does not, of course, preclude trying to identify those component parts and to understand their interactions. Again, however, quantitative methods are of limited value. Neither task is initially suspectible to this type of approach, although at a second stage quantitative techniques can (in principle) play an essential verificatory role.

The pitfalls of starting from a quantitative approach are illustrated by the examples presented which show how, in various ways, we are missing the point by falling back on *a priori* assumptions to frame our analytical categories. Much of the information we have to draw on has, by default, been generated on the basis of received wisdom (not to mention political orthodoxy); for there has been little or no rigorous work to check whether these assumptions are relevant or sufficient for identifying, measuring and explaining inter-ethnic differences.

Thus, in the case of racial harassment, assumptions are made about who will be the victims and who will be the perpetrators; about what type of activity constitutes harassment; and about the significance of the numbers of reported cases. In the case of general victimisation, assumptions are made about the social and demographic factors which 'explain' different levels of victimisation and which, in turn, may 'explain away' apparent ethnic differences. Yet, far from demonstrating that the 'real' explanations are non-racial, the ways in which these factors *combine* to the detriment of ethnic minorities is essentially racial: that is, it represents that particular and disproportionate burden of general disadvantages which have classically been defined as 'racial disadvantage'.[10] And, finally, as has already been shown, the crime figures are interpreted in the light of two sets of factors (socio-demographic and 'legal') as though these were objective measures. Yet these variables are, of themselves, open to various interpretations; they are given different weight by different individuals and in different areas; and – not least for these reasons – they have very different implications for separate groups.

All of this suggests that there is a need for much more good quality, rigorous *qualitative* research in the field of race and crime. Such research must be prepared to challenge received wisdom where appropriate, whether this is the politically received wisdom (of the left or the right) or the academically received wisdom which works with paradigms which fail to reflect ethnic diversity. Its main function must be to frame appropriate research questions and to identify the range of variables which must be covered if research data are to be interpreted satisfactorily. By the same token, it is essential to shaping relevant and practical policy recommendations based on the findings of research. A wide range of qualitative techniques will be not only appropriate but also necessary to discover:

1 First-hand accounts of the experiences and perceptions of those on the receiving end of the criminal justice system.

2 First-hand accounts of the experiences and perceptions of the agents of the system.
3 Relevant features of the organisational context within which criminal justice decisions are made (in terms of both ethos and structures).
4 The influence of external social and political factors on the ways the criminal justice agencies operate; and the impact of their social environment on the perceptions of the different parties referred to.

Qualitative approaches will also be needed to be able to identify variations on these four axes across areas, within them and over time.[11]

It is within the framework of this type of qualitative work that quantitative approaches can, in principle, play a number of essential roles. Yet, even here, a number of practical limitations must be understood from the outset so that appropriate allowances may be made, whether in generating the data or in interpreting it. Two of the most important of these limitations relate to the ethnic categories available and the question of sample size.

The 1991 census asked a direct question on respondents' ethnic origin for the first time. To interpret ethnic differences in criminal justice data, it is essential to be able to make comparisons with national and (where appropriate) local data; and it is also important to be able to compare the representation of different ethnic groups at different points throughout the system. Any arguments that the census categories are inappropriate, therefore, are by now otiose: these categories are the basis for the most up-to-date, extensive and authoritative benchmark data which have yet been available; they will not alter for at least ten years; and, meanwhile, the Labour Force Survey, which provides useful (albeit limited) updates between censuses will be using the same categories as the census.

Yet the census categories cannot adequately represent the reality of ethnic identity as it is, on the one hand, experienced by individuals and, on the other, perceived by others. Nor did any of the range of classifications they must now replace. The census categories simply represent the outcome of the quest by the Office of Population Censuses and Surveys (Sillitoe, 1987) for a new, improved question which would be (a) susceptible of statistical analysis;[12] and (b) less unacceptable than any other to respondents at the time and in the necessarily artificial circumstances in which it is asked. Analysts and policy makers need to understand clearly, therefore, that categorical forms of 'ethnicity' can never be more than extremely crude approximations. If they fail to take this into account, the examples given in this chapter suggest that they will similarly fail to get to grips with the real issues and with the ways in which these, in turn, may vary.

The second set of practical limitations on quantitative approaches concerns sample size and the range of variables which needs to be accommodated. Given that non-white minority ethnic groups only make up about 5 per cent of the total population, sample surveys are unlikely to pick up sufficient numbers for useful analysis unless (a) their total sample is very large; (b) they are conducted in areas of high minority ethnic concentration; or (c) special measures are taken to over-sample minority respondents. Even the availability of large data sets such as the prison statistics, which cover whole populations, would not entirely overcome the practical difficulties. Despite the size and in-built over-representation of particular groups, absolute numbers in some cells might still be quite small. The problems of collecting the full range of variables which need to be taken into account, therefore, are related not only to the enormousness (and resource implications) of the task; there are so many that it is almost impossible to envisage an analysis which would not collapse under their full multivariate weight. For, ideally, the data would need to cover the following:

1 A sufficiently refined range of ethnic groups to distinguish not only between those of African, West Indian, Indian, Pakistani and Bangladeshi origin but also much smaller groups, such as the different refugee communities. It should, in turn, be able to distinguish between the immigrant and subsequent generations. And entries in the 'Black Other' and 'Other' categories would need to be coded and analysed to pick up those of different 'mixed' origins and the emergence of other, currently uncoded groups over time.

2 All relevant socioeconomic and demographic variables, including: age; sex; employment history over a meaningful period; family circumstances and background; area of residence and relevant characteristics thereof (including ethnic make-up); housing tenure; educational attainment and history; as well as other relevant personal factors such as medical and psychiatric history.

3 All relevant legal variables, such as: number and nature of previous convictions; area of arrest and trial; plea; type and quality of legal representation; court of trial (and reason); whether bail refused (and reasons); number and nature of charges; number (and ethnic origin) of co-defendants; factors cited in mitigation; and recommendations of social inquiry reports.

This shopping list is patently impractical and, at the same time, incomplete. As such, it demonstrates clearly that, even with more extensive statistical data across a wider range of criminal justice agencies, we could find ourselves with an ever more complex range of ethnic differences to explain and still with insufficient tools to set about the task.

The implications for quantitative methods, however, are not completely negative. They strongly reinforce the argument that such approaches need to be complemented (and, indeed, informed) by qualitative research; but they do not suggest that the latter can ever be a substitute for 'hard' data. For qualitative research itself has serious limitations. It can identify the problem in ways which statistics cannot; but it is incapable of demonstrating the scale of the problem and may ultimately prove less appropriate for systematically exploring its dimensions. And the bottom line of this, of course, is that 'hard' data make a more compelling claim on the attention of policy makers and on the resources they control, not least because they are replicable. That is, policy makers can, if necessary, obtain objective verification of the results of quantitative research before committing money to implementing recommendations based on them. Moreover, the research can, in turn, be replicated subsequently to quantify the effect of these interventions (a point which is taken up further below). Where findings are based on qualitative research, neither of these safeguards is available and policy makers, therefore, take much greater risks in choosing to act upon them.

As such, quantitative approaches might yet be used more effectively in a number of ways. The argument here implies that the available data should be extended both to cover a wider range of criminal justice decisions and to include as wide a range of relevant variables as is practicable. It also follows that statistics should be better contextualised. While their limitations should be acknowledged, their inconclusiveness can be overstated: tentative findings and questions raised which appear to merit further study can be reinforced by cross-referring to other relevant research findings, including those of qualitative research. In sum, quantitative approaches are essential but not sufficient. What is needed is 'triangulation'.[13]

In conclusion, it is worth considering whether quantitative approaches have failed to realise their potential in the field of race and criminal justice because their role has been misconceived. Instead, we might usefully understand the role of statistics in two ways.

The argument here has been that statistics have inappropriately been assumed to hold the key to identifying problems and the reasons for them. This has led (to confound Jefferson's original metaphor) to a wild goose chase: the answer is always just around the corner and perpetually hangs on technicalities such as one or more missing variables or the need for a larger sample. Cynics can all too easily interpret this as a pretext for inaction; for they rightly claim that there is extensive evidence from other areas of social policy that direct and indirect discrimination persist, along with the effects of racial disadvantage. It might, however, be more appropriate – as well as more profitable – to take as a premise that the criminal justice system is no more likely to be exempt from these problems than any other agency. That is, we should stop trying to reinvent the wheel by testing statistically for proof of discrimination. We should assume that of two possible working hypotheses, the hypothesis that there is discrimination (albeit unconscious, indirect and various in its manifestations) is much more plausible than its opposite. And, from this starting point, we can adopt a triangulated approach to test our hypothesis, using qualitative research, double-checked against both statistical data and the experience of other disciplines.

Following from this is a further, and perhaps more important, role for statistical approaches. A triangulated approach is essential for identifying the problem; and qualitative methods are likely to be most appropriate to understanding *how* the problem arises. These two processes establish a sound, empirically validated basis for changing policy and practice. It is also possible and, some would argue, necessary to make such changes on the basis of common-sense assumptions about what is wrong without waiting for the outcome of research. Where statistical approaches may come into their own is in evaluating the impact of changes in policy and practice, whether such changes are research-based or grounded in intuition (or politically driven). For, at its simplest – even in the absence of most other 'relevant' variables – if these interventions resulted in statistically significant changes in ethnic differences this would constitute a powerfully persuasive form of validation. And, by the same token, if they did not, there would be strong grounds for calling them into question.

Additionally, collecting statistical information to check whether the problem was being tackled effectively could offer an effective riposte to the cynics. For the figures currently on offer can only serve to substantiate the complaint of ethnic minorities that, although data have been collected on them for years, the problem of their over-representation in prisons has got steadily worse.

Acknowledgements

I am indebted to a number of people who looked at earlier drafts of this chapter. Even where I have ignored them – or failed to do them justice – I would like, in particular, to acknowledge the very helpful comments of Nigel Fielding and Mike Hough.

Notes

1 A study of the effectiveness of anti-discrimination legislation commissioned by the Home Office drew attention to the persistent failure to address issues of indirect discrimination (McCrudden et al., 1990).

2 The research, which resulted in the publication of the DoE's 'Guide to Good Practice' (1989) was based on in-depth studies of policy and practice to deal with racial harassment in six local housing authorities. I was the coordinator for the project and conducted three of the local studies.

3 It often seemed possible, however, that some incidents and disputes might have blown over or been resolved informally had the parties been of the same ethnic origin.

4 The area analysis used in the BCS was based on 11 classifications of types of neighbourhood (see Mayhew et al., 1989, Appendix G).

5 Thus surveys of political and other attitudes have shown important differences within the same ethnic groups according to whether they live in areas of high or low ethnic minority concentration. And both Smith (1983) and Walker et al. (1990) suggest that their experience of policing is also likely to be different.

6 The classification system used by the Metropolitan Police has employed five categories (White, Black, Asian, Other and Unrecorded) based on visual assessment. Labour Force Surveys have used self-classification based on ethnic origin and has presented results for nine groups (Indian, West Indian, Pakistani, Bangladeshi, African, Chinese, Arab, Mixed and Other), although these are sometimes aggregated. The census is based primarily on a nine-fold classification (White, Black Afro-Caribbean, Black African, Black Other, Indian, Pakistani, Bangladeshi, Chinese and Other).

7 In June 1990, persons convicted of drugs offences accounted for 10 per cent of adult male prisoners but 28 per cent of adult female prisoners. The proportion of women had risen from 22 per cent in 1986.

8 In 1987–89, Indians comprised 30 per cent of the non-white ethnic minority population. The figure for Pakistanis and Bangladeshis combined was 21 per cent.

9 Thus, for example, different stereotypes are held of different groups. And the British Social Attitudes Surveys (Jowell and Witherspoon, 1985) have shown different levels of prejudice against Asians and Afro-Caribbeans.

10 Classically, the Home Affairs Select Committee report of 1981 defined racial disadvantage as: 'a particular case of relative disadvantage within society. With the exception of racial discrimination, the disadvantages suffered by Britain's ethnic minorities are shared in varying degrees by the rest of the community. Bad housing, unemployment, educational underachievement, a deprived physical environment, social tensions – none of these are the exclusive preserve of ethnic minorities. But the ethnic minorities suffer such disadvantages more than the rest of the population, and more than they would if they were white' (Home Affairs Select Committee, 1981: x, para 12).

11 This does not necessarily imply waiting for longitudinal data. Some inferences might already usefully be drawn from intergenerational differences revealed in large data sets such as the census.

12 Ease of statistical analysis has required categories to be mutually exclusive. One

consequence has been that the 'mixed' group was not included in the 1991 census and is to be dropped from the Labour Force Survey.

13 Bulmer (1984: 32) describes triangulation as 'the combination of two or more different research strategies in the study of the same empirical units'.

4

Race Issues in Research on Psychiatry and Criminology

Deryck Browne

To tease out the complex web of issues involved in both the psychiatric and criminal justice systems is an arduous task. To do so with the added factor of focusing specifically on race issues within these two broader constructs is extremely difficult. This is not because race itself is an issue of great complexity: racism is for the most part about power and oppression and is easily understood, particularly by those who suffer it. It is because those very powerful institutions (the psychiatric and criminal justice systems) have developed, grown and adapted in ways which are automatically designed to buttress them against criticism from without and to withstand even the most qualified calls for change and progress.

In Britain, these institutions have grown up in a regimen which dictated that white was correct and supreme and things black at best questionable. In short, it is impossible to examine the performance of any large established institution in Britain without at least appreciating its historical context. For example, it would be pointless to attempt any examination of British (or western) psychiatry without appreciating that for several hundred years psychological sanction was given to the enslavement and captivity of all people of African descent.

These racist philosophies were in turn given the full sanction of the penal code. Have these institutions changed, and how much? Do they provide an equitable service for black[1] people? Researchers have attempted to answer these questions with varying degrees of success, partly determined by factors that stand outside the researchers' control: mundane factors such as lack of ethnic monitoring, uncoordinated record keeping and the cooperation of the agency or the system under investigation. These factors in themselves partly answer the question for us. The obvious difficulty here is that those research subjects that open their arms to investigation are usually those who have least to hide, lose or fear. What is clear is that for any researcher simply to 'pitch in' to any study concerned with race and the fields of criminology and/or psychiatry/psychology without considering the historical context is, of itself, methodologically unsound, as this is bound to lead to distortions.

Previous research illustrates the fact that black people's experience of psychiatry in Britain is largely a negative one. In 1981 it was found, in a study focusing on southern England, that the number of first admissions for schizophrenia among black people was more than three times the norm (Dean, 1981). A study carried out in northern England concluded that people born in the 'New Commonwealth' were up to four times more likely than white people to reach the psychiatric services either through police involvement or via that of a mental welfare officer (Hitch and Clegg, 1980). And Littlewood and Lipsedge (1979) found that black patients were at least twice as likely to have been formally admitted under the Mental Health Act 1959 as any equivalent white group. It has also been shown that in one inner-city locality the young (16–29 years) migrant Afro-Caribbean admission rate under Part II of the Mental Health Act 1983 was 17 times that of whites (while the British born Afro-Caribbean rate was about half that of their migrant counterparts). Also, under Part III of the Act (that which concerns patients involved in criminal proceedings), it was found that young British born Afro-Caribbeans were detained at four times the white rate. Young migrant Afro-Caribbeans registered at 25 times the rate of young whites (Cope, 1989). Evidence also points to black patients receiving increased doses of medication and being controlled with greater levels of physical restraint than other (white) patients. One need only examine the incidence of black deaths in institutions such as Broadmoor Special Hospital to realise this.

It is necessary to place these findings in some historical context because it is only here that it makes any (if tragic) sense. During the period of slavery in which Europeans made captives of African peoples for some four centuries, a European psychology set about dehumanising Africans; thus eradicating the need for Europeans consciously to contemplate the damage they were inflicting. For example 'Drapetomania' was conceived, a category of 'mental illness' whereby any captive African who attempted to flee was diagnosed as mentally ill, the rationale being that to flee such a 'benign' institution must surely be a sign of some mental instability. The economic utility of the availability of this psychiatric designation will be readily appreciated.

In the 1930s Jung expounded on the cultural pollution of Europeans as a result of the influence of jazz music; and Carothers in *The African Mind in Health and Disease* (1953) maintained that African peoples were not capable of experiencing depression. We must ask ourselves how far things have moved on from this depiction when current research findings tell us that black people are less likely to receive therapeutic forms of treatment for mental health problems, such as psychotherapy and counselling, and more likely to receive (increased levels of) medication in secure settings.

It seems that the various agencies active in the public and social domain, such as the education system, social services and health care, are as efficient, if not more so, in controlling or policing the lives of black people as is the police force proper. The role of the police, courts and indeed the whole criminal justice system is of prime importance here also, as all of these agencies can (and do) induct black people into psychiatric 'careers'. Certainly the work of these agencies, the processes involved, the procedures used and the decisions arrived at (and the criteria used) are of paramount importance to the black community, and as such are worthy of investigation and research. The key factor here remains what type of research needs to be done and what kind of methods employed.

Previous Research on Race and Psychiatry

Research carried out over previous decades in the field of criminology has illustrated the fact that black people's experience of the criminal justice system is certainly more of a negative one than that experienced by their white counterparts (see Chapters 1 and 2). Much of the research that has been carried out in the field of psychiatry and black people's experience in Britain has endeavoured to illustrate that there is black over-representation among patients in psychiatric hospitals (or coming to psychiatry). Detailed studies have shown that most of these hospital admissions are accompanied by diagnoses of serious mental illness or schizophrenia.

The reasons given for these abnormal phenomena are contentious and interesting. It was initially conjectured that supposed higher rates of mental illness among black people were a consequence of the migration process. The argument was that either there is something about the type of people who choose to migrate that makes them susceptible to mental illness, or something about the process itself. (This argument was not confined to black immigrants to Britain; it had been used with regard to differing groups of migrants to various countries.) However, subsequent studies had to abandon this theory when it became clear that second generation black people in Britain were being admitted to psychiatric institutions at a rate as high as the first, and sometimes higher: ethnicity now replaced place of birth as the key variable in relevant studies.

Subsequent works claimed that the cause of black over-representation lay in genetics, adverse reactions to white racism or some culture dichotomy between black patient and white practitioner. But what all of these theories seemed to have in common was that they were based upon the assumption that there existed an ethnic vulnerability to mental illness and that this was separate from either the quality of the professional service that was on offer or, to a lesser extent, institutional process. Examples of this type of research can be found if one examines the literature of the early to mid-1970s.

Bagley (1975) provided an overall view of the adjustment of West Indians to society in Britain. He argued that stress factors contributed to the 'apparently' higher rates of mental illness among black people, and that limited opportunities for advancement (caused by racism) were major causes of stress. Bagley also discussed problems of adjustment that West Indian immigrant children and adolescents might face within the education system. He pointed to the higher rate of behavioural deviance found in this group than in native children. Indeed, this is the subject of a further study involving Bagley (Rutter et al., 1974). In this research educational disadvantage and racial discrimination are identified as stress factors producing behavioural problems in West Indian children at school which are *not* found in the same group within the family home. Milner (1971) discusses the nature and implication of problems of identity in minority group children in Britain. It is argued that racial prejudice and discrimination produce stress which may in turn lead to black children rejecting their own racial group and identifying with the white group. The confused sense of identity which can result, it is agreed, can lead to types of behaviour associated with juvenile delinquency. In a study of juvenile delinquency among Asians, Batta et al. (1975) focused on the identity confusion of children of mixed Asian and British parentage. These children, it is contended, feel alienated from both British and Asian cultures and consequently form a 'high risk' group.

These studies would appear to be typical of their day; answers were being sought to extremely pertinent questions, but the basic premise that black people were somehow more deviant, in whatever respect, was not really questioned. Solutions were merely sought to explain 'why'. The gap, in terms of research, at this stage is obvious. What was needed was some method of investigation which interrogated those systems and the professionals making key and far-reaching decisions on and about black people. Although we are here primarily concerned with mental health, this would also involve schooling and the education system, policing, the courts, the whole criminal justice system and other areas of health care and social services. The reason for this is because they can all, at various junctures, feed into the mental health or psychiatric system. How this happens is equally important but it is not within the remit of this chapter to map out.

Research from the mid-1980s to the Present

In the main, studies carried out in the late 1980s and (to date) in the 1990s have been considerably more far reaching than their fore-runners, though this is not to say that all of the relevant questions have been addressed. Studies have continued to focus on the over-representation of black people within the psychiatric system; some have made capital out of this factor alone, while others have sought to explore the phenomena behind this and question the process at work.

The process of compulsory admission to psychiatric units has been given considerable attention, for it is here that perhaps the most blatant example of the disservice rendered to black people by the statutory services lies. Typically, Section 136 and the possible abuse of this by the police has been contentious. Dunn and Fahy (1990) looked into this: between October 1983 and December 1985, 268 patients were brought in by police to a psychiatric hospital in South London. Comparisons were made between black and white people on several clinical and demographic variables and it was found that, while the vast majority of admissions received a psychiatric diagnosis, an excess of black admissions was recorded, black men were younger, more likely than whites to be given neuroleptic drugs, and more likely to be put on compulsory orders. Also, black men were more likely to receive a case note diagnosis of schizophrenia or drug-induced psychosis. It was found that the differences in clinical management between ethnic groups could, at least partially, be accounted for by these differences in diagnoses.

Pipe et al. (1991) also examined the use of Section 136: social, demographic and clinical information was collected retrospectively on all 99 people referred to a South London hospital in 1986 under this section. Afro-Caribbeans were over-represented (largely young men under 30 years). Also black people, it was found, were more likely to be perceived as threatening, incoherent and disturbed, although less clearly diagnosed with a mental illness.

Various other studies have attempted to examine the phenomenon of the abnormal rate of black admissions to psychiatric units. Harrison et al. (1988) conducted a prospective study examining all patients of Afro-Caribbean origin with a first onset psychosis presenting to the psychiatric services from a defined catchment area in Nottingham. Utilising several diagnostic classifications, rates for schizophrenia were found to be substantially increased in the

Afro-Caribbean community, and especially in the second generation British born.

McGovern and Cope (1991) looked at young Afro-Caribbeans and whites diagnosed as suffering from schizophrenia upon first admission. It was found that Afro-Caribbeans, as well as being over-represented, were more likely to be admitted compulsorily, especially on forensic orders. They were less likely to make and maintain voluntary contact with the services. There appears to be little difference in the physical treatment given to both groups, but the Afro-Caribbean group was more likely to be readmitted in subsequent years and one-third of the Afro-Caribbean males were treated at some time in forensic units.

In an earlier study, Cope and Ndegwa (1990) compared white and Afro-Caribbean patients admitted to a Regional Secure Unit on a number of psychiatric and forensic variables. Afro-Caribbean patients were admitted in numbers greatly in excess of their representation in the local population, and were significantly more likely to be referred from the prison system while on remand; in contrast, white patients were more often admitted from NHS and Special Hospitals. Significantly, more Afro-Caribbeans than whites were socially isolated, had a previous criminal history and a history of previous compulsory admission. They were also significantly more likely to be diagnosed as schizophrenic and to require transfer while on remand in custody for urgent psychiatric treatment. Also, a larger number of black patients received restriction orders. The possible reasons for these findings are considered by the authors; they also discuss the prison system, the association between psychiatric illness and arrest and the role of the local psychiatric and the forensic psychiatric services.

In a 1991 study Moodley and Perkins examined the pathways to psychiatric inpatient care in an inner London borough. Data were collected from a series of 52 consecutive admissions of adults to the psychiatric wards serving the area. The most striking feature of the results was the variety of routes taken to inpatient care, combined with a high level of police involvement (23.1 per cent of admissions) and low referral from general practitioners (GPs). There were no significant differences found in the routes taken by Afro-Caribbean and white people or by men and women. But higher proportions of Afro-Caribbeans received a diagnosis of schizophrenia; higher proportions of Afro-Caribbeans considered themselves to have nothing wrong with them but were compulsorily detained. Interestingly, higher proportions of whites were diagnosed as depressed and considered themselves to have physical problems rather than psychiatric ones. However, results clearly indicated that it was ethnic status rather than diagnostic category that accounted for the higher rates of compulsory detention of Afro-Caribbean people. The study also considered the implications of the findings for service development and delivery.

Various studies conducted during the 1980s appeared to show that class was perhaps as important a variable as race. Harrison et al. (1984a) examined the distribution of inpatient psychiatric admissions throughout the city of Bristol during the period 1979–81. High rates were found from central urban areas of low social class and areas with a high immigrant population. The findings suggest that 'immigrant' groups (mainly of West Indian origin) are no more likely than others living in the city centre to become psychiatric hospital inpatients. But, significantly, this group was found to require compulsory admission more regularly than other groups. In a follow-up study, Harrison et al. (1984b) compared three groups of patients (from populations with markedly different rates of compulsory psychiatric admissions) on a range of social and clinical data. West Indian and white patients from inner-city areas differed in many respects but they were both more likely than other patients to be referred to the psychiatric services through the police, with little GP involvement, and were often admitted from public places following disturbed behaviour. However, levels of violence and threatening behaviour were no higher among inner-city patients of either colour, and once admitted these groups showed similar treatment compliance to white patients who had been admitted compulsorily from suburban areas.

Lack of GP involvement in black admissions was nothing new. In 1980 Rwegellera examined the differential use of the psychiatric services by West Indians, West Africans and the English population: 290 West Indians and 73 West African patients were identified and matched against 204 and 53 English (white) patients respectively. Results showed that significantly more 'migrant' patients were *not* referred to hospitals by their GPs, also that more of this group showed disturbed behaviour prior to psychiatric contact and that more were admitted to hospital compulsorily.

The above studies are typical of the types of research that have been carried out in the field of race and psychiatry during the past decade. Sometimes, the results are conflicting but this is to be expected in independent research with all its attendant vagaries. But unanimously, these studies (and there are many more) are saying that something is going seriously wrong for black people in the relationship with the psychiatric services. This itself is a source of some consternation for the black community which, justifiably, sees itself as somewhat over-researched. This annoyance might not be so great if the main thrust of the bulk of the research being conducted was aimed at practical solutions as opposed to highlighting or even sensationalising what might be termed 'recognised problems'.

Research into Race and Psychiatric Remands

The author conducted a small-scale study into race and psychiatric remands in an inner-city location (Browne, 1990)[2]. The aims of the research were threefold:

1 To investigate the extent to which black people were remanded for psychiatric reports when appearing before magistrates.
2 To enquire into the nature and outcome of these psychiatric remands.
3 And to consider the implications for the provision of services to black people who have passed through the remand process.

These broad objectives point to a basic problem with many research briefs (involving race issues and otherwise) – that is, to attempt to cover a very wide spectrum in limited time. Certainly, in hindsight, the brief for this project was sufficiently broad to discourage study of any depth, given that the time scale was one year. It would be unrealistic to expect research to be immune from the restraints and constraints of the market place and there is an inevitable tendency for researchers and consultants perhaps to promise more in terms of delivery than the competition. One would only hope that quality would win over quantity every time. But it is perhaps not as cut and dried as this. Perhaps it is the case that larger organisations with more resources at their disposal, more of the right kind of 'contacts' with funding bodies, and almost exclusively white run, will win out in bids over the smaller community-based voluntary sector agencies, often black, who will continue to get the crumbs of, say, local authority joint finance revenue to 'tell us your problems' in small-scale, short-term and ill-funded feasibility and research studies.

One way to restrict the scope of work involved is to do so geographically. This was done in this instance by focusing upon a research area that quite neatly comprised a microcosm of the wider construct of the psychiatric services and the criminal justice system (i.e. local magistrates court, established statutory and voluntary sector psychiatric and mental health services, local prison) as well as a long-established local black community. Clearly, all research must define its boundaries geographically, methodologically and with regard to objectives, but curiously therein lies a further problem: no matter what the arguments for a specific focus there will always be claims from some quarters that, as a result of limited geographical focus, it is invalid to draw general conclusions or that conclusions drawn are invalidated due to a lack of comparative work. These are general problems which a study covering any topic might come up against. The study *Black People, Mental Health and the Courts* did, however, present certain other problems and research considerations which merit discussion.

Access to the local magistrates court was initially granted, thus giving access to court registers disclosing certain limited information on all recent (past five years) cases coming before this court. One year's records were initially manually examined (approximately 38,000 cases) and those which magistrates had logged as remanded for psychiatric assessment were extracted and investigated in greater detail. This process was extremely time consuming but was effectively the only way to proceed: there existed no computerised archive of case details. Apart from the time spent examining thousands of individual cases a further concern was that this retrospective look at one year's cases, despite the thoroughness with which it was conducted, would possibly 'miss' some relevant cases and thus lead to an undercount of the actual number of psychiatric remands. This was a result of the varying methods by which psychiatric remands might be requested and the methods by which this was (or in some cases was not) recorded by magistrates: 'Private' psychiatric reports which were arranged by defence lawyers during the course of an ordinary (non-psychiatric) remand may not have even been presented when the case returned to court. This will largely have depended on how useful to their clients' defence lawyers deemed them to be. And even when 'private' assessments were used by the defence it is likely that this factor will have gone unrecorded as the initial remand was not for that specific purpose. Thus this particular study will not have picked up any such cases. Although this factor will have led to a reduced sample, it was considered important to document the lack of record keeping and explain in the text of the report the effect that this had on the study.

A further problem arose when researchers were confronted by the fact that magistrates had varying methods of recording the same information. Thus a remand for psychiatric assessment on a defendant might be logged in the court register as 'remand for reports', 'remand for medical reports', 'remand for mental and medical reports' etc. As a result any entry that could possibly have constituted or included a remand for psychiatric purposes was investigated and the irrelevant cases not followed through when positive proof was gained that there was no psychiatric involvement.

Although the above processes took up a good deal of research time (perhaps half of the time allocated to field work), the main obstacle was yet to come, in that none of the cases (eventually 70) extracted for the study was identified by race at the court stage. It was obviously crucial that ethnicity was identifiable as the trends around the treatment of black remandees was the crux of the study.

In order to gather some breakdown of race it was decided to investigate three possible sources of information. Defendants were followed through to:

1 the prison establishment to which they had been remanded;
2 the local psychiatric hospital where they had invariably been assessed if remanded on bail;
3 the probation office that had handled their case.

This was not a foolproof method. The only agency of the three which systematically monitored race was the local male remand prison. Prison records eventually yielded information on 16 members of the sample of 70. A further 24 were traced to the local psychiatric hospital where sporadic ethnic monitoring ensured that approximately half of these were assigned some racial classification. The majority of the 70 remained 'unknown', but probation was able to supply information which eventually led to 52 defendants in total being assigned some racial classification.

Because of the diversity of sources of information about race and the largely random method of monitoring used by most agencies involved, it was decided to keep ethnic classifications broad and assign individuals to relevant categories. The classifications used were simply Black, Asian and white. The breakdown achieved is shown in Table 4.1. For the purposes of the study the term 'Black' was used for anybody of African origin whether or not they happened to be born on that continent, in the Caribbean or in Britain.

Table 4.1 *Incidence of requests for psychiatric assessments of defendants by race*

	No.	%
Black	23	33
White	27	39
Asian	2	3
Not known	18	25
Total	70	100

The issue of ethnic classifications and which to use is often a vexing one, but also one which has been used to detract from the negative experiences of black people at the hands of large institutions. This has been possible because the continuing debate about which classifications are politically correct can often stand in the way of using any classifications at all; and, furthermore, when the 'correct' classifications are deduced it is most unlikely that these will dovetail with the often broad-based classifications used by long-established institutions. The politically 'right-on' researcher thus has a problem. Does he or she use crude classifications which mirror those used in the investigated agency's monitoring system, or a more sophisticated system that does not? The answer must lie with the researcher and an assessment of what he or she is trying to investigate.

In an investigation of psychiatric hospital records, the author found the method of ethnic monitoring in a particular hospital extremely haphazard, often being recorded in some shape or form in doctors' or nurses' medical notes, or sometimes on a partly filled in ethnic monitoring form. As I wanted to achieve a detailed examination of what was happening to particular ethnic groups, and also those born in Britain and those born abroad, I posed a four-tiered race question on the pro forma designed to gather information. I asked for race (black, white, Asian and other); ethnicity (African, Caribbean, Indian, Bangladeshi, Irish etc.) and place of birth (Africa, Caribbean, Ireland, Cyprus etc.). I also included a question on whether or not refugee status applied to the individual. Unravelling medical notes proved a time-consuming exercise, but generally a good deal of this information was available in a high incidence of cases. It was not thought that there was a large margin of error as researchers were working with factual information often stated only too clearly by doctors. None the less it must be remembered that this information was *as recorded* by medical personnel. There was more than one instance of conflicting information in the notes. One woman, for example was described as 'Mauritian' in one set of medical notes and 'Indian' in another. Cross-reference information eventually proved her true ethnicity.

Face-to-face interviews (semi-structured) were also carried out with criminal justice personnel as part of the research for *Black People, Mental Health and the Courts* (Browne, 1990). There are general rules which apply to these: they are generally time consuming, but they do yield a high response rate (as opposed to questionnaire type methods). The general drawback is that they may lead to unstandardised questioning which may limit the comparisons that can be made across responses. In the area of race issues a further complication lies: the race of the interviewer might significantly affect the response that the interviewee gives. Resources allocated to the study in question did not allow for variation of interviewers to attempt to minimise participant bias. Thus one black researcher carried out all interviews. A strongly asserted neutral stance and assurances of confidentiality with regard to personal identification allowed fairly good quality information to be gathered on what for many of the personnel involved (magistrates, psychiatrists, court clerks, probations officers) was a 'sensitive' issue. For example, one magistrate felt able to say 'It's an Afro-Caribbean trait perhaps to laugh and smile and they're not meaning it's all a great big joke', thus declaring his own employment of stereotypical images.

It is arguable that any research which wants to investigate the true impact of race on decision-making must not reveal its objective to the respondent and any racial trends should be recorded alongside other variables, such as lack of accommodation, previous criminal record etc. This, of course, is valid but may yield little information on the actual topic you are interested in (i.e. race) while supplying lots of useful but possibly irrelevant information. The strength of the method employed in the study in question was that, by setting out the issues for discussion, where personnel were willing to speak frankly this yielded much good quality information. The obvious drawback of this method was that it was dependent on the frankness of respondents.

The same issues were raised for NACRO in work carried out by the Mental Health unit. In the work of the 'Diversion Project' (a Home Office/Mental Health Foundation funded initiative to develop methods whereby mentally disturbed offenders might be diverted from the criminal justice system to health and social services settings) interviews were carried out with personnel in the relevant agencies across three areas. A different development officer was assigned to each area. Responses to questions on race and equality of opportunity for the one black development officer were significantly less informative than those recorded by his two white colleagues. (This was not further tested; so it is possible, though perhaps unlikely, that practitioners from this particular locality were generally reluctant to discuss this issue. A very high degree of all practitioners interviewed were white.)

In a sense what appears to be the most telling account of the ways in which race influences the decisions of professionals comes not from their own reports, but from the account of the (black) people about whom these decisions are made, for it is here and only here that we will begin to understand the nature of racist practice – in the very violent effect it has upon ordinary people's lives. The case studies in *Black People, Mental Health and the Courts* (Browne,

1990) were culled from court archives, but they still provided the most convincing accounts of the negative experiences of black people caught in the coils of these systems.

In further work carried out on the impact of race on the procedure used on people on compulsory civil sections of the Mental Health Act, 1983, individuals were largely left to provide (with the assistance, if desired, of group work leaders) their own accounts, and these tell similarly violent, moving accounts of the injustice they have experienced and give good insight into the nuances of decision-making and procedure and the ways in which these can adversely affect people.

Conclusion

There are innumerable methods by which research on race, criminal justice and psychiatry can be carried out. It is, of course, vital that the methods used are adapted to suit the research question and not vice versa. Whatever the methods it is crucial that any work is placed within its true historical context so that issues are not examined in a vacuum, that ethnic classifications used are sufficiently sophisticated to provide the detailed information required and that sufficient store is placed on the account of black people themselves, whether these be the professionals or the client/user groups.

Notes

1 In this chapter the term 'black' is used to refer to people of African origin whether born on that continent, in the Caribbean or in Britain. Where studies referred to have described findings with reference to other terms (e.g. Afro-Caribbean or West Indian) then I have used these terms.

2 This was a NACRO initiative supported by the Afro-Caribbean Mental Health Association and the Commission for Racial Equality.

5
Approaching the Topic of Racism: Transferable Research Strategies?

Loraine Gelsthorpe

> They behave this way not because I'm black but because they are white.
>
> (Alice Walker, *Possessing the Secret of Joy*)

Any white researcher approaching the topic of racism or racial discrimination I suspect does so with a degree of trepidation and anxiety, for neither the terms and boundaries nor strategies and politics are clear. My intention in this chapter is to reflect on some of my own experiences in researching race and gender issues in the preparation and presentation of social inquiry reports.[1] Indeed, it is to tell you something of the story of my attempt to study such issues. But the chapter is also informed more generally by previous research on women and girls in criminology and in the criminal justice system when at one point I joined the pressing trail on the search for sexism. Some reflections along that particular journey, which encouraged the realisation that sexism is a complicated concept which requires considerable theoretical and methodological sophistication, subsequently led me to take a different route and a route which has some relevance for doing research on racism. What is offered here, however, is not so much a route map and a set of prescriptions, as a few signposts, cautions and encouragements. No hard and fast rules for conducting research in this area can be provided.

Race and Gender Issues in the Preparation and Presentation of SIRs

Social inquiry reports have frequently provided a focus for analysis. They have been approached in a number of different ways: in a historical perspective (McWilliams, 1986; White, 1978); in terms of their use by different criminal justice system and allied agencies (Shaw, 1982); the ideological views of the writer (Hardiker, 1975); the recommendations in reports in relation to the outcome (Hine et al., 1978); their content (Godson and McConnell, 1989; Perry, 1974) and their language and style (Horsley, 1984). Bottoms and Stelman (1988) have usefully added another dimension by considering differing theoretical rationales.

In contrast, there has been relatively little work which has focused exclusively on race and gender issues in reports and report writing, though the research that has been carried out is deserving of our attention. (For race issues, for example, we might turn to Hudson, 1989b; Mair, 1986; Pinder, 1984a; Shallice and Gordon, 1990; Waters, 1990; Whitehouse, 1983. For gender issues, see Allen, 1987; Eaton, 1986; Jackson and Smith, 1987; Mair and Brockington, 1988; Worrall, 1990.) Needless to say, this is not an exhaustive list of research, merely an indication of the rich sources of data that exist. But the research is complicated, not least by the very different research methodologies employed and by the fact that researchers have started from very different vantage points: some from involvement in writing reports as practitioners, some from large-scale empirical data sets and some from ethnographic research, for example. The research which I describe in this chapter, therefore, was conceived and carried out against a background of general research on reports, and race and gender issues in relation to reports, which has produced very mixed conclusions. Some studies pointed to discrimination, others were equivocal on this point.

There were six main objectives in the research which I carried out between 1989 and 1991:[2]

1 To examine whether or not the content of social inquiry reports (SIRs) differed according to ethnicity and gender considerations.
2 To assess whether or not there were any gender or ethnic related differences in the recommendations made in SIRs.
3 To assess whether or not there were differences across gender and ethnicity in the sentencing by magistrates, particularly when considered in relation to SIR recommendations.
4 To examine whether or not there was variation between probation officers in terms of the role that race and gender might play in the preparation of an SIR and its recommendation.
5 To explore magistrates' perceptions and use of SIRs and to consider whether or not their concerns and questions cut across race and gender considerations.
6 To consider what impact, if any, gatekeeping procedures had on the preparation and interpretation of SIRs.

From the outset, then, the research was designed to include both quantitative and qualitative components. It involved three probation areas in England and Wales (two areas in the first instance), analysis of 1,152 reports (in terms of overall content and recommendation in relation to sentences achieved), a more detailed content analysis of 128 reports and 71 interviews (37 with probation officers and 34 with magistrates, split between two of the areas involved in the study). If there was a model for the research it was that of George Mair (1986) whose study was based on 1,173 cases in the areas of Leeds and Bradford. While this research is generally hailed as empirically sound (with its analysis of report recommendations and sentences achieved in the courtroom), it is recognised that the low proportion of cases from ethnic minority groups meant that any conclusions drawn may be rather tenuous. The aim of the current study was to remedy some of the deficiencies in this respect.

As I became engaged on the research after the study had started, my preparation time was relatively brief. The main problems that I was faced with in the first weeks concerned (a) a lack of data, especially on women, and (b) problems in persuading probation service personnel to participate in the research by completing questionnaires on the ethnicity of offenders. Problems in the first category were largely overcome by extending the research to include a third area and by extending the data collection periods. The second area of difficulty was more problematic and perhaps never satisfactorily resolved. In a sense, this was the starting point for the story of this research and, more particularly, ultimately confirmed my strong suspicions that the research was complex, and that racism and racial discrimination, like sexism and sex discrimination, cannot be neatly packaged in categories and picked off the pages.

In 1990, Simon Holdaway and Janet Allaker reported that over 75 per cent of all probation services (42 out of 56) claimed that they monitored the ethnic origin of people for whom a social inquiry report was prepared. A further eight services at that time claimed that they had plans to set up some sort of monitoring. Broadly speaking, Holdaway and Allaker found that there were five different systems of ethnic classification in use in different areas. Eleven areas were using direct or slightly modified versions of the Commissions for Racial Equality recommended classification scheme (i.e. the Office of Population Censuses and Surveys General Register classification scheme which contains 9 categories of ethnicity: White, Black Afro-Caribbean, Black African, Black Other, Indian, Pakistani, Bangladeshi, Chinese and Other ethnic group). A further 10 areas employed a similar classification but produced a four-fold as opposed to a nine-fold system. Other services had larger classification schemes, developed to accommodate local population groups. In two areas the categories used were simply Black and White. Until January 1991, therefore, when the Home Office announced that ethnic monitoring would be required throughout the probation service, following a commitment from the Home Office and Lord Chancellor's Department to a policy of racial equality and to the elimination of racial discrimination (Home Office, 1992b), there was no common system of classification. Such variation was clearly borne out by the data collected as part of this study.[3]

In area A, my predecessor arranged for the probation service to record ethnic category on a revised monitoring form from which details of offenders could be abstracted. The probation service had for some time recorded whether or not clients were Black, White or Other (giving scope for specification within this latter category). In the preliminary stages of the research, following extensive discussions with senior probation officers and a service race monitoring committee, the codes of Afro-Caribbean, Indian, Bangladeshi, Pakistani, Irish and White European were added. In area B, the probation service routinely completed an elaborate monitoring form on clients – devised within their own service – and I gathered that ethnicity was recorded by probation officers for every client. The data collection period, however, October 1989 to March 1990, saw a slight change in their monitoring codes: before January 1990 – Black Afro-Caribbean, Black Asian, White and Other (to be specified); after January 1990 – Black Afro-Caribbean, Black Asian, Black Other, White European, White Other and Other.

In area C the prescribed codes were Black, White and Other. The recording of ethnicity was not a routine matter in this probation service and, although the codes were formally agreed for the purposes of the research (in theory the information was to be collected by probation officers in consultation with their clients), in practice very little information was collected by the service and I resorted to contacting clients individually by letter to ask if they would mind indicating how they saw themselves in terms of ethnicity so that I could examine whether or not there was any discrimination in report-writing practices or indeed in sentencing. I sent out some 86 letters in this way indicating the codes of Black, White and Other, but encouraging participants to specify how they saw themselves in terms of ethnicity. I received 62 responses to my letter.

This is a long but necessary introduction to some of my reflections. The task of dealing with ethnic categorisation was, at the time, a lengthy, thought-provoking and painful experience and one which changed my approach to the research. Unwittingly, I found myself embroiled in continuing disputes between the Home Office, National Association of Probation Officers (NAPO) representatives and black probation officers (some of whom were members of the Association of Black Probation officers) about the role and importance of ethnic monitoring by researchers and practitioners. In the course of negotiations and discussions with probation researchers and practitioners I was variously charged with being a 'Home Office lackey', racist and unthinking in my approach. 'How much evidence of racial discrimination do you need for God's sake?' I was asked by a black probation officer who had just refused to participate in the research. 'You're a white academic who can know nothing about discrimination' challenged another. Their words were to remain with me. How much indeed? And what counts as evidence anyway? What is racial discrimination? Can it be uncovered by the coding of ethnic categories and monitoring? What do the ethnic categories mean? What do they mean to the people who record them? How are they recorded? Do the categories used bear any relation to the way in which people see themselves? What do different categories matter if all involved in criminal justice look simply at skin colour? Could I ever, as a white academic, understand *anything* about racial discrimination?

Such challenges marked the beginning of a process of learning. This is not to suggest that I had not already reflected on forms of oppression and how oppression can be measured, nor is it to suggest that I had not previously addressed issues of difference and discrimination, such issues had been taxing in relation to women and notions of sexism. I also had some basic grounding in the research on racial discrimination and acknowledged in a general and perhaps distant way that criminology is not only a subject dominated by men, but that the criminal justice system perpetuates racism. I had also at times noticed my anxiety to be 'politically correct'. But from this point onwards the issues were to strike me in a different way and I was thus forced to reflect on the research and the research strategies set out for me – not as an 'experienced researcher', but as a 'white, female researcher' – as someone who had experienced varying degrees and forms of 'otherness', but not an 'otherness' defined in terms of race or ethnicity.

Let me return to ethnic categorisation. To gloss over differences in the use of ethnic categories is problematical because such variations may themselves signal commitment to one or other political ideology. At least, the use of one set of categories over another may be interpreted in this way. The term 'black', for example, is frequently used as a generic term: NAPO has suggested that it is an important term because it very powerfully marks the distinction between white and other groups. NAPO members have argued that to break down the category of black into sub-categories perhaps masks the central point that *black* generally denotes unfair treatment. Indeed, it may be argued that categorisation beyond a simple black/white distinction amounts to an intentional negation of the political point to be made.

Equally, it is important to recognise the limitations of the term 'black' as a generic term. There is no one black identity – to use the term may suggest that there is. There is further criticism that the use of the generic term may imply that Asians are required to subordinate their own identity to one forged by persons of African descent. Modood (1988), for example, has argued that the implications of using the term 'black' is that Asians are required to accept African leadership in the struggle against racism even though they constitute a majority of those in Britain who are its victims. There are further difficulties. I realised that even to use the term 'Black and Asian' implies African leadership by placing the constituent terms in an order which defies the normal convention of alphabetical ordering and places the numerically more numerous of the two groups in a secondary position.

If the category 'black' is inappropriate because it masks different ethnic identities, we could suggest the term 'ethnic minorities' as an alternative. It is a very convenient phrase, but even this is beset with difficulties. First, there are many ethnic minorities in Britain who are not by any definition black (for example, Irish people) and they are not typically intended to be included in the designation, but technically they are an ethnic minority. Secondly, the term fails to accommodate those situations where members of black communities in places such as Liverpool or Nottingham are culturally indistinguishable from their white neighbours. Thirdly, there is a problem with the term minority, as it is often interpreted to imply that the designated group is politically and morally less significant than the majority. There are also difficulties with the term 'ethnic' itself. We hear of 'ethnic' pottery and fashion, for instance, and this signifies the way in which white people are apt to see ethnicity as an attribute only of others, something that distinguishes 'them' from 'us'. And then there is the ordering of the phrase: should it be 'ethnic minorities' or 'minority ethnic groups' to get over the 'them and us' problem and to signify that we are all ethnics?

As I cast around looking for a solution to my dilemmas in how to proceed with research which required some form of ethnic classification, the difficulties appeared insurmountable. Another problem concerned the conflation of *category* and *identity*. (Indeed, I found some classification schemes which mixed skin colour, religion, language, ethnicity and geography, though they are clearly not one and the same thing.) In this research I was faced with *client cultural identity* in one area, *ethnic codes* (categories) in the second and *self-identified race* in the third area and out of these I was expected to produce meaningful comparisons. The problems were compounded when it was not clear who had actually completed the monitoring forms which indicated such information. A small resolution to this difficulty was to think in terms of *group identification* taking place among those *inside* an ethnic boundary and *categorisation* from the *outside*, where it is a matter of external definition. How this squared with what had actually been done in terms of the information given to me as part of this research I do not know, but the resolution is one which I have employed to good effect in subsequent research.

The issues of ethnic categorisation were never fully resolved in this research. At best, what was achieved was an uneasy compromise. Following this research I might argue that self-designated identity is the preferred option and that this should take precedence whenever one is trying to record ethnicity. However, as a researcher I would have to argue that one researcher cannot interview 1,152 defendants in 28 different courts at the same time. Perhaps the lesson to be learned here is that the meaning of ethnic categorisation has to be clarified in research and that researchers should seek to ensure that there is consultation between clients and recorders of ethnicity from the outset. The difficulties experienced in this context, however, perhaps added to the research rather than detracted from it, for my searching examination of the use of categories highlighted some of the difficulties in interpretation and forcefully drew attention to the limitations of research of this kind. Ultimately, there are perhaps circumstances when the social researcher or policy maker may have to use ethnic categories which seem appropriate whether or not they coincide with the common-sense definitions or identities embraced by people themselves. Indeed, this may be an important strategy in examining how people categorise one another; the application of categories may provide a telling clue to discrimination. It is the use to which such information is put which is important. Ethnic categorisation can be helpful to draw distinctions between different groups of people, to identify the focus of discrimination, to illuminate patterns of disadvantage and domination and to assess the impact of changes in policy and practice. Without such data on ethnicity, discriminatory policies and practices may remain unchallenged.[4]

The struggle to achieve a compromise with regard to ethnic categorisation subsequently led me to focus more on the qualitative aspects of the research than was originally planned. Indeed, the uneasiness about categorisations led to some increased dissatisfaction with 'paper monitoring' as whole. For it seemed to me that discrimination could not be measured simply by looking at social inquiry report recommendations and sentences; nor could it be easily measured by looking at the content of reports, for analyses of 'finished reports' or of statistical findings can give only a partial picture of discriminatory practices which are perhaps now rarely conscious and overt, but rather unconscious and covert. In the course of this research, as once before in the 'search for sexism' (see Gelsthorpe, 1986, 1989), I became more and more aware of the need to look beyond the surface appearance or non-appearance of discrimination to the exigencies of organisational life. In this sense, my research strategy shifted from 'documented and documenting discrimination' to 'unravelling and understanding how discrimination occurs'.

As I have indicated, the study included a small number of interviews to try to record how probation officers and magistrates approached social inquiry reports in terms of writing them and reading them, respectively. This could easily have been a task conceived in terms of recording discriminatory comments. Instead, I saw the task as a broad one in which I might delve beneath the spoken word to try to understand the standpoint of the interviewee in an organisational context with competing demands and claims. The interviews then included questions on report allocation, the issue of home visits, gatekeeping procedures and other policy and organisational constraints which may have unintended consequences that can be construed as racist or sexist. Two examples are briefly described here.

Towards an Understanding of Discrimination

First, of the 128 reports randomly selected for detailed analysis, half had been prepared by male and half by female probation officers. However, looking at the figures more closely I found that it was predominantly male officers who had prepared reports on black males, predominantly female officers who had prepared reports on black females, predominantly female officers who had prepared reports on whites and, by a margin of under 3 per cent, predominantly females who had prepared reports on white males. The figures are not significant in themselves, but they perhaps become significant if there is a suggestion that male and female probation officers approach their work differently or have different interests.

Clearly it is important to give some attention to allocation procedures since there is at least scope for discrimination, not as a reflection of conscious partiality but as an unintended consequence of a particular organisational practice. From the interviews with officers it would be fair to report that most (though not all) perceived and experienced report allocation to be a genuinely democratic affair, with senior officers intervening only to spread the workload fairly, to protect over-worked officers and perhaps to provide newly qualified officers with an appropriate range of clients. Despite these claims, however, some officers were well aware that they 'picked out' offenders who interested them. Everyone in the team might have to take their share of 'run of the mill' cases (for example, drink driving offenders), but there was scope to pursue individual preferences.

Leaving aside the important influences of staff availability and workloads, 'scope to pursue individual preferences' may lead to different client groups being perceived rather differently. Indeed, the interest shown in particular client groups may well reflect the social, gender and racial composition of a particular probation team. This is not to suggest that this is not desirable (or avoidable), nor is it to suggest that there are clear-cut distinctions across groups of officers (with white officers being most interested in white offenders and so on), but it is to suggest that the composition of the probation team may be an important influence on the allocation of reports. Far from specialisms being a hindrance to probation work, they are perhaps an essential part of it and make for sound professional practice. But if there are distinctions between 'run of the mill' or 'bread and butter' cases and cases which are 'more challenging' or 'more interesting', then it may be important to look at which clients fall into which category (on the basis of their offence) and any differences in approach which ensue.

It also appeared from this research that the rarity of the female offender makes her attractive to probation officers, particularly to female officers. While the fact that most reports on females were prepared by females may be explained away by workload allocation and the sex distribution of officers in each team, it is less easy to dismiss the comments of officers on this point which suggest that their approach to report writing for female offenders (white or black) is quite different from the approach to report writing on males. As one officer said: 'It's harder to do reports on women but ultimately more satisfying, especially if you end up supervising her. You can do some real work – old fashioned casework – call it what you like, but at the end of the day you feel you've actually done something.' Needless to say, current debates about the changing emphasis in probation work from a loosely conceived 'advising, assisting and befriending' to 'supervising offenders in the community' has particular implications for officers who find the more traditional approaches to probation work more satisfying. But the broader point here is that reports on different groups of clients may be shaped differently to reflect the differential concerns and interests of report writers.

The second example concerns home visits. The study showed that in 43 per cent of cases involving women and only 6 per cent of the cases involving men were there home visits. A number of officers claimed that they would visit women in their homes because of the difficulty of persuading female offenders to come to the office, and also because of their child care responsibilities. Some officers viewed the whole issue of home visits with scepticism, believing them to be of little use in the task of report writing. Most of those interviewed, however, reported that there were either formal or informal team policies which prohibited (or at least limited) opportunities for probation officers to visit single men in their homes unless they were already known to the service. Some officers claimed that the restrictions only applied where defendants had been charged with offences involving violence; others claimed that there was general reluctance to visit men on large housing estates. Perhaps the important point in all this is that it seemed significant to me to question whether or not these policies meant that black or Asian defendants were less likely to receive home visits on the grounds of safety or because of where they were living. It would be misleading, of course, to suggest that whether or not a home visit had been carried out was the determining factor in the shaping of reports and on the sentences given, but there was potential for discrimination here which seemed worthy of further investigation.

These are but two small examples of organisational constraints that might affect report-writing practices, but they nevertheless serve to point to the need to focus much more on the organisational context in which reports are prepared as well as on reports as 'finished products'. 'Paper monitoring' and statistical analyses of findings may be thus limited and limiting in terms of measuring discrimination; first, we gain only a 'surface' picture and not an account of how the picture has been created and, secondly, it may be tempting to assume that discrimination is not occurring unless it can be clearly documented and 'captured' as part of statistical findings. In this regard the hard won battle to establish monitoring within the criminal justice system under the Criminal Justice Act of 1991[5] may be double-edged. On the one hand, it may be seen as a reflection of the concerns about discrimination and symbolic of the need to address racism and sexism and other forms of discrimination; on the other hand, the focus on statistical monitoring may not only mask deeper forms of discrimination but lead to complacency.

The research route taken so far then has involved some questioning of ethnic categories and how they are recorded, and some realisation of the limitations of 'paper monitoring' and of the need to penetrate the exigencies of organisational life in order to approach the task of unearthing hidden forms of discrimination and understanding discrimination. My challenger's words, however, required a much more extensive journey of reflection. It is one thing to question what counts as evidence, it is quite another to question whether or not I could ever understand and accurately record aspects of discrimination. Once again, therefore, I had to face the question of whether or not I could ever, as a white academic, understand *anything* about racial discrimination.

Transferable Methodologies?

It was at this point that I turned to previous work on feminist perspectives in criminology and particularly to debates about so-called feminist strategies. Indeed, I consoled myself with recollection that, along with others, I had once argued that men could do feminist research. If men can do feminist research I reflected, surely a white woman could do research in an area which required some investigation of racism.[6]

It is generally agreed that feminism can inform research in two main ways: in terms of the choice of topic and in terms of the research process, though neither of these is unproblematic (Gelsthorpe, 1990; Reinharz, 1992).[7] With respect to topic, for example, many feminist researchers have chosen areas relevant or sympathetic to women. Indeed, it might be argued that a 'conscious partiality' is one of the central tenets of feminist research since researcher, researched and the knowledge produced in the transaction taking place between them are all historically and culturally specific and societally situated; there can be no 'objective' research in the traditional sense, because the impartial, detached, decorticated researcher is a figment of liberal mythology. Feminist research is thus candid about its political project which is the identification and elimination of the forces which work to oppress women in society.[8] For some, the concern to make women visible has led to the unequivocal commitment that research should be 'on, by and for' women. Much of the research on differential law enforcement and sentencing disputes (Chesney-Lind, 1973, 1977; Edwards, 1984) demonstrates these concerns.

However, researchers have also found this dictum problematical and some have indicated that none of these criteria is adequate as a test of whether or not research is feminist (Stanley and Wise, 1983: 17–21). Rather, they have suggested that it is more appropriate to place the criteria in a social and political context (Cain, 1986a). Thus it becomes possible to determine 'how, why and when' the 'on, by and for' criteria should be used (Gelsthorpe, 1990). In particular, this dictum has been criticised with regard to the extent to which it excludes men. The issue of feminist research *on* men is perhaps easier to deal with than feminist research *by* men, but it is precisely this which is relevant to the issue of research on racism by a white researcher. First, though, I will deal with the point about feminist research *on* men for there is relevance here too. I address the issue of feminist research *by* men at a later point.

In some ways it would be difficult to envisage much feminist research in the field of criminology if research on men were excluded, for so much of the criminal justice system revolves around men: it is mainly men who are labelled offenders, mainly men who police offenders and mainly men who are imprisoned. Maureen Cain (1986a) has explained how it became possible for her to envisage doing research on men by accepting their involvement on the basis that feminist criteria are satisfied if those researched remain *active* and *gendered* subjects. And Carol Smart's (1984) research on lawyers and Kathleen Daly's (1989) research on defendants both demonstrate that there can be feminist research on men.

But the point is much wider than this: women cannot be studied in isolation from men or from gender considerations. Thus if we want to understand, say, women's oppression, we obviously need to understand the part that men play in this. More generally, researchers have to consider how gender shapes and influences women's (and men's) lives and, to paraphrase David Morgan (1981), 'taking gender into account is "taking men [and women] into account"'.

In the context of research on race and gender issues in the preparation and presentation of social inquiry reports there are some clear parallels. If we want to understand racial discrimination this must surely involve focusing on black and white people in relation to one another. Indeed, all too often race relations have been conceived in terms of 'them' causing a problem or no problem as the case may be (see Genders and Player, 1989; McDermott, 1990), rather than the problem of racism and the ways in which powerful, white organisations and groups of people oppress minority groups. My concern to focus on *processes* of discrimination, then, as much as, if not more than the *end product* (that is, the social inquiry reports themselves) seemed to be an appropriate concern and one in keeping with the need to look at *relationships* between black and white people.

With respect to the research process and choice of methods, some feminist writers have been quite prescriptive in setting out what is and what is not acceptable. My view is that researchers should strive to use whatever research methods seem appropriate to the task, but that they should always be used sensitively and with awareness of their limitations (Gelsthorpe, 1992).[9] It would be fair to say, though, that feminist researchers have promoted small-scale ethnographies and and interview research which to some degree (at least) allow research participants to speak for themselves (see for example, Carlen, 1985; Eaton, 1993), with the assistance of a researcher/analyst, rather than their words and experiences being translated into meaningless tables and 'academicspeak'.[10] All these points, of course, might be relevant for the researcher intent on focusing on racism, if the concern was to do good research and to reflect sensitively and accurately some aspect of racism, and so I do not wish to dwell on them here. Rather, I wish to turn to the thorny question of whether or not men can do feminist research, for it is here that we can discern a direct parallel with the white researcher seeking to do research on racism.

A distinctive feature of much feminist research is that it generates its problematic from the perspective of women's experiences. Some feminist writers, therefore, (notably radical feminists) have argued that men's biology and/or psychology prevents them from becoming feminists or doing feminist research. There is a 'womanly capacity that men do not possess' (Pateman, 1986: 7), for example, and women's voice is 'in a higher register' (Gilligan, 1982); they are perceived to have access to a privileged means of knowing and, consequently, to a superior knowledge. Needless to say, this smacks of essentialism. While accepting that women do share certain experiences based on their gender, the idea of a 'shared conscious-ness' is problematic in that it implies a common unity among all women. This is clearly not the case; age, class and race cut across gender distinctions, dividing women just as they do men (Clegg, 1975) and so the 'conscious experiences' of women vary greatly. A less limiting definition of feminism, as I have indicated, is that it involves the recognition that women are oppressed on the basis of their sex and attempts to end that oppression (Radcliffe Richards, 1982). Thus, although women directly experience oppression to varying degrees, men can recognise its existence. Men cannot be feminists in the sense that women can be, but they *can* hold a feminist perspective that is sufficiently sympathetic to women's position. However, as Cain (1986a) states, such empathy can only arise from *active* involvement in the issues.

This point has been emphasised by David Morgan (1981) in his reflections on men, feminism and research. After taking part in a British Sociological Association summer school on feminism and research, he felt that he began to 'know' feminism rather than 'know about' it. Also, he suggests that the experience led him to question his own 'taken-for-granted' gender (1981: 84). Morgan, therefore, argues that it is vital for men to be involved with feminist research in order to question their attitudes about themselves and develop greater understanding of gender issues. To argue that men cannot do feminist research would be tantamount to arguing that only teachers can study teaching practice or other teachers, or that only prisoners can study prisoners. The researcher is rarely in exactly the same position as the research subjects in terms of class, cultural and social experiences. The ability to produce an effective analysis is not simply achieved by being a teacher or a prisoner. Similarly, the ability to contribute to feminist understanding is not something achieved by virtue of being female. The 'women's experience' from which the feminist problematics arise need not necessarily be the experience of the researcher herself/himself.[11]

There are three further points to be made in support of feminist research in criminology *by* men. First, there is clear evidence that men have made significant contributions (John Stuart Mill, Karl Marx and Friedrich Engels, for instance, are all cited by Harding (1987) as having made positive contributions, though this is not to suggest that their contributions are unproblematic, few are). The work of Lee Bowker, Tim Beneke and Russell Dobash are perhaps more obvious examples.

Secondly, if feminist work is to extend beyond research on women, then the suitability of either male or female researchers will have to be considered in the light of the chosen research topic. (Male researchers may have greater access to male-dominated groups – prison officers, police officers and football fans all spring to mind – whereas female researchers may be more suitable for research concerning female-dominated groups – rape victims or battered spouses.) Finally, it is simply illogical to criticise men for ignoring women and then to insist that they are incapable of contributing anything.[12] There is much here that is relevant for the white researcher seeking to understand racism. To seek to know is not the same as knowing, but the process of coming to know, of wanting to understand, provides the researcher with a starting point. But we can pursue the arguments further.

For Stanley and Wise (1983) feminist research involves the possession of a 'feminist consciousness' which is rooted in the experience of being a woman in a sexist society. However, it is the position adopted in 1990 which they call 'fractured foundationalism' which is of more interest here (Stanley and Wise, 1990). Their position is 'fractured' because they do not wish to espouse any form of essentialism, that is, belief in the existence of a pre-social, metaphysical essence of 'woman' and of 'man', a true, authentic self, without and beyond time and space, transcending all culture and history. Such a position, however, developed to its compelling, albeit extreme, conclusion, would make any inter-subjectivity whatsoever impossible. The argument would be that sex/gender is not the only, nor even the most salient, characteristic of any individual, considered within any given historical–cultural context. On the contrary, sex and gender are mediated by other factors such as class, race, age, religious and sexual preference, and ethnicity, and it is only a mixture of these factors, occurring within specific sites of struggles which constitute a person's worldview (or formative contexts, Unger, 1983); the grid of knowledge, beliefs, sentiments and desires are always in fact contingent no matter how embedded in social practices. Moreover, the argument runs, it is fallacious to contend that, for instance, sex/gender is or may be the equivalent of racial oppression, since no two historically and culturally specific sites, structured by varying configurations of the 'master censures' (Sumner, 1990), produce an equivalence in subjectively experienced oppression.[13] The logical conclusion of this line of argument would appear to be that no one can understand anyone else; we are all ontologically separate beings, with a historical specificity constituted by a wealth of personal experience which only we can begin fully to comprehend and explicate, each for ourselves.

But inter-subjectivity can perhaps be rescued by recognising the existence of shared cultural experiences which mediate between individuals and facilitate communication and understanding. Thus we arrive at standpoint epistemologies which assert that women's position in patriarchal societies gives them a special standpoint from which to perceive and understand systems of oppression, as a prelude to using the knowledge so gained to effect an overthrow of these oppressive systems. This does not mean, however, that all women harbour revolutionary consciousness, far from it. On the contrary, although women's oppression affords them a privileged route to the feminist standpoint, this can only be achieved through political struggle, that is (in Marxian terms) through 'praxis': a mixture of hard work, commitment and pain.

Sandra Harding (1987), Nancy Hartsock (1987) and Dorothy Smith (1988), among others, have explained that feminist epistemology is more than women's world viewpoint. It is a method, a mode of enquiry which lays emphasis on the experiences of women and on the actualities of their everyday worlds (Harding, 1987). This justificatory approach parallels the way in which Hegel developed the 'proletarian standpoint' of Marx, Engels and Lukacs. The behaviour of two groups of people, men and women, is shaped by social and material life. Consequently, their respective visions and 'knowledge' are invariably different. In a system of domination, knowledge emerges for the oppressed through struggles to overcome that domination. It is out of this that feminist standpoints emerge. Needless to say, there is no one common standpoint. This is clearly not so at two levels. First, we cannot assume that black/white, young/old, working class/middle class and so on experience life in the same way. Secondly, standpoints are chosen by individuals and may change over time; they are transitional. Thus we are all likely to hold more than one at any single moment. As a consequence, we may begin to question how the concept of standpoint can help rather than hinder research. But it does help. Once we use experience to generate problems, hypotheses and evidence, and once we place the researcher on the same critical plane as the research subject, traditional epistemological assumptions can no longer be made. The old agendas raise questions such as 'who can be knower?' and 'do subjective studies count as knowledge?'. Feminist researchers who have attempted to answer these questions through conventional epistemological tests have found their position uncomfortable. In contrast, the concept of feminist standpoint theory makes explicit multidimensional experiences of reality for both the researcher and the researched; for example, it draws attention to how everyday worlds are 'shaped and determined by relation and forces external to them' (Smith, 1988: 110). Correspondences can thus be drawn between the material world and the everyday world as 'lived experience'. Further, researchers can identify the place from which they are creating knowledge and hence can deal with the 'epistemological inevitability of site-specific (or value-laden) knowledge' (Cain, 1986b: 8).

The question is can men attain a feminist standpoint? Jaggar (1983) explicitly says that they can, although it will never be easy for the oppressor fully to comprehend his complicity with the systems of oppression, and to relinquish all the benefits that accrue to him. On the other hand, it may be argued that patriarchal society oppresses the oppressors, by foisting limiting and destructive sex/gender identities upon them; and that recognising this fact and engaging in a struggle against it is part of a feminist project in which men can fully participate (Avi-Ram, 1989; Brod, 1990). Research by men would then contribute to an emancipatory politics designed to facilitate human flourishing.

What is of relevance here for the white researcher is the need to recognise that standpoints are constituted by politics, theory, theoretical reflexivity and choice (of site), not by biology, skin colour or ethnicity. In this way, the standpoint of the researcher features alongside those of the researched; this is not to suggest that the white researcher can ever provide an informed 'insider' account of racism within the criminal justice system, but s/he can look to change the behaviour which causes and sustains racism, starting with ourselves. Comprehension of knowledge production – of racism – thus requires both theoretical and personal reflexivity.

Conclusion

This account then of a white female researcher's attempts to grapple with some aspects of research on racism within the criminal justice system is telling of some of the difficulties involved. It is not intended to be justificatory, though I imagine it could be read that way; nor is it to suggest that dilemmas in developing research strategies are easily resolved. There are many difficulties not included in the reflections here or to which I have made only passing reference: the meaning of racism and whether or not people define themselves as members of a racially or ethnically dominated group; subjective versus objective experiences of racism and whether or not subjective experiences of discrimination have to be validated in any particular way for them to 'count'; different forms of discrimination and how one can simultaneously comprehend the complex operation of different forms of oppression, for example, have continued to trouble me following the research on social inquiry reports. I have touched on only three particular reflections: the limitations of 'paper monitoring', the need to look at 'processes' of discrimination as well as 'finished products' and, finally, a possible starting point for the white researcher who, as an 'outsider' will not be able fully to comprehend racism, but who wishes to 'know'. In seeking to describe something of my experiences in this research I have drawn certain parallels with feminist research and research on sexism, but I see these parallels as a small contribution in the process of 'coming to know', not as a determining principle for research on racism.[14]

Acknowledgements

I would like to thank Jane Morris for her helpful comments on this chapter, and the editors for their patience and encouragement.

Notes

1 Under the Criminal Justice Act 1991 which came into force on October 1, 1992, social inquiry reports became 'pre-sentence reports' to reflect their main purpose in providing background information on the offence, offender and possible penalties to the court.

2 I took over the project some months after it had started, the researcher who was initially involved having left the project to begin a new post. I thus took over at a point when the research objectives had been set and negotiations with probation services for research areas were in progress. It would have been difficult to have changed the research agenda at this point and I was in many ways obliged to be faithful to the research proposal already agreed with the Home Office who were funding the research.

3 Since the project's completion, a system of ethnic monitoring of probation staff and offenders has been agreed between the Home Office, ACDP, NAPO and ABPO.

4 I benefited greatly from discussion with Navnit Dholakia of the Commission for Racial Equality on these points.

5 Section 95 of the Criminal Justice Act 1991 states: '1) The Secretary of State shall in each year publish such information as he considers expedient for the purpose of (a) enabling persons engaged in the administration of criminal justice to become aware of the financial implications of their decisions; or (b) facilitating the performance by such persons of their duty to avoid discriminating against any persons on the ground of race or sex or any other improper ground. 2) Publication under subsection 1) above shall be effected in such manner as the Secretary of State considers appropriate for the purpose of bringing the information to the attention of the persons concerned.' Section 95 was a late addition to the Act following determined pressure from various interest groups and organisations who were concerned about racism.

6 I should also note here that, as a contract researcher, I needed the job since my previous contract had come to an end. There may, of course, be ethical objections to my having agreed to pursue research on racism and sexism in social inquiry reports, but as the research was initially conceived it did not strike me that any special skills would be needed over and above sensitive interviewing skills, ability to carry out a detailed content analysis of reports and statistical analysis. Few contract researchers are ever in a position to choose exactly what they would like to do; nor indeed are they in a position to refuse work.

7 The meaning of feminist perspectives in criminology have long been debated (Gelsthorpe and Morris, 1990; Smart, 1976). The 'lowest common denominator' of feminism might be that a feminist perspective means 'accepting the view that women experience subordination on the basis of their sex and working towards the elimination of that subordination' (Gelsthorpe and Morris, 1990: 2), though clearly not all feminists would be happy with this definition. Moreover, there are problems in establishing who holds a 'feminist perspective'; there are a number of criminologists who would either not see their work as exclusively feminist (e.g. Carlen, 1983, 1985, 1988) or whose work would not be seen by others as such, but who have nevertheless contributed to the construction of an alternative feminist body of criminological knowledge (e.g. Jones et al., 1986). Equally, there are a number of feminist writers who would not see themselves or be seen by others as criminologists but who have also made significant contributions to this body of knowledge (e.g. Brownmiller, 1975; Cain, 1989; Kelly, 1988; Smart, 1989). Indeed, criminology has for many feminist writers and researchers been a constraining rather than a constructive and creative influence.

8 This does not make it any less 'objective' than traditional research, however, since that too must have (albeit unacknowledged) political objectives and consequences, often contributing to the maintenance of the status quo.

9 Some writers have suggested that quantitative methods are inconsistent with feminist values, for example, since they have objective appearance. But large-scale surveys have provided important background data for feminist, as for other, researchers. The problem is perhaps not quantification itself, but insensitive quantification (Eichler, 1988). Others have expressed a preference for interview research, but not interview research as traditionally conceived; rather, there is rejection of the idea of an interview as a one-way process (Stanley and Wise, 1983; see also the review of feminist interview research in Reinharz, 1992). There has also been concern to explore, and take responsibility for, the potential impact of participating in

research which may be distressing for research subjects, whether as offenders, victims, defendants or practitioners (Kelly, 1990; Oakley, 1980).

10 See Farran (1990) for a good description of how 'data collection' in traditional research is effectively 'data construction'.

11 Diana Woodward and Lynne Chisholm (1981) provide a good example of this. They carried out research on the lives of female graduates with children whose husbands were in employment. The researchers say of themselves that they were young, career-orientated feminists and only one was married. In their view, they had little insight into the women's experiences of marriage, parenthood or husbands' employment. They argue, however, that the research did not suffer because of this, but rather it was enhanced by the fact that the women had to explain in more detail the reality of their lives.

12 This is very much the point that Harding makes in her defence of men's involvement (1987).

13 I am grateful to Paul Roberts for drawing these points to my attention.

14 There are perhaps more obvious parallels to be drawn between sexism and racism than those touched on in this chapter: as processes, for example, racism and sexism may be quite similar; ideologically, they both construct common sense through reference to what is 'natural' and 'biological' – reference is made to 'essential' differences; concepts of race and gender are both socially constructed and there have been attempts to ameliorate both racism and sexism through legislation, for example, (see Brittan and Maynard, 1984 for an exploration of some of these points).

6

Theoreotyping: Anti-racism, Criminology and Black Young People

John Pitts

A first rate theory predicts, a second rate theory forbids.

(Aleksander Kitaigorodski, *Molecular Crystals and Molecules*)

In this chapter I look critically at the contemporary debate about race, crime and justice in criminology and social work in Britain, and the implicit and explicit assumptions which inform it. Having attempted to account for the upsurge of academic interest in race and crime in the early 1980s and the intellectual struggles which ensued, I chart the contours of the contemporary debate. One curious characteristic of this debate is the frequency and duration of the gaps, which ought to be filled with contemporary empirical evidence but are usually papered over by rhetoric or outdated and irrelevant truisms. I argue that, by and large, British criminology has relied on unexamined stereotypes and false analogies and that the 'anti-racism' industry has attempted to impose the straightjacket of a 'correct', sanitised version of events on the ways we think about these issues.

Like most of the people who write about these issues, I stand relatively close to the cultural and economic centre of British society, a place I am able to occupy, I believe, only because other people, many of them black, stand on the social margins. It follows that 'where I stand', my proximity to the 'centre', will shape my point of view and the analysis which proceeds from it. My account of events comes from somewhere near the centre and so it 'tells it', not necessarily 'like it is', but the way it appears to me. That is my disclaimer, what of other people's?

Disclaimers

Virtually every text which concerns itself with questions of race, crime and justice includes a disclaimer to the effect that:

> Even though in some places, at some times some 'black' young people appear to be disproportionately involved in particular types of crime, there is little hard evidence to indicate that, in general, 'black' young

people are more prone to involvement in persistent and serious offending than white young people.

Though broadly correct, rather than explaining why the author is about to ignore the subject, this disclaimer almost invariably serves as the springboard from which s/he dives head-first into it. Robert Harris (1992), writing under the sub-heading 'Black People as Offenders' states: 'we cannot discuss these issues in a simple empirical way because we simply do not have sufficient hard data to do so'. The obligatory disclaimer having been lodged, he then proceeds to discuss the involvement of black people in crime at some length. Given the paucity of empirical evidence we might well ask why, since the early 1980s, so many criminologists, journalists and politicians have concerned themselves with these issues at all. But, of course, the debate is not, first and foremost, about criminological 'facts', but about political anxieties.

What started out in the early years of the Thatcher administration as a fear of 'race riots', involving impoverished black young people and directed against prosperous, middle-aged, white ones had, by the 1990s, become a concern about the cost-effective management of social disorder on the social margins. The race, crime and justice debate in Britain began, effectively, in the spring of 1981 in the wake of the Brixton disturbances. It is a product of the peculiar politics of the 1980s, the decade in which, with increasing frequency, working-class young people from 'areas of disrepute' took to the streets of British towns and cities, with bricks, home-made fire bombs and latterly firearms, to do battle with the police. Brixton's distinction is that it was the prototype for such collective expressions of dissent.

Riots and Uprisings

Whether they were 'riots' or 'uprisings', the events of spring 1981 in British inner cities moved us onto a new and uncharted political terrain. Suddenly, it *could* happen here. There was looting, violence and plenty of wanton destruction but the central issue to emerge from the disturbances was a political, not a criminological, one. Here we had some white, but more black, young people, fighting in the streets with a police force which they claimed, was arbitrary and lawless in its dealings with them. What started out as a fight between young people and the police came, within a very short space of time, to be represented by the police, the media, politicians, social scientists and black 'spokesmen' as a conflict between the police and the 'black community'. The Socialist Workers Party, never slow to exploit an opportunity to 'sell the paper', rushed out a special edition depicting the 'riots' as a working-class uprising against capitalist oppression; but in vain. A chain of events, which could have been 'read' in a variety of ways and at a number of different levels, had been irredeemably racialised.

This is not to deny the bitter history of relations between the police and black people in the area nor that decisions about the policing of 'black neighbourhoods', made at the highest levels of the Home Office and government, proceeded from the explicit assumption that black Britons were a volatile group of people who were potentially subversive to public order (Pitts, 1988). The point is that questions of generation, social class and, indeed, gender were, quite literally, edited out of the story within hours of the first reports of the disturbances. Symbolic events are simplified events and, for very different reasons, the police, the government, opposition parties, some criminologists and black organisations, preferred to represent the Brixton 'riots' or 'uprisings' as a bi-polar conflict between black people and the police; a symbol of the parlous state of contemporary race relations.

But, as we have already noted, this was not a debate about criminological 'facts', indeed, strictly speaking, it was not a debate at all. As the argument unfolded over the following weeks and months, evidence that black young men robbed people in the street was countered by evidence that the police were using the 'sus' laws to stop, search harass and arrest inordinate numbers of innocent black adolescents. While the police and political protagonists of the right denounced the violent offences of black young men, some criminologists and political protagonists of the left and centre denounced the violent offences perpetrated against them by police officers.

The debate, such as it was, had been politicised, simplified and polarised and in the process 'radical criminology' found itself torn between its political affiliations and its intellectual ones. In response to the events in Brixton and elsewhere, many radical criminologists had assumed a posture which can best be expressed thus:

> Black young people do not, contrary to the assertions of the agents of the state, commit a disproportionate amount of street crime and burglary, and in view of the poverty in which they are forced to live and their lack of access to opportunity, it is hardly surprising that they do.

As political activists they had chosen sides and were fighting their corner with the weapons at hand. As social scientists who came from the tradition established by Marx, and elaborated by, among others, Lenin, Gramsci, Husserl, Fanon and Althusser, they could hardly ignore the fact that, in Auden's phrase, 'those to whom evil is done' (sometimes) 'do evil in return'.

Whose Side are We On?

Arguably their dilemma was the logical outcome of the radical criminological project, the precepts of which had been laid down almost a decade and a half before by Howard Becker in his seminal paper, 'Whose side are we on?' (1967). Becker enjoins sociologists to recognise the impossibility of discovering an objective social 'reality' 'out there'. Confronted with a plurality of accounts given by actors who have differential power to impose their definition of the situation on events, and political and administrative practices which favour the definitions of the powerful, social scientists will, he says, by default or design, have to choose sides. If, then, sociological research must inevitably represent the subjective experience of only one of a plurality of groups and individuals, sociologists should, Becker argues, make an ethical choice to 'tell it like it is' on behalf of the powerless and the oppressed. For Becker and his successors, to be a social scientist is to be partisan. There is no neutral ground on which to stand, no vantage point from which a broader view may be grasped. One is on the side of the powerful or the powerless, part of the problem or part of the solution.

'Whose side are we on?' crystallised the political posture of the 'radical criminology' which developed in the 1960s and early 1970s in Britain and the USA. Radical criminology rejected the role of 'handmaiden of the status quo' in which conventional criminology was cast. It would offer no comfort to 'the MAN' (i.e. the establishment) and instead aligned itself with liberationist struggles, adding its voice to the voices of the oppressed; the prisoners, the psychiatric patients and the squatters, who were struggling to get 'out from under'. Refusing to regard 'deviant' acts as pathological, it re-presented them as acts of resistance, rebellion or revolt against the established order. While the political posture commended by Becker was adopted by British radical criminologists in the 1970s, their political analysis owed far more to Marx than to labelling theory.

The Debate within Marxism
It was against this backdrop that the argument surrounding *What is to be Done about Law and Order?* (Lea and Young, 1984) unfolded. This was not an academic debate about the 'evidence', of which there was very little, but an acrimonious political row about 'praxis', about the way Lea and Young, as radical criminologists, have conducted themselves (Gilroy and Sim, 1985).

The central strands of the argument developed by Lea and Young asserted that: in certain neighbourhoods impoverished black young people committed a disproportionate amount of crime; that its victims tended to be other poor black people; that, as such, rather than an expression of resistance to oppression, such crime simply compounded their victim's oppression and that socialists and radical criminologists cannot, in any straightforward way, simply be 'on the side' of the socially deprived perpetrators.

Their critics replied that by their acceptance of the category of 'black youth crime' as the 'problem', a category generated by the control culture, they had broken with a central tenet of the radical criminological project and given comfort to the MAN. By assisting in the transformation of black young people into 'folk devils', it was argued, they were contributing to the mystificatory process of political displacement in which the crisis in the social relations of production is transformed into a crisis of race relations. Put simply, they had changed sides.

For their part, Lea and Young argued that for too long radical criminology had denied politically inconvenient aspects of social reality. It had, they claimed, espoused a romantic and idealistic view of the world, which while 'politically correct' was factually and espistemologically flawed. They called for the abandonment of illusions and a return to realism. *What is to be Done about Law and Order?* attempted to delineate the territory which radical criminology could inhabit in this radically changed political environment. In espousing 'realism' Lea and Young tried to seize the political initiative by articulating the concerns of the working-class victims of crime and mounting an assault upon police inefficiency and governmental indifference.

This was a struggle between a Marxism which 'read' street crime as a fabrication of the ideological state apparatus and one which viewed it as apolitical, egotistical behaviour generated by poverty and status frustration. Whereas Paul Gilroy and his colleagues utilised the structuralist schemas developed by Louis Althusser, John Lea and Jock Young found their theoretical inspiration in a Marxism mediated via 'opportunity theory'. What they shared was a belief in social structure as the primary determinant of human behaviour and class struggle as the motor of social processes.

Das Kapital's Unwritten Epilogue

In *What is to be Done about Law and Order?* Lea and Young (1984) employed the 'opportunity theory', developed by Richard Cloward and Lloyd Ohlin in the USA at the end of the 1950s, to explain the upsurge in civil disorder and 'crimes of poverty' in Britain at the beginning of the 1980s. Opportunity theory tells us that when an ideological fantasy of an open, meritocratic society, in which everybody is free to strive for socially valued goals, is overlaid upon the social reality of a class-divided society in which opportunity is apportioned on the basis of social rank rather than ability, it will create social 'strain' at those points in the social structure where the discrepancy between ends and means is felt most keenly.

In Britain in the postwar period governments attempted to deal with this problem in two ways. On the one hand, they pursued social and economic policies which aimed to bring greater opportunity to the poor, while on the other they attempted to reduce, or at least obscure, discrepancies of wealth, opportunity and privilege (Habermas, 1976). With the election of the Thatcher administration of 1979 this strategy was abandoned. Instead, discrepancies of wealth were fostered, and paraded in the belief that this would act as a stimulant to entrepreneurism and higher productivity.

The confidence with which this approach to social inequality was embraced derived from real changes in the distribution of political power which had taken place in Britain in the preceding decade. The protracted economic recession, which began in Britain in the late 1960s had precipitated the erosion of Britain's industrial base and, with it, the power of the trades unions. Through the introduction of automation, internationalisation and ever more restrictive industrial relations legislation, British industry had attempted to stave off recurrent economic crises and stabilise the falling rate of profit. In the ensuing 'struggle' between the employers and the unions both sides incurred enormous losses and irreparable damage. The collapse of the Miners' Strike in 1985 marked the moment when, to all intents and purposes, the struggle was resolved in favour of industry.

The Withering Away of Class Analysis

The major effect of these economic and political changes was the reversal, in the late 1970s and early 1980s, of the postwar tendency towards a narrowing of the gap between rich and poor and the growth of both relative and absolute poverty. Yet the deepening of class divisions and social inequalities also saw the fragmentation of the political constituency, in the labour movement, parliament, welfare, education and the academy, which had espoused a class analysis. In consequence, the language of 'social class' fell silent. This had nothing to do with its explanatory power; indeed, it had seldom been more relevant. Within a few years, political and academic discourse was purged of references to social class, poverty and inequality and a new language which reflected the analysis of a newly powerful political constituency took its place.

The Rise of Managerialism

For welfare professionals in general, and those working in the justice system in particular, the defeat of organised labour in the mid-1980s was paralleled by the collapse of the political and theoretical paradigm which, up to that point, had ascribed meaning to their professional endeavours. These were the people by whose professional efforts the postwar dream of a well-educated, open and equal social democratic society was to be realised. Conceived in the shadow of Durkheim rather than Marx, it was none the less a project predicated on the materialist premise that inequitable social structures generated forms of anti-social behaviour which could only be remedied by social re-structuring. The planners, the social workers and the probation officers were the 'social engineers' who would do this. This was a paradigm which although almost always at variance with reality, gave coherence and purpose to the efforts of the professionals who worked within the welfare state.

In the mid-1980s in the welfare and justice systems, professional workers whose job it had been to devise solutions to social problems were pushed to one side by professional managers who identified their primary task as the 'delivery' of 'tightly targeted' cost-effective public services to their 'customers'. Managerialism narrows the focus of reform. Turning away from sociological abstractions like social structure, social class and anomie, it concerns itself with the detail of policy, practice, beliefs and values in an organisation, a school or a local authority. Eschewing broader political concerns it intends that organisations should put their own houses in order. It is concerned with the responses of organisations to individual customers and this concern extends neither beyond that individual's contractual involvement with the organisation nor to similarly afflicted individuals who have no such involvement. These developments were nowhere more evident than in the juvenile justice system in the 1980s:

> if the period from the mid-1960s to the early 1970s can be characterised as the era of *professionalism*, the period from the late 1970s . . . could be characterised as the era of *managerialism*. In this period, 'being on the side', or acting in the interests of young people came increasingly to be defined in terms of the minimisation of professional intervention in their lives. The development of professional practice came gradually to take second place to the development of policy, and social imperatives were increasingly subordinated to economic ones. As a result, interventions by managers which aimed to limit the involvement of welfare professionals in people's lives came to assume the mantle of radicalism while practitioners who insisted upon seeking out new 'needs' were portrayed as reactionaries. (Pitts, 1991: 7)

From the mid-1980s, the government attempted to fashion a 'rational' cost-effective justice system. In doing so it adopted the radical 'scientific' managerial style pioneered in Wandsworth and Westminster; describing its mission in terms of outcomes, targets and performance indicators. In the process, the socio-political analysis, which had previously informed the endeavours of public professionals, was supplanted by an alternative paradigm which cast 'cost-effective service-delivery' as an ultimate virtue. When confronted with problems which, in an earlier era, had been attributed to 'social injustice', welfare and justice agencies, in managerialist mode, simply developed equal opportunities policies and talked about 'targeting'. Thus structural inequalities were transformed into administrative anomolies for which bureaucratic solutions could be devised (Pitts, 1992).

Managing Racial Oppression
Racial oppression may well have been real, pervasive and morally repugnant but it was as a dysfunctional organisational residue that it became the target for the managerialist crusade which was transforming the welfare–justice nexus in the 1980s. In the process, racial oppression was de-contextualised, simplified and transformed into 'anti-racism'.

By the late 1980s every agency and institution within what had been the welfare state and the criminal justice system had, or was in the process of developing, anti-racist statements, anti-racist policies, anti-racist strategies, anti-racist codes of practice and sanctions for breaches of same. The enthusiasm of the Home Office, the probation service, the Central Council for Education and Training in Social Work, and a multiplicity of other public sector organisations and agencies, for anti-racism was paralleled only by an almost universal vagueness about what it was.

On the face of it, anti-racism was an uncontentious and inexpensive strategy. As a managerially led 'negative' reform, it needed only slight changes in attitudes and behaviour, and the modest reorganisation of existing resources, for its realisation. It required neither a redistribution of wealth nor a realignment of power relations. Whereas the political programme which emerged from a class analysis required, in its fullest form, the transfer of the means of production, distribution and exchange to public ownership for its realisation, in the final analysis, anti-racism merely asked us to change our minds.

Anti-racist Epistemology

The implicit theory underpinning anti-racism reverses the materialist account of cause and effect which was a central tenet of the class analysis it supplanted. In this new formulation black people are denied access to educational opportunity and lucrative high-status work roles by 'institutionalised racism'. Institutionalised racism is a product of imperialism. It involves the imposition of unexamined, eurocentric evaluations of the proclivities and capacities of black people by relatively powerful white ones. Such evaluations have come, over the period, to structure individual attitudes, social practices and social institutions. In consequence, black people are structurally disadvantaged in the competition for educational, vocational and material resources. Whereas an earlier politics saw racism as a product of structural inequality, anti-racism sees structural inequality as a product of racism, and attitude change as the process whereby such inequality will be eradicated.

Slavoj Zizeck (1989: 88) in his account of the process of ideological transformation observes that:

> the multitude of 'floating signifiers' of proto-ideological elements, is structured into a unified field through the intervention of a particular 'nodal point' (the Lacanian *point de capiton*) which 'quilts' them, stops them sliding and fixes their meaning . . . What is at stake in the ideological struggle is which of the 'nodal points' . . . will totalise, include in its series of equivalences, these free-floating elements.

The ideological quilt which overlay the welfare–justice nexus was reworked and totalised around a new nodal point which located what came to be called the 'oppressions', as a product of an administrative malfunction in an otherwise increasingly open, classless, meritocratic society, analogous to John Major's 'Opportunity Britain'. In this formulation, such a society might be realised if only we will subordinate ourselves to the necessary managerial disciplines. Pre-eminent among the 'oppressions' from which managerialism was to deliver us was racism.

The Limits of Anti-racism

The logic of this position, were it to be argued through, would be that as 'anti-racist practice' became established, Britain's black population would experience greater occupational mobility. As some black commentators have observed, however, the late 1980s and early 1990s, the period in which anti-racist practice began to permeate the public services, also witnessed a slowing down, and in many cases a reversal, of the trend towards upward occupational mobility for black professionals in the public sector.

Although this was an experience shared by other social and racial groups, for whom the late 1970s and the early 1980s had been a period of upward occupational mobility, a central precept of the anti-racist project, that any attempt to explain the reversals of fortune experienced by black people in terms of the social class location they share with other similarly economically fragile groups, is regarded as an attempt to marginalise the question of race (Mullard, 1991). As a result, any investigation of the oppression of black people is destined to start from the premise that it is the product of 'racism' alone. Anti-racism does not set out to discover the factors which have contributed to a black person's predicament but to explain how, in any given situation, racism has created that predicament. It starts with an answer and works its way back towards the question. As Ian Craib (1987: 45) has observed:

> Theoretical work becomes a matter of demonstrating that the single beloved cause is at work behind all phenomena, however unlikely that seems, and however strongly the evidence points in the other direction . . . Any theoretical position which adopts a monocausal position takes on the air of an evangelical religious belief; there are attempts to convert the heathen and innumerable *ad hoc* hypotheses formed . . . [but] the theory cannot be proved wrong, it does not respond to evidence.

The argument developed here is not that racism, the practice of using power to act in a discriminatory way against people simply on the basis of their race, is not central to an explanation of the social and economic predicament of black people in Britain. Nor is it that social practices and social institutions in Britain, by default or design, either fail to operate in, or actively work against, the interests of black people. The argument is that racism and institutionalised racism are both necessary and central elements in an adequate explanation of black people's predicament, but they are not, of themselves, sufficient. Anti-racism, by adopting an idealistic paradigm and a simplistic view of racial oppression, has steered us away from those questions which could enable us to develop an adequate explanation of the phenomenon. An adequate explanation must account for the interplay of race, class, gender, social structure, culture and biography, and the ways in which they shape the chances and choices available to groups and individuals in similar structural locations (Critcher, 1976; Mills, 1959).

Racism and Criminology

Anti-racism has found a solid base in social work and has had a significant impact on practice and policy in juvenile justice and the probation service. Its impact on other parts of the justice system and on criminology is more oblique. For its part, mainstream criminology in Britain effectively abandoned its concern with the aetiology of crime in the mid-1970s and settled instead for an administrative criminology bent upon an evaluation of government policies which, in the 1980s, were increasingly inspired by the 'gut-level' feelings of cabinet ministers. The perspective shifted from the rehabilitation of individual offenders to, what were in effect, evaluations of the cost-effective management of aggregates of offenders and attempts to 'target' interventions more 'accurately' in order to ensure that the apparatus of justice 'delivered' a 'quality service' to the courts and a less expensive one to the government. Thus, while there was no 'anti-racist criminology', 'administrative criminology' which constituted the mainstream, was infused with the same managerialist preoccupations.

It was against this backdrop that criminology responded to the increasingly urgent demand from black activists, and students and practitioners in the welfare–justice nexus, for ideas and evidence about race, crime and justice. This has meant that as the 1980s progressed British criminology paid increasing attention to these questions. However, the paucity of empirical evidence, uncertainty about how the involvement of black young people in crime should be handled theoretically and politically by a largely white profession, and the flight from class analysis, discussed above, ensured that the emphasis on social reaction and the neglect of aetiology which characterise both anti-racism and mainstream administrative criminology was perpetuated. As a result, most criminological studies in this area tend either to ignore the question of the involvement of black young people in crime or to utilise strategies which create historical or geographical distance, addressing the 'there' and 'then' rather than the here and now.

As people who are dependent upon the criminal justice and social welfare systems for their livelihood, criminologists are often constrained to search for answers to questions formulated by those who administer those systems. These questions, as we have seen, increasingly concern the cost-effective management of problem populations rather than the eradication of social problems. Add to this the implicit injunction upon all researchers in the post-1979 British welfare and justice systems that if they cannot bring good news they should not bring any, and it should not surprise us that there are significant gaps in our knowledge which nobody seems particularly keen to fill and that some of the material we do have lacks the ring of authenticity.

Criminology has tended to develop its arguments about race and crime on the basis of an idiosyncratic epistemology, an over-reliance on American data, a simplistic perception of 'blacks', a neglect of the 'whites' who appear to share a similar predicament, a muddled view of culture in general, a romanticised perception of Asian culture in particular and a pejorative view of the Afro-Caribbean family. More importantly, perhaps, like the anti-racism industry, it appears to have abandoned the concept of social structure.

Epistemological Dualism

The little evidence there is about the involvement of black people in crime tends to concern young men of Afro-Caribbean descent, and it suggests that those who are involved in serious crime tend to be involved in different kinds of crime which tends to be concentrated in particular localities (Burney, 1990; Jefferson, 1991; Pratt, 1980; Stevens and Willis, 1979). But the peculiar nature of the offences committed and the localised nature of the offending is also a characteristic of the drug-related robbery, 'lager loutery', 'joy-riding' and 'football hooliganism' perpetrated by some white young people. Thus we must ask whether 'black youth crime' is a distinctive phenomenon or a particular form of another phenomenon.

We have already noted the way in which the Brixton disturbances of 1981 were immediately 'racialised'. We do not know who the white young people who were involved in the Brixton disturbances were. They gave no interviews and no 'spokesmen' articulated their discontents. We do know that when the story of the summer of 1981 is retold these politically inconvenient figures, who constituted a significant minority of those initially involved in the fighting, have fallen victim to collective, selective amnesia.

The remarkable similarity between the accounts of relations with the police given by black young people in Brixton in 1981 and those of white young people in dilapidated housing estates in Salford, Bristol, Burnley and Carlisle in 1992 might suggest a consideration of how police perceptions of particular young people and neighbourhoods as disreputable are constituted and how this determines their subsequent behaviour towards them. But it is extremely unlikely that these events will be linked in this way. We know that, on average, black young people are stopped and searched by the police four or five times more often than white young people, but we also know that the incidence of white stop and searchers in 'areas of disrepute' is the same as the black figure (Smith, 1983).

In his study of prisoners entering Rochester allocation Borstal Colin Guest (1984) observed that the unemployment rate for the black entrants was in excess of 60 per cent, a figure similar to that for young black people in the areas from which they were drawn. However, the unemployment rate among white entrants was also over 60 per cent, although the figure for white young people in the areas from which they were drawn was nearer 25 per cent.

This suggests that there are white working-class young people in Britain who are, by definition, not subject to racism, yet are located in a similar socio-structural position, and subject to pressures and risks similar to those experienced by black young people. While it is reasonable to assume that police perceptions of disreputability are related to race and colour and that racism in employment contributed to high levels of unemployment among black entrants to Rochester Borstal, racism alone is not a sufficient explanation of the processes at work in these situations.

On the basis of this evidence, it is at least arguable that the race, crime and justice debate might be fruitfully broadened into a debate about social and economic marginalisation, its causes and consequences. Perhaps we should resuscitate that sub-field of empirical criminological enquiry concerned with the highly localised and distinctive patterns of crime perpetrated by members of socially marginalised adolescent peer groups, which has fallen into disuse since the advent of administrative criminology in the mid-1970s (Cloward and Ohlin, 1960; Downes, 1966; Parker, 1974; Pearson, 1987; Shaw and McKay, 1942; Smith et al., 1972; Whyte, 1943).

Lyric and Epic Criminology
The difference in the ways offending by black and white young people is approached in contemporary British criminology is reminiscent of the distinction Hegel draws between *Lyrical* and *Epic* modes of understanding. Lyricism seeks the essence of all things in the meticulous investigation of the detail of one thing. The Epic mode, by contrast, is the attempt to forge diverse phenomena into one totalising conceptual schema in order that its true nature may be revealed.

In its dealings with black young people, criminology abandons its traditional inductive, positivistic *modus operandi*. For good or ill, most criminology has been based upon the assumption that if one is able to gather together data on the biological, genetic, dietary, social, economic, psychological or educational characteristics of enough individual perpetrators one might build a picture of the characteristics of an entire category of offenders. In their dealings with black young people, however, most criminologists reverse this process. They proceed deductively, developing explanations of what makes black young offenders 'tick' on the basis of their understanding of extrinsic socio-cultural factors like 'black child-rearing patterns', 'black culture', 'black history' or 'black politics' rather than the empirical and quantifiable characteristics of the young people concerned (Cashmore and Troyna, 1982; Pratt, 1980; Wilson, 1975). The characteristics which black robbers share with white robbers in terms of age, social class, educational attainment, family structure etc. are ignored in favour of racialised explanations which, in fact, stress the characteristics they share with the vast majority of black young people who have never robbed anyone. This tendency, on the part of British criminology, to invoke an Epic mode of explanation is nowhere more evident than in its frequent recourse to the American analogy.

The American Analogy

A problem which dogs the political and academic debate about race and crime is the implicit, and sometimes explicit, assumption that what happens in the USA today will happen in the UK tomorrow. Thus, in the spring of 1992, Bernie Grant, the MP for Haringey, erroneously predicted 'Los Angeles-style riots in the streets of London this summer'. Utilising a similar device, Robert Harris (1992), while acknowledging that his argument is not supported by any home-grown evidence, none the less invokes data from the USA to prove his point. He writes:

> The *per capita* offence rate of blacks in the United Kingdom is *almost certainly* higher than that of whites however, though less starkly than either official figures or popular stereotypes suggest . . . Nevertheless, in North America, where the research is *better* than in Britain the data, though they differ on points of detail show *clearly* that most minorities . . . are significantly more crime-prone. (Harris, 1992: 108–9; emphasis added)

The clear implication of this passage is that 'black crime', whether in the UK or the USA, is of a piece. If this is correct, it follows that the American data can be used, unproblematically, to demonstrate the veracity of the author's argument about 'black crime' in Britain.

In the area in England and Wales with the highest crime rate and the highest murder rate is a secondary school in which organisational development techniques are being used in an attempt to minimise the victimisation of pupils. There is bullying, intimidation and racial abuse, but nobody has been killed there and, with the exception of a few trips to the casualty department, nobody has been hospitalised as a result of this behaviour (Pitts, 1993).

Denise Gottfreidson (1987) used a similar strategy in a high school in inner-city Baltimore, she writes: 'Tragic incidents resulting in student deaths and serious injury were not uncommon . . . One shooting incident resulting in death occurred only days prior to the researchers first planning meeting with the school staff.' It is not simply that Denise Gottfreidson has access to better data but rather that, in terms of the behaviour she confronts, she lives in a different world, dealing with problems people in Britain can barely imagine. The behaviour in the UK school appears to be similar but slightly worse than that reported in 'tough' secondary schools in Stockholm and Amsterdam and about the same as in Paris. It simply defies comparison with the behaviour described by Gottfreidson. The data are not analogous.

With a *per capita* murder rate ten times higher than that of the UK, it is clear that both the form and extent of crime in the USA is profoundly different. Afro-Americans are massively over-represented in most categories of serious crime and even more heavily represented in penal establishments in general and on 'death row' in particular (Lea and Young, 1984).

The 'American analogy' offers British criminologists a repository of data with which to make good the paucity of domestic material and allows a decent degree of equivocation about the domestic experience. It also offers some academic and political protagonists a symbol of an apocalyptic future with which to spice up their arguments. But we must not be seduced by American dreams or American night-mares. The problems of Britain's post-colonial legacy are more akin to those of France or The Netherlands than the problems of race relations in the USA (Rushdie, 1982). The strategies adopted in Europe are also more relevant than those deployed in the USA (King, 1991). In the USA, both crime rates and discrepancies of wealth and opportunity are far greater than in Europe where an established social democratic tradition has mediated the impact of the socially divisive policies of the 1980s:

> Try as the Thatcher government might, it has been unable to impose an American-style political culture upon the English public. According to the opinion polls, the public persists in the belief that the state should intervene not only to rectify the most obvious injustices but also to create, and guarantee, the conditions which make for a decent life for all citizens irrespective of wealth or ability. (Pitts, 1992: 185–6)

Recourse to the 'American analogy' has 'muddied the waters' and allowed British criminology to avoid the politically uncomfortable, and methodologically complex, business of discovering what is really happening in Britain.

Who Are the 'Blacks'?

In their appropriation of American data British criminologists appear to have ignored James Baldwin's warning that 'You can't tell a black man by the colour of his skin.' The US data cited by Robert Harris, for example, also shows that Afro-Caribbeans in the USA are less crime-prone and far more likely to achieve educationally and vocationally than indigenous Afro-Americans and this raises the question of which 'blacks' we are actually talking about?

Are we talking about the hundred or so members of Afro-Caribbean 'posses' from Lambeth who perpetrate the lion's share of street crime in Brixton, Clapham, Streatham and Oxford Circus (Burney, 1990)? Or are we talking about the smaller number of Afro-Caribbean young people from Tower Hamlets and Newham who are members of predominantly white gangs which victimise Bengalis? Or do we mean the all-Bengali self-styled 'Rock Street' Mafia (not the real street name) who, in response to this victimisation are now 'getting their retaliation in first', and perpetrating a great deal of affray, assault and actual bodily harm along the way?

There is no evidence, but it is almost certainly true that the amount of street crime perpetrated by 28-year-old, male, British Afro-Caribbean chartered accountants is the same as that perpetrated by 28-year-old, male, British Caucasian chartered accountants, namely 0.0 per cent. This is so obvious that it would be a totally trivial observation were it not for the fact that in its dealings with black populations, in marked contrast with its dealings with white populations, criminology almost invariably fails to distinguish between black people on the basis of their social class, education, gender, age and income. Yet, these are the factors, alongside the way he was brought up by his mum and dad, which determine that our Afro-Caribbean chartered accountant will stay on the straight and narrow.

This tendency to treat as homogeneous groups of people whose only common characteristic is that they are not Caucasian is not only thoughtlessly ethnocentric, it is poor scholarship and it leads to the denial of complexity which, Richard Titmuss warned us, is the essence of tyranny.

Culture

Similar criticism may be levelled at the way in which the concept of 'culture' is used in the debate. Culture is dialectical, inasmuch as we are shaped by it, through our ideas and actions we also shape it. Culture is not some atrophied monolith which dictates our deeds. One and a half hours spent watching *My Beautiful Launderette* should be enough to alert us to the fact that, culturally speaking, things ain't what they used to be, if indeed they ever were. Culture is a continually changing means of adaptation carrying within it traces of what we have been and intimations of what we can become. Yet, all too often in the race and crime debate, 'culture' is invoked as if it were a timeless and inexorable determinant of behaviour.

Cashmore and Troyna, for example, in their attempt to explain the involvement of black young people in street crime in Birmingham in the 1970s tell us that: 'there is a penchant for violence within the West Indian culture *probably* stemming from the days of slavery' (1982: 32–3; emphasis added). What they fail to tell us is how this cultural penchant has survived the years since the abolition of slavery, why it has leapt at least three generations, why most black young people don't do it, why some white young people whose ancestors were never enslaved do, and why it arrived in Birmingham in the late 1970s to afflict a small group of black British adolescents who had never set foot on a Caribbean island. Nor does it explain why Afro-Caribbean chartered accountants seldom hit people.

It is not that culture is unimportant in shaping behaviour but that, in offering culture up as an explanation in this way, it denigrates and pathologises it. The denigration of Afro-Caribbean culture finds its corollary in the idealisation of Asian culture. Tony Jefferson writes:

> Though I have no space to explore this properly and in truth *little research exists* to help here *it seems clear* that we will need to look towards certain cultural factors (*probably* those to do with family and community structure and religion) for an explanation. (Jefferson, 1991: 181; emphasis added)

Cultural stereotyping permeates both the mundane discourses of everyday life and the esoteric ruminations of the race, crime and justice debate. As Bryan (1992) has suggested, in both, the fantasy of the Afro-Caribbean family is of a rudderless ship pitching and tossing in a turbulent sea; of children abandoned by their fathers, often before they are even born, and condemned to the erratic care and discipline of a mother who, when she is prepared to tear herself away from her lovers at all, visits harsh and inconsistent punishment upon her children. It follows from this that Afro-Caribbean boys grow up with no self-discipline, only able to understand control when it is imposed from without.

The fantasy of the Asian family, by contrast, is of a tranquil house built upon the solid rock of tradition. Each member of the family understands exactly where authority lies, in the hands of the male elders, and they know their rights and obligations and the penalties which will be imposed if they fail to live up to these obligations. The costs in terms of loss of individual autonomy are outweighed by the benefits in terms of warmth, stability and self-discipline.

But the figures who populate the fantasy are strangely familiar for they are, the *deserving* and the *underserving poor*. A nineteenth-century imagery is imposed upon a complex contemporary reality. It is an imagery which evokes echoes of the id and the super-ego, of heaven and hell. This is a world of stereotypes not people, of symbols rather than flesh and blood and, as such, it tells us more about the ideological baggage and inner worlds of white people than it does about the families of black people.

Culture or Acculturation?

One of the few things we know with any certainty about the relationship between race and crime is that levels of crime among immigrant groups, and their descendants, almost always rise to those already pertaining in the neighbourhoods in which they settle (Lambert, 1970; Shaw and McKay, 1942). This is an important observation, suggesting that crime rates are neither a simple product of the proclivities of individuals nor of the cultural penchant of particular ethnic groups but, rather, a product of the chances, choices and solutions available within the milieu they enter. The rise in the crime rate among the second and subsequent generations of an immigrant group is a product of acculturation; the process whereby people make an accommodation with, and establish ways of being within, a new social environment. In the process, some 'incoming' young people will adopt the strategies and behaviours of the established social groups who are the culture carriers. These are the people who set the pace and dictate the terms on which the struggle for space will be conducted. They are, themselves, trapped in the area and share the same deprivations as the incoming families which are forced, by economic necessity, to share their neighbourhood and their social predicament. This said, however, it would be erroneous to infer that any more than a handful of these young people will become involved in serious or persistent offending.

Areas of Disrepute

These neighbourhoods are, invariably, areas of disrepute but the people who inhabit them have considerable economic and ideological utility. In his study of crime and policing in East London, Dick Hobbs (1989) argues that the prosperity and security of Westenders is, and always has been, contingent upon the relative poverty and economic fragility of Eastenders. Excluded from 'steady jobs' in the City of London's economic mainstream, Eastenders developed their own distinctive occupational style. He writes: 'With few exceptions the only occupations open to East Londoners were [a] heavy manual work paid at piece- or gang-rate, [b] street trading; or [c] a craft trade that required no apprenticeship, was not subject to workshop discipline, and amenable to self-employed status' (1989: 97). Short-falls in legitimate earnings were made good by a bit of 'ducking and diving' and over the period an elaborate illegitimate opportunity structure, with its own sophisticated division of labour, was overlaid upon the legitimate economic activity of the East End (Cloward and Ohlin, 1960).

In the economic history of Britain in the post-war period working-class black people have performed a similar function to that fulfilled by their white neighbours in areas of disrepute. Together, they have served as an expansion tank and a safety valve for an economy perpetually lurching from boom to slump and back again. Recruited initially to remedy a shortfall in the supply of cheap labour during the economic expansion of the 1950s, the combined effects of racism and recession have consigned many of today's black young people to the ever-expanding pool of 'flexible, expendable, un-unionised, surplus labour on the margins of the economy' (Hunt and Mellor, 1980; Pryce, 1979).

Transition or Immobility?

Shaw and McKay (1942) observed that when members of an immigrant group and their descendants moved on from the 'zone of transition' to more prosperous and prestigious neighbourhoods, their rate of recorded juvenile crime diminished. The gradual absorption of successive waves of 'immigrants' into the 'mainstream' of British society has a long history. It is, however, a process which appears to work only for white immigrants. Within one or two generations the Huguenots, Jews, Irish, Italians and Poles have, to all intents and purposes, disappeared into the cultural and ethnic mainstream. Not so Asian and Afro-Caribbean Britons, the majority of whom appear to be socially immobilised in the areas of disrepute on the margins of the economy.

Immobility and Protracted Adolescence

Adolescence is a period of transition but how long it lasts and when it ends depends upon whether a young person has the social and economic wherewithal to proceed to the next stage in the life-cycle. In his study, undertaken in the USA during the great depression, W.F. Whyte (1943) 'hung out' with a group of 'corner boys' in an Italian neighbourhood. As the book proceeds, we realise that Doc and the Nortons are not teenagers but men, some of them in their mid- to late twenties and that they have been hanging out on the same corner for over 10 years. They have been doing this because, having no steady jobs, they have no money to pay rent, buy furniture and do all the other things one would need to do to become a 'family man' in Cornerville. They are, as a result, frozen in a state of perpetual adolescence.

In East London in the early 1990s, black juvenile justice workers observed that the upper age of members of the local Afro-Caribbean 'posse' had risen to over 30. One of the consequences of this has been that the older members have introduced some of the younger ones to more serious crime. Like Doc and the Nortons, these men could not make the transition from adolescence to higher status adult roles because they simply did not have the means to do so.

Enforced adolescence means that young people, black and white, in areas of disrepute on the social and economic margins are, quite literally, prevented from growing up. This has important implications for their involvement in crime because all the evidence we have suggests that 'growing up', the assumption of adult roles, rights and responsibilities, also means growing out of crime (Rutherford, 1986).

It is against the backdrop of this expanding pool of economically marginal, reluctant adolescents that the violent public disorder which is coming to characterise areas of disrepute throughout Britain, and for which Brixton 1981 was the prototype, must be understood. These young people are condemned by poverty and unemployment to inhabit overcrowded, under-resourced, high-crime neighbourhoods. They are compelled by social structure and culture to be less than whole people trapped in a limbo world somewhere between childhood and adulthood long after the 'developmental tasks' of adolescence have been completed. Moreover, they are fixed ideologically, destined to serve as folk devils, to provide the screen upon which the fears and fantasies of those near the social centre are projected.

Conclusion

If a century of sociological studies of crime in cities has any validity, it would be astonishing if we did not find that the crime rate among the young people who inhabit the poorest sections of our inner cities was not disproportionately high. We would expect this to be the case irrespective of their race, religion or hat size. The fact that a disproportionately large number of young black Britons are located in such areas would suggest that their crime rate would, in consequence, be higher than average. This is a plausible hypothesis but, for reasons already discussed, it is a hypothesis which remains more or less untested. This is because the political issue, 'race and crime', has detached itself from the empirical reality about which, let us remind ourselves, we know very little and mainstream criminology would apparently, like us to know even less. To insist, therefore, that the plight of those black young people who inhabit the poorest sections of our inner cities, who are prone to a multiplicity of social, educational and economic deprivations, are most likely to become involved in crime but are also most likely to be wrongly accused of such crime, and victimised by it, must be explained in a wholly different way from the plight of similarly located, similarly crime-prone, frequently 'framed', often victimised white young people is, at best, naive.

The assertion of the anti-racism industry that 'racism' is the pre-eminent, indeed exclusive, analytical category and explanatory schema for the multiplicity of disadvantages which afflict black people in Britain is a political posture rather than an credible intellectual proposition (Mullard, 1991). It attempts to make good the limitations of an analysis which was 'totalised' around social class by placing racism in a similar 'totalising' role. In separating racial oppression from social inequality and poverty, it requires us to forget most of what we know about the involvement of dispossessed black and white young people in crime and civil disorder, to desist from discovering more and to stay silent about our experience. To that extent, it sacrifices the interests of those young people to political expediency.

Rather than the competition between 'perspectives' and 'isms' which the anti-racism industry is fostering, we need a theoretical synthesis which can grasp the complex and ever-changing relations between race, class and gender on the social margins, and the ways in which they are mediated by structure, culture and biography (Critcher, 1976; Mills, 1959). Such a synthesis would embrace the idea that the social world has an ideological centre and a hierarchical structure which reflect both historically determined racial and class relations and economically determined contemporary power relations.

It would resist the temptation to assuage its anxieties about the complexity and 'unknowability' of the world by developing a new totalising schema and, instead, pursue a theoretical agnosticism in which the interplay between the categories of race, class, gender, structure, culture and biography could promote fruitful coexistence in place of the arid conflict which characterises contemporary debate. It would acknowledge that social structure and ideology affect the consciousness of the oppressed, their oppressors and those who investigate oppression. Beyond this, it would come to grips with the uncomfortable possibility that oppressed people, by a process of internalisation, may themselves become the oppressors of those whose predicament they share.

Such an approach would lead us to a consideration of the aetiology of particular forms of individual and group behaviour rather than the virtually exclusive concern with social reaction which characterises the lion's share of research in this field. It would recognise that racial oppression has social, economic and existential consequences more serious and more pervasive than the misrecognition and maltreatment of black people by misinformed or malevolent agents of public services. It would remind us that even when every last employee of every agency in the welfare and justice systems in Britain has at last become 'racially hip', the factors which ensure that the greatest injustice of all, that so many black children and young people in Britain can see no future for themselves, will remain untouched.

7

Constructions of Black Criminality: Racialisation and Criminalisation in Perspective

John Solomos

The question of race and crime has played an important role in the politics of race in contemporary British society. There is little doubt that over the past two decades political debates about racial issues have been deeply influenced by concerns about crime and the potential for criminality among sections of the black communities in inner-city localities. Additionally, it seems quite clear that within institutions such as the police force we have seen the development of specific ideologies about this issue and particular types of police response. This process was given added impetus in the 1980s by the phenomenon of urban unrest in many inner-city areas, which led to the entrenchment of racialised ideas about crime and disorder.

This chapter analyses the processes through which this racialisation has come about. It will look particularly at the changing forms of debate about race and crime during the past two decades. Arguing for the need to put the question of race and criminality in a broader socio-political context, the chapter is organised around a discussion of the key debates on this issue. It begins by looking at the period from the late 1960s and early 1970s, and then looks more specifically at trends and developments during the 1980s. It concludes by looking at the question of how this issue is likely to be perceived in the future.

Race and Criminality

Along with the broader processes of racialisation, the 1960s saw a growing focus on questions of race and crime, and continuous attempts by the police and by government to deal with the danger of conflict between the police and black communities (Keith, 1993; Solomos, 1988). The concerns at this stage were about the growing number of complaints of racial discrimination by the police against blacks, the future of young blacks, and the fear that racial violence and disorder could be reproduced in major cities.

In July 1967 the Home Office issued a circular to all Chief Constables on *The Police and Coloured Communities*, which advised them to appoint, particularly in areas of black settlement, liaison officers whose task would be to develop better relations with black communities and educate the police themselves on the dilemmas of policing such areas. This was followed by a number of consultative meetings to discuss the policing of particular localities and to analyse the long-term prospects of future conflict between the police and black communities.

The police themselves began to recognise, somewhat hesitantly, the need to develop an understanding of the context of policing in multiracial areas. In 1970 a conference of US and British specialists and practitioners was held under the auspices of the Ditchley Foundation to discuss 'police–community relations' on both sides of the Atlantic (Clarke, 1970). Other meetings and seminars were also held to discuss this issue, and from 1970 onwards the annual Reports of the Commissioner of Police of the Metropolis contain some discussion of the specific issues related to the policing of multiracial areas.

This debate was carried forward in the national media, as well as in specialised race journals like *Race Today*, which was at the time published by the Institute of Race Relations. The public nature of the debate helped to politicise the question of race and policing to a new level during the early 1970s, particularly as pressure mounted from within the black communities for investigations into cases of harassment by the police, and for 'greater equality before the law' (Hall et al., 1978; John, 1970). It should also be remembered, of course, that it was during this period that the question of 'immigration and race' came to occupy a central role in debates about domestic social policies at both a national and a local political level. This broader process of racialisation helped to increase the impact of the policy debate about the inter-relationship of crime and race, since this issue served to give further credence to the Powellite warnings that immigration was undermining the whole of the social fabric of the inner cities. The imagery of black involvement in criminal activities and in public order offences helped to fuel and give a new direction to the increasingly volatile public debate about race relations.

Crime and Ghetto Life

In 1970 Gus John published his influential study of Handsworth called *Race in the Inner City*, and in the same year John Lambert published a study of *Crime, Police and Race Relations*. Both studies attracted attention because they came out at a time when the issues of relations between the black communities and the police and the involvement of young blacks in crime were the subject of much concern. During the same period a number of feature articles and reports in the press discussed various aspects of the growing tension between the police and the black communities, both at a national level and in relation to specific communities. The complaints against the police by the black communities themselves, which had been articulated as early as 1966 in Hunte's *Nigger Hunting in England*, reached new levels during the early 1970s and were rapidly becoming a political issue.

John's study of Handsworth was a particularly important document in this period. Written by a black researcher, who had spent some time living within the black community in Handsworth, it highlights the question of policing and the position of young blacks as the core concerns of local residents. It was written at a time when the police themselves were discussing their role in the policing of multiracial inner-city areas and formulating their ideologies and practices on this issue (Humphry, 1972). Additionally, media coverage at the time talked of the growing tensions between the police and black communities, and 1969–70 saw a number of minor street confrontations with the police in areas such as Notting Hill.

John began his account of Handsworth with an analysis of the area and the contrasting perceptions offered by local residents of the postwar period. But the core of his report, and the issue which gave rise to a full debate in the press, was the description which it offered of relations between the local black community, particularly younger blacks, and the police. John reported that one police official had pointed out to him that the 'growth of black crime' in the area was the work of a 'hard core' of 40 or 50 youngsters (John, 1970: 20). But his own perceptions of the situation were more complex, and he summarised them as amounting to three main issues:

1 The prevalence of rumours, fears and explanations of black involvement in criminal activities.
2 A tendency by police to blame the 'hard core' of young blacks for 'giving the area a bad name'.
3 Deep resentment by older and younger blacks with their social position and the discrimination they had to endure.

Additionally, he warned that there were signs of 'a massive breakdown in relations between the police and the black community', and that if nothing were done the situation was likely to lead to confrontations between black residents and the police and outbursts of urban unrest:

> In my view trends in Handsworth are a portent for the future. A decaying area, full of stress and tension, which also happens to be racially mixed, is going to find it increasingly difficult to cope with the root problems because racial animosities and resentments have taken on an independent life of their own. The problem is not, and can never be, simply one of law and order. (John, 1970: 25)

It was this context, argued John, which explained why both young blacks and the police saw the situation in the area as one of open 'warfare' (1970: 28–9).

Evidence from black communities across the country highlighted three particularly contentious issues. First, complaints by young blacks that they were being categorised as a problem group by the police, and that they were therefore more likely to be questioned or arrested. Secondly, allegations that the police used excessive physical force in their dealings with black suspects. Finally, it was argued that such attitudes and forms of behaviour by the police were helping to fuel popular rumours about the involvement of young blacks in crime, and to drive a wedge between the police and the black communities.

Perhaps most significantly the shifting emphasis on young blacks as a problem category for the police and for society as a whole was being framed increasingly around the question of crime. The shift became particularly clear when (a) the question of policing was investigated by the Select Committee on Race Relations and Immigration during 1971–2, and (b) popular and media debate focused on the involvement of young blacks in forms of street crime which were popularly defined as mugging.

As argued above, the politicisation of the question of crime in relation to young blacks is best seen within the broader context of official and public concern with the interplay between ghetto life, the social position of young blacks and criminal activities. The Select Committee on Race Relations and Immigration's investigation of *Police/Immigrant Relations*, which was carried out during 1971–2, represents a useful starting point for understanding the concerns of the state, the police and the black communities in relation to policing and law and order.

The Committee's report, two substantive volumes of evidence, and the government response to its recommendations were, in effect, the first coherent official statement on the inter-relationship between race, crime and policing. Young blacks were a central issue in the deliberations and the conclusions of the Committee, since it was the younger generation who were both popularly and officially seen as the 'source of the problem'. The Committee took evidence from community groups, police officials, local authorities and government departments on the causes of 'growing tension' between the police and sections of the black communities. Although the popular press and John's report on Handsworth had shown that police on the ground perceived a section of blacks disproportionately involved in criminal activities, the Committee concluded that this claim was not supported by the evidence:

> The conclusions remain beyond doubt: coloured immigrants are no more involved in crime than others; nor are they generally more concerned in violence, prostitution and drugs. The West Indian crime rate is much the same as that of the indigenous population. The Asian crime rate is very much lower. (Select Committee, 1972, Report: 71)

It did point out, however, that there was one major source of conflict between the police and black communities: namely, the 'explosive' relations between the 'younger generation of West Indians' and the police. The source of this conflict was seen as lying in a combination of factors, most notably in the situation of young blacks themselves and the attitude of the police (1972: 68–9).

On the question of allegations that the police were engaged in practices including harassment, assault, wrongful arrest and detention, provocation, fabrication, planting of evidence and racial insults, the Committee was much more reticent to come to any conclusions. It accepted that much of the evidence submitted to it by the Community Relations Commission contained claims that such practices were common in many localities (Select Committee, 1972, Evidence: vol. II: 65–8; vol. III: 716–35, 765–71). While accepting that these claims were believed by many black people, it found it impossible to 'prove or disprove' them, with the truth lying somewhere in between the claims of the police and their critics (Select Committee, 1972, Report: 20–21). Rather, it saw these claims and counter-claims as the natural outcome of a lack of communication between the police and sections of black youth. This lack of communication helped to build stereotypes and to reproduce situations of conflict.

The Committee recommended that a programme of action should be implemented to improve communication, including more training and schemes to improve relations with the black communities in problem areas (1972: 92–5). It concluded that such a positive programme of action could ensure that better relations were re-established between young blacks and the police: 'If the best examples of leadership in police and immigrant relations prevailed throughout forces in the United Kingdom, many of the difficulties we have dwelt upon would, within a reasonable space of time, diminish. In some places they could wither away' (1972:92). From this perspective the situation in some localities, although 'explosive' and dangerous, could be defused if the pressures which produced tension between young blacks and the police were dealt with.

This was a hope which was to remain unfulfilled throughout the 1970s, since the production of the Select Committee's Report on *Police/Immigrant Relations* coincided with a marked politicisation of the debates about black youth, and police and crime during the late 1970s and 1980s. This politicisation, occurring as it did at a time of upheaval about race and immigration more generally, was reflected in frequent media reports, official documents, and speeches by politicians, police officers and other opinion leaders. From the early 1970s it focused particularly on the supposed involvement of young blacks in the form of street crime popularly defined as mugging.

Mugging, Social Control and Young Blacks

The social construction of the question of mugging and black youth during the early 1970s represents perhaps the clearest example of how the politicisation of debates about race and crime came about. The genesis and development of official, police and media ideologies about mugging have been analysed and commented on from a number of angles during the past 15 years, and I do not want to retrace the steps of existing accounts. I shall focus instead on one aspect of this phenomenon: namely, the interplay during the early 1970s of images of black youth and mugging and the consequences of this process for policy and practice in relation to young blacks.

The history of the media and popular response to the mugging issue has been analysed in some detail by Hall et al. in *Policing the Crisis* (1978). The premise of this study was that the construction of black communities as social problems was the ideological bedrock on which the black youth/urban deprivation/street crime model of mugging was constructed during the early 1970s. Mugging as a political phenomenon, according to Hall et al. became associated with black youth because they were seen as: (a) a social group which suffered the most direct impact of the cycle of poverty, unemployment and social alienation which afflicted inner city areas; and (b) suffering from the added disadvantage of belonging to a racial group with a 'weak' culture and high levels of social problems, such as broken families and lack of achievements in schools (Hall et al. 1978: ch. 10). The power of these images according to this study derived partly from popular common-sense images about race and the inner cities, but also from the feelings of uncertainty which were developing within British society as a whole about the position of black communities and their role within the dominant institutions (Hall et al., 1978: 346–9).

Hall et al. note, for example, that even in areas where young blacks were a small minority of the total youth population, the issue of crime on the streets became intimately tied with the category of black youth. This ideological construction became possible because during the period from the early 1970s onwards a dominant concern about the 'ghetto areas' focused on the supposed drift of young blacks into a life of crime and poverty. According to Hall et al.:

> For all practical purposes, the terms mugging and black crime are now virtually synonymous. In the first mugging panic, as we have shown, though mugging was continually shadowed by the theme of race and crime, this link was rarely made explicit. This is no longer the case. The two are indissolubly linked: each term references the other in both the official and public consciousness. (Hall et al., 1978: 217)

This convergence of concerns about race, crime and the ghetto areas onto the category of black youth thus involved a combination of images which linked particular areas of specific types of crime, and these crimes to a specific category of the local population. The definition of 'criminal areas' in everyday police practices thus gained a clear racial dimension, which was in turn accentuated by the wider social and economic processes which confined black communities to inner-city areas and excluded them from equal participation in the labour market and in society more generally.

During the 1970s it also became clear that everyday confrontations about minor issues could easily escalate into open conflict and acts of collective protest on the streets. This phenomenon had already been noted in media coverage and in the Select Committee's 1971–2 Report, but the level of tension mounted during 1973–6 in a sequence of incidents which can now, with the benefit of hindsight, be seen as presaging the larger-scale disturbances during the 1980s. This included the widely reported confrontation in June 1973 between black youth, the police and the wider black community in Brockwell Park, South London. The events were widely reported in the popular and serious press, and in black journals such as *Race Today*. One of the features of the reporting of this event centred on the image of the events as a 'race riot' and as a sign of larger riots and disorders on the horizon. This theme became more pronounced once it was clear that the Brockwell Park incident was not merely an isolated incident, and that outbreaks of a similar kind were becoming part of the everyday experience of many inner-city areas.

Another factor which helped shape the politicisation of the mugging issue was the wider picture of societal concern about disorder and a breakdown of law and order in British society. Although this phenomenon was not always linked to popular and official perceptions of race, crime and policing, the volatile racialisation of political debate during the early 1970s helped to bring the two issues together in popular discourse.

Policing, Racialisation and Black Crime

Since the 1970s other preoccupations about black crime have come to the fore, which involve broader issues about race relations as well. First, the growing politicisation of debates about the social and economic conditions within the black communities broadened concern out from a preoccupation with young blacks as such towards the wider communities within which the younger generation lived. In this sense debates about black crime signify concern about the crisis of the 'urban black colonies' (Hall et al., 1978: 338–9). Secondly, the period since the mid-1970s is one in which the question of black youth has become intimately tied to the broader issues of disorder and violent protest, particularly in areas of high levels of black settlement.

The period of the late 1970s saw a number of examples of the material importance of these shifts in political language. The most important was the attempt by Enoch Powell and other politicians to politicise the debate about black crime, and the occurrence of small-scale riots in areas such as Notting Hill in 1976 and 1977, and in other localities from 1977 onwards (Keith, 1993). As a result the issue of black crime was firmly placed on the political agenda. A number of stages in this process were particularly important.

First, the release in January 1975 by the Metropolitan Police of figures from a study of victims' descriptions of assailants in the Brixton area of London. This claimed to show that 79 per cent of robberies and 83 per cent of offences of theft from the person were carried out be black people. This study was widely reported in the media and helped to attract attention to the 'growing problem' of black involvement in crime and the destabilising role of young disillusioned blacks. Secondly, in May 1975 Judge Gwyn Morris jailed five young West Indians for mugging offences in South London. In sentencing them he commented: 'These attacks have become a monotonous feature in the suburbs of Brixton and Clapham, areas which within memory were peaceful, safe, and agreeable places to live in. But immigration resettlement, which has occurred over the past 25 years has radically transformed that environment' (*The Guardian*, May 16, 1975). He went on to argue that youngsters such as them were collectively a 'frightening menace to society', and that they represented 'immense difficulties' for those interested in the maintenance of law and order.

Thirdly, and perhaps more important in terms of its public impact, Enoch Powell's speech of April 1976 about mugging being a 'racial phenomenon' helped to articulate a wider undercurrent of concern about the inter-relationship between race and crime. Powell's speech was in turn linked to the evidence submitted by the Metropolitan Police in March 1976 to the Select Committee on Race Relations and Immigration. The Committee was investigating *The West Indian Community* (1977). In its evidence to the 1972 Select Committee Report on *Police/Immigrant Relations* the Metropolitan Police had not raised black crime as a major problem, but the intervening period had obviously transformed their image of this issue. In the very first paragraph of its evidence the Metropolitan Police mentioned the 'uneasy nature of the relationship between police officers and young blacks' in some localities. Although the memorandum did not argue for a direct link between crime and race, and it mentioned the social disadvantages that were common in such areas, it went on to argue that:

> It is not part of our position that there is a causal link between ethnic origin and crime. What our records do suggest is that London's black citizens, among whom those of West Indian origin predominate, are disproportionately involved in many forms of crime. But in view of their heavy concentration in areas of urban stress, which are themselves high crime areas, and in view of the disproportionate numbers of young people in the West Indian population, this pattern is not surprising. (Select Committee, 1977, Evidence vol. II: 182)

Whether surprising or not, this analysis was to prove extremely controversial, and was directly criticised in the evidence submitted by the Community Relations Commission, to which the Metropolitan Police responded with additional evidence to support their claims. The public debate over these statistics helped to push black crime onto the political agenda in a way which gave legitimacy both to popular concern about crime on the streets and to the arguments of politicians such as Powell who called for 'repatriation' as the only solution to crime and disorder.

As argued above, the symbolic threat of violent disorder was a theme in official political language about young blacks from the late 1960s onwards. But in August 1976 it became a material reality on the streets of Notting Hill. During the annual Carnival in the area a major confrontation took place between young blacks (and to some extent young whites) and the police. Other confrontations took place in other cities. Although not on the same level as the disturbances of the 1980s, the symbolic significance of this event was clear at the time and has been reiterated with some regularity ever since. The unstated issue which links all these events together was that the confrontations mentioned all involved young blacks in one way or another. Other less major confrontations also took place in November 1975 in Chapeltown (Leeds), and in other areas. During this period police activities under the 'sus' legislation and by the Special Patrol Group led to frequent instances of lower level confrontations between the police and young blacks (AFFOR, 1978; Demuth, 1978; Hall et al., 1978). More broadly, the concern with the 'growing problem' of black crime helped to make the police on the ground suspect all black youngsters, and particularly those who congregated in groups. The imagery of violent street crime combined with that of violent street disorders and confrontations to make every young black, or particularly groups of them (such as Rastafarians), a potential suspect in police eyes. They were suspect not only because of social perceptions about their involvement in street crime, but because they were black, because of the areas in which they lived, their style of dress and social contact, and their leisure activities. This is certainly how an increasing number of younger blacks, along with their parents and independent researchers, saw the situation in many inner city localities, particularly those that were seen as 'immigrant areas'.

It was because of this 'growing problem' that Robert Mark, the Metropolitan Police Commissioner, chose to highlight in his annual Report for 1975, even before the Notting Hill disturbances, the fact that there was a tendency within black communities 'for groups of black people to react in violent opposition to police officers carrying out their lawful duties' (Report of the Commissioner of Police of the Metropolis for the year 1975, 1976: 12). This was a theme taken up in articles in police journals and by official police documents during this period. The widely publicised Metropolitan Police evidence to the Select Committee investigation on *The West Indian Community* stated the official police wisdom and common sense on the subject when it noted that:

> Recently there has been a growth in the tendency for members of London's West Indian communities to combine against police by interfering with police officers who are affecting the arrest of a black person or who are in some other way enforcing the law in situations which involve black people. In the last 12 months forty such incidents have been recorded. Each carries a potential for large scale disorder; despite the fact that very few situations actually escalate to the point where local police are unable to cope. Experience indicates that they are more likely to occur during the summer months and that the conflict is invariably with young West Indians. They can occur anywhere in the Metropolitan Police District, but are of course more likely in those areas which have a high

proportion of West Indian settlers. (Select Committee, 1977, Evidence, vol. II: 178)

This perception was repeated across the country in the areas where confrontations between young blacks and the police, and growing tension between them, had become a major issue. Within this context references to urban disorder and street violence became a synonym for confrontations between young blacks and the police.

Apart from the national trends discussed above, it is also clear that the response of the police in areas such as Notting Hill, Brixton, Handsworth and Moss Side further accentuated the stereotype of young blacks (or at least a section of them) as members of a 'criminal sub-culture'. At a common-sense level, the everyday contact between young blacks and the police was interpreted through police ideologies as involving a clash between the cultural values of the majority community and those of the minority communities caught up in a web of poverty, unemployment, racial disadvantage and alienation. But such notions about the nature of the 'racial problem' which the police faced in many urban localities were in turn supported by common-sense notions about the localities in which the black communities tended to be concentrated and the socioeconomic conditions which confronted young blacks in inner-city areas. This helped to create symbols which the police could easily identify as the source of the problem whether at the individual level (in terms of 'criminal' young blacks) or at the level of geographical localities ('criminal areas'). This process in turn helped to give further support to the notion that the source of the problem lay in the culture and attitudes of young blacks, with racism and discrimination seen as playing only subsidiary roles.

Race, Crime and Statistics

The 1970s then witnessed a complex process by which young blacks came to be seen as intimately involved in (a) particular forms of street crime and (b) confrontations with the police which represented a challenge to the maintenance of law and order. The early 1980s in turn were an important period in the racialisation of debates about law and order, crime and policing in at least two ways. First, the politicisation of the black youth unemployment issue helped to focus attention on the inter-relationship between unemployment and crime. Secondly, the riots during 1980–81 and 1985 forced the issues of black crime and violence on the streets onto the mainstream political agenda. The widespread coverage given to the issue of race in connection with the riots helped to open up a wider debate about issues such as mugging and black crime under the wider concern of the future of British society.

In the aftermath of the 1980–81 riots in Bristol, Brixton, Toxteth and elsewhere, one of the most important public debates about 'race and crime' took place during 1982–3. It followed the decision of the Metropolitan Police in March 1982 to release a racial breakdown of those responsible for street robberies, a statistical breakdown which it had not published previously, although it had been collating such statistics for some time (Scotland Yard, Press Release, March 10, 1982; *The Guardian*, March 11, 1982). The police statistics showed a marked rise in street robberies, but the crucial statistic which the press and the media picked on was concerned with the 'disproportionate involvement' of young blacks in street crimes such as mugging, purse snatching and robbery from stores. The press reaction to the press release varied from sober commentaries on the nature and limitations of the statistics to sensational headlines about black crime, including *The Sun*'s 'The Yard Blames Black Muggers'. But a common theme was the argument that the statistics, along with the riots during 1980–81, were further evidence of the consequences of letting in alien communities to settle in the very heart of Britain. *The Daily Telegraph* articulated this argument succinctly:

> Over the 200 years up to 1945, Britain became so settled in internal peace that many came to believe that respect for the person and property of fellow citizens was something which existed naturally in all but a few. A glance at less fortunate countries might have reminded us that such respect scarcely exists unless law is above the power of tribe, or money, or the gun. But we did not look; we let in people from the countries we did not look at, and only now do we begin to see the result. Many young West Indians in Britain, and, by a connected process, growing numbers of young whites, have no sense that the nation in which they live is part of them. So its citizens become to them mere objects of violent exploitation. (*The Daily Telegraph,* March 11, 1982)

Such an argument amounted to a direct link between race and crime. A similar tone was adopted by papers such as the *Daily Mail* and *The Sun*, which went even further in their use of images of mugging – harking back to Powell's 1976 definition of mugging as essentially a black crime. A year later the intervention of Harvey Proctor, the right-wing Tory MP, helped to secure the release of similar figures by the Home Office and led to a similar wave of articles in the press about the 'rising wave' of crime in areas of black settlement. Since then the Metropolitan Police have been much more reticent about publishing such statistics (although they continue to be kept), because of their potentially volatile political impact.

Not surprisingly, however, the issue of the involvement of young blacks in criminal or quasi-criminal activities became a key area of concern for the police and other institutions, both locally and nationally. Because of this climate of official concern the issues of crime and violence remain central to the full understanding of how contemporary ideologies about young blacks as a social category were formed and how they are being transformed.

Crime and Policing after the Riots

This emphasis became clear in the aftermath of the riots of 1980–81, and particularly after the widespread disturbances of 1985 (Benyon and Solomos, 1987). The construction of the riots as a form of criminal activity became a way of understanding them not as a form of protesting against the unbearable social conditions of inner-city areas or the actions of the police, but a criminal act or a 'cry for loot'. This was an argument put most succinctly by Geoffrey Dear, Chief Constable of the West Midlands Police and by Douglas Hurd, the Home Secretary, in relation to the 1985 riots in Handsworth (Dear, 1985). Another argument was that the outbreak of violence in Handsworth and Brixton, in particular, was brought about by drug barons who saw the police attempting to curb their activities and control their territory. Numerous examples of this line of argument can be found in Dear's report on Handsworth, and in a number of major press stories published during the riots.

The attack on criminal acts and the emphasis on order, resonated through a long debate in Parliament on October 23, 1985, on urban disturbances. Rejecting the Labour Party's call for an independent inquiry into causes of the riots, the government succeeded in pushing through the following resolution:

> That this House recognises the crucial importance of the maintenance of public order; applauds the courage and dedication of the police and responsible community leaders in restoring order; and welcomes Her Majesty's Government's commitment to early effective action in the light of the recent urban disturbances. (*Hansard*, vol. 84, 1985: col. 388)

A measure of how the law and order argument was used can also be found in the numerous calls made by Douglas Hurd for people to rally round the police in order to defend the rule of law, and the acceptance by virtually all the media that, in the short term at least, the restoration of police authority on the 'streets of fear' was the first priority.

Taking the specific argument about the role of drugs and drug barons in stimulating the riots, this seems to have served two purposes. First, it distanced the riots from the social, economic, political and other grievances which had been linked to them, by locating the cause outside the social problems of inner-city dwellers and in the simple greed of the drug barons to accumulate. Secondly, just as Dear's image of a few hundred 'young black criminals' was used to explain what happened in Handsworth, the problem of drugs was used to explain what happened at a national level. The issue of drugs provided an everyday image, already a national issue through saturation media coverage and public debate, around which the police, the Home Office and other institutions could de-socialise the riots.

What is clear, therefore, is that the public pronouncements branding the riots as criminal acts and a cry for loot were only one element of a wider ideological construction of the events around the theme of a drift towards crime. While the branding of the riots as criminal seemed to depoliticise them, it is quite clear that a more complex analysis of why crime and disorder were a growing phenomenon exercised an influence on police and other official ideologies.

The theme of outside agitators had been widely used to explain the 1980–81 riots, but 1985 saw a massive explosion of this imagery and its use to explain the causes of the attacks on the police. Take, for example, the treatment by the press of Bernie Grant, and other black and white local Labour Party leaders. They were labelled by Douglas Hurd as the 'High Priests of Race Hate', and then followed lurid press stories which attempted to show how 'GLC leftists', 'black activists' or plain 'reds' were behind a campaign to undermine the police, to stimulate urban violence and to bring about a collapse of law and order. Such stories served a double function. First, they unmasked the forces behind the riots and gave credibility to claims that even if they were not pre-planned they had been sparked off by agitation from leftists and other folk devils. Secondly, they helped to decontextualise the riots from the issue of racism and the social position of inner-city black communities by laying the blame for race hate squarely at the door of the extreme left and black activists. Indeed, according to Ronald Butt, a regular columnist for *The Times* and other papers on race issues during 1980–81 and 1985, race had become a new weapon in the class war.

If blaming assorted types of reds for the outbreak of street violence had taken on new forms in 1985, the traditional outside agitator themes of masked men and foreign agents did not exactly disappear. A classic of its own kind is the following story from the *Daily Express* of October 8, 1985 about the death of PC Blakelock on Broadwater Farm:

> *Moscow-trained hit squad gave orders as mob hacked PC Blakelock to death.*
> The thugs who murdered policeman Keith Blakelock in the Tottenham

riots acted on orders of crazed left-wing extremists. Street-fighting experts trained in Moscow and Libya were behind Britain's worst violence.

The chilling plot emerged last night as detectives hunted a hand-picked death squad believed to have been sent into North London hell-bent on bloodshed.

They include men and women from Commonwealth countries like Jamaica, Barbados and Nigeria, who have been trained in Russia and Libya in street revolutionary tactics.

A number of similar stories resonated through the pages of the popular press, even when there was no evidence supplied or when the links seemed to be a matter of assertion. Looking for the 'men behind the riots' turned out to be less a matter of the individual 'leftists' who were named in such stories but of the construction of symbolic cues about the threat posed to Britain by 'outside agents', 'men and women from Commonwealth countries'. In fact, what is interesting about the *Daily Express* story, apart from the classic headline, is the way it highlights the supposed use of 'immigrants' by Russia and Libya to undermine order and stability.

The symbolic political value of such metaphors has been noted in studies of riot response in the USA, where the 'outside agitators' argument was used to deflect attention away from social, economic and policing issues (Edelman, 1971; Lipsky and Olson, 1977). The experiences of 1980–81 and 1985 in Britain suggest that such an analysis needs to be contextualised against a broader historical perspective, since 'outside agitator' type of arguments do not seem to have any relation to the 'facts' of the riots as such. They seem to form part of a wider use of symbolic political language to help make sense of the crises facing British society. Ambiguous political situations such as riots help engender anxieties about the role of external threats to order, but they do not create such beliefs. But when they are contextualised against the background of wider political debates about race and immigration in post-1945 Britain it becomes easier to see the interconnections between images of outside agitators and the popular stereotypes of blacks as 'alien'.

The notion that the growth of street violence was the product of a combination of social problems leading to the emergence of a 'criminal element' and 'hooliganism' was one of the main themes in accounts of the 1980–81 riots, as pointed out above. But in the responses to the 1985 riots we see not only a common-sense use of such ideas but a more sophisticated use of such an explanation by sections of the police. Some reference to this development has been made in relation to Dear's report on Handsworth. A more developed version was offered in the aftermath of the 1985 riots by Sir Kenneth

Newman, Commissioner of the Metropolitan Police. During the period of 1982–5 he had already made a series of influential speeches on the issue of disorder and the growth of violence in British society. In a paper delivered in 1983 he had warned that in many inner-city areas the police were under threat and unable to maintain order: 'In many multi-ethnic areas police encounter not merely apathy and unhelpfulness when making enquiries or engaging in order mainten-ance, but outright hostility and obstruction' (Newman, 1983: 28). He warned that such a situation could result in a cycle of increasing crime, law-breaking, police inability to maintain order and the reinforcement of urban decay. He argued that increasingly policing was not an isolated service but part of a wider set of agencies which helped to maintain social stability and order and prevent a drift towards crime and lawlessness. He saw such agencies as particularly important in the areas of education, health and social services, housing and environment, and employment.

In the aftermath of the 1985 riots Newman extended his analysis by arguing that crime and the fear of crime helped to reinforce attitudes towards the police and society which allowed violent protests to break out and challenge the legitimacy of the established order (Newman, 1986a,b). Crime, according to Newman, provided not so much a causal explanation for riots, but one element in a broader crisis of social policy and control. He saw this as particularly important in areas of a 'multi-ethnic' nature where cultural and political hostility towards the police was growing.

Racialisation and Criminalisation in the 1990s

What has also become clear during the 1990s, however, is that the trends outlined above have by no means reached a conclusion. The criminalisation of black communities has proceeded apace and has taken on new forms in the current period. There is widespread evidence that the criminal justice system is now one of the key mechanisms by which ideas about racial difference in British society are reproduced. Evidence about this can be derived from studies of the number of young Afro-Caribbeans prosecuted for indictable offences, the number of prisoners from minority backgrounds and other studies about the involvement of black people in the criminal justice system generally (Keith, 1993; Reiner, 1989). There is also a wealth of evidence about racist attitudes and beliefs within the police. Several studies have shown that racist values play an important role in the everyday culture of the police at both rank and file, and command levels (Graef, 1990; Keith, 1993; Reiner, 1991; Young 1991). Though this evidence in itself cannot necessarily fully explain the criminalisation of black communities, it is worth noting that, despite the efforts made over the past decade to tackle the prevalence of racial prejudice in the police force, racism clearly persists.

Such trends have aroused concern within many local communities about the future. Moreover, it is clear that the policing of black communities is an issue that is by its nature already heavily politicised and is becoming more so. In many inner-city areas the question of policing is now at the forefront of local political debate. This is for a number of reasons, but it remains the case that in many areas the question of 'black crime' is at the heart of both popular concerns and of the concerns of the police. In the context of recent social and economic changes this concern with 'black crime' is likely to become an increasingly politicised issue over the next decade.

In the early 1990s an increasing preoccupation of public policy and political debate has been the question of new forms of public disorder which are not constructed in 'racial' terms. This happened particularly in the summer of 1991 when disturbances of various kinds took place in places as diverse as Oxford and North Shields (Waddington, 1992). Since 1991, similar outbursts have occurred in other regions and have led to widespread public debate about the political instabilities caused by the growth of an 'underclass' in British society. Given these new developments it is still important to note that in many parts of the country the issues of 'race and crime' and 'race and disorder' have not disappeared from the political agenda. The public furore about the 'underclass' is in many ways heavily racialised and it is likely therefore that the rest of this decade will see new moral panics about race and crime emerge, although not necessarily along the same lines as the 1970s or 1980s.

Conclusion

Successive shifts in political language about race since the early 1970s have involved the issue of policing and black crime as a central theme. Whether in terms of specific concerns about mugging, street crime, or with the question of urban unrest, the interplay between images of race and crime has remained an important symbol in political language. Since the late 1970s, and particularly after the 1980–81 and 1985 riots, political debates about the black crime issue have also been overdetermined by the phenomena of urban unrest and civil disorder. This also helps to explain the increasingly politicised nature of the response to the two issues. The ideological construction of the involvement of young blacks in mugging and other forms of street crime provided the basis for the development of strategies of control aimed at keeping young blacks off the streets and keeping the police in control of particular areas which had become identified both in popular and official discourses as 'crime-prone' or potential 'trouble spots'. It also helped to bring to the forefront a preoccupation with the social and economic roots of alienation and criminal activity among young blacks. This was reflected in the debate about the impact of unemployment on young blacks. But it was also reflected in the increasing preoccupation of the police and other agencies with crime in the context of inner-city areas and with the growing racialisation of the public debate about crime.

In the present political environment of economic dislocation and social exclusion, the public debate about race and crime is likely to remain an important part of the political agenda. Recent developments in areas as diverse as London, Birmingham and Manchester have shown that the prospect of further violent confrontations involving the police remains as likely as in any period since the early 1970s.

Acknowledgements

I am grateful to Les Back, Clive Harris and Michael Keith for various discussions that have helped to clarify my ideas and allowed me to express them more clearly.

8

Racism, Citizenship and Exclusion

Dee Cook

This chapter will examine the utility of the concept of citizenship in understanding both the ideological and material conditions under which black[1] people live their lives in Britain, and under which they receive discriminatory treatment within the criminal justice and penal systems. Citizenship is essentially about *inclusion* and membership: it will be argued that, for black people in the 1990s, formal and informal mechanisms of *exclusion* serve to deny them their full social, economic and political rights of citizenship. Exclusion manifests itself through the denial of legal citizenship (effected through immigration policies) and denial of social citizenship through the experiences of poverty and racism. In addition, black people may be constituted as 'other', as *non-citizens* in powerful popular and political discourses which stress the importance of membership which some may win through a form of 'cricket test', but which implicitly involves exclusion for many others. After a brief discussion of the terminology of citizenship, the concept will be analysed with particular reference to the legal and social dimensions of citizenship, realised through immigration and social policies which both generate and reinforce exclusion. Finally, contemporary political and popular discourses around 'citizenship' will be critically examined.

Citizenship in Theory

Marshall (1950) outlined three elements which constituted citizenship: the civil, political and social. The civil element is associated with the rule of law: liberty of the person, freedom of speech and the right to justice; the political element concerns the ability to participate in the electoral process, as representative or voter; the social element concerns 'the whole range from the right to a modicum of economic welfare and security to the right to share to the full in the social heritage and to live the life of a civilised being according to the standards prevailing in the society' (Marshall, 1981: 10). The realisation of full citizenship therefore involves three different sets of social institutions: the criminal justice system, parliamentary institutions and those institutions concerned with the provision of education and social welfare. But their contributions to citizenship are to a degree interdependent because 'A political system of equal citizenship is in reality less equal if it is part of a society divided by unequal conditions' (Barbalet, 1988: 1).

A universal franchise, for instance, therefore appears to mark equal political citizenship, but this may be rendered meaningless in the context of unequal social and economic conditions which effectively disempower poor and marginalised groups. Implicit within citizenship theory is the assumption that citizenship itself has the capacity to erode such inequalities. Marshall (1950: 84) held that 'citizenship and the capitalist class system [are] at war', a war in which citizenship may unite a society divided across class lines and impose 'modifications' on class (1950: 84). Yet, at the same time, citizenship may provide a basis of *apparent* equality upon which the structure of (capitalist) inequality could be built: 'The rights of citizenship inhibit the inegalitarian tendencies of the free economic market, but the market and some degree of economic inequality remain functionally necessary to the production of wealth' (Marshall, 1981: 12). Citizenship is seen to unite where class divides, but the apparent unity gained through equal legal and political citizenship rights serves to conceal the fundamental economic inequalities inherent within (and functional for) capitalist societies.

Leaving functionalist arguments aside, the important issue here is that full and equal citizenship (involving the elimination of social inequality) appears incompatible with the operation of free market economics. It is therefore deeply ironic that the leading proponents of the free market (New Right politicians) were to 'rediscover' and re-work the theme of citizenship throughout the 1980s and subsequently add it to their own political lexicon. Just as Margaret Thatcher had 'hi-jacked' the rhetoric of 'freedom' from the left, so her successors have continued her adaptation of the language of citizenship for their own political usage. Hence, whereas in the 1950s T.H. Marshall had defined citizenship as 'a status bestowed on those who are full members of a community. All who possess the status are equal with respect to the *rights* and *duties* with which the status is endowed' (Marshall, 1981: 11, emphasis added), 30 years on, the New Right re-worked the concept in order to emphasise the *duties* of citizenship, a theme later central to John Major's 'Citizen's Charter': 'citizenship is about responsibilties – as parents, for example, or as neighbours – as well as our entitlements' (Citizen's Charter, 1991). Within this perspective the 'entitlements' of citizenship are conferred only upon those who are *responsible* and active in carrying out their duties as citizens.

But for theorists and campaigners from the left, the *rights* of citizenship remain the paramount concern. For them, citizenship is defined in social as well as political and legal terms: it denotes the ability to participate fully in the social and political life of the community. But the ability to participate fully may be limited by social inequalities, as Ruth Lister argues: 'Poverty is corrosive of citizenship. For women and members of black and minority ethnic communities living in poverty, the exclusion from full citizenship is often compounded' (Lister, in Cohen et al., 1992: vii). Before discussing the 'corrosion' of social citizenship through the operation of the welfare state and the experience of poverty, it is first necessary to outline the processes whereby *legal* citizenship (the precursor to all other rights) may be formally and informally denied on racial grounds.

Citizenship in Practice: Immigration and Exclusion

'In a legal sense, citizenship was and essentially still is a device for the administration of immigration control, an aspect of policy whose principal aim has been to keep as many black people as possible, whether Asians or Afro-Caribbeans, out of the country' (Gordon, 1991: 77). Although this is not the place for a detailed history of such policies, key themes do emerge from the historical and political literature which help to explain the ways in which the status of citizenship is still formally and informally denied to black people. The first theme concerns *the racialisation of the immigration issue*.

In the period from 1945 to 1962 'immigration' became synonymous with 'race' in political and popular discourses. The British Nationality Act 1948 had created a new category, 'Citizen of the UK and Colonies', which extended legal and political rights to all Commonwealth citizens. At the same time, the state was encouraging the use of migrant labour (particularly from Europe) to meet labour shortages, but when migrants from the colonies started to arrive they were immediately perceived as a 'problem'. The publicity surrounding the arrival of 417 Jamaicans on the *Empire Windrush* in 1948 'Helped to obscure the fact that the majority of immigrants continued to come from the Irish Republic, from "white" Commonwealth countries and other European countries' (Miles and Solomos, 1987: 89). In short, 'Commonwealth immigrants' were only seen as a problem if they were black, and the racialisation of the political debate on immigration controls clearly influenced popular beliefs since 'despite the continuing scale of white immigration, popular common sense perceived all immigrants as black' (Miles and Solomos, 1987: 91).

There was, and still is, a discrepancy between the promise and the actuality of according British citizenship to black Commonwealth citizens, but history indicates it was always likely to be thus:

> Citizenship was, in the Roman Empire, a prize for the most subservient and most able of the conquered. The British were more magnanimous. As all imperialists must, they robbed Indians, Africans and all other people lucky enough to be conquered by marauders sailing under the British flag . . . But in the fine spirit of British generosity, they gave citizenship free to all their new subjects . . . [who], ran the theory, could hardly complain so long as they could call themselves British citizens. The concession had the added advantage of costing nothing. (Foot, 1965: 125)

Paul Foot's view suggests a deeply cynical use of formal citizenship, as conferred by Britain, an imperial token gesture which was not expected to have any profound effects upon the Mother Country. But, when *black* colonial subjects exercised their legal right to come to live in the Motherland, the implications were far reaching.

A second theme arising from the literature on immigration centres upon the use of Commonwealth immigrants as a *reserve army of labour*. It is worth emphasising that the flow of migrant labour into post-war Britain was not a hostile 'invasion': the British Empire offered a solution to the problem of acute home labour shortages. For instance, London Transport recruited bus crews in the West Indies and, as Minister of Health (1960–63), Enoch Powell encouraged the recruitment of West Indian and Asian nurses to staff British hospitals. Indeed, for some, the prospect of losing this cheap source of immigrant labour was worrying:

> In the hot and heavy industries such as foundries – never popular in times of full employment with the home labour force – they frequently constitute the only available pool of labour. [In the textile industry] it has been claimed that nightshifts would be forced to close down entirely without them. (*The Times*, August 4, 1965)

Although essentially racist, such sentiments acknowledge the important part immigrant labour played in the booming economy of the early 1960s, but, at the same time, show the historically vulnerable position of black labour in British society. When economic boom is followed by recession, the 'reserve army of labour' is hardest hit, as the poverty experienced by black people in Britain in the 1990s shows.

Thirdly, racialised responses to immigration influenced *popular and political responses to incidents and events involving black people*: reactions to the Notting Hill and Nottingham 'race riots' in 1958 (when black immigrants were the victims) reconstituted the 'problem' as evidence of the negative and inevitable consequences of black immigration and settlement. After Notting Hill and Nottingham, legislation to control immigration was justified in terms of the difficulties experienced by the host society in assimilating 'coloured immigrants' (Miles and Solomos, 1987). Over the next two decades racial discourse shifted from the emphasis on immigration and 'the enemy without', to black communities as 'the enemy within' (Solomos, 1988: 233). (See Chapter 7 for Solomos' discussion of the differing ways in which black youth has, over the past 20 years, been constituted in political discourse as a threat to social order.)

Commonwealth citizens, therefore, first became subject to immigration controls in 1962 with the passing of the Commonwealth Immigrants Act. The Act introduced a hierarchical 'voucher system' for applicants who were categorised according to whether they had a job to come to in Britain, possessed a skill which was in short supply or were 'other' applicants, priority being given to those who had served in the British armed forces. The goal of the Act was to reduce the numbers of black immigrants and marked an important phase in the *politicisation of race through the 'numbers game'*. Between 1963 and 1973 (when the voucher system was abolished), the number of successful applicants fell from 30,130 to 2,290, yet similar controls and reductions were not sought on the entry of citizens from the Republic of Ireland and elsewhere in Europe (Solomos, 1988: 93).

Paul Gordon has remarked that 'Immigration is always presented as a threat, and it's never talked about in terms of this country's moral, legal and historic obligations' (*The Guardian*, January 6, 1993). In the same article, Diane Abbott MP made a simple but crucial observation: 'Immigration policies flow from racism, not the other way round. If we weren't in a racist society, people wouldn't mind how many black people there were in this country.' Although an obvious point, it is none the less vital to recognise the racist foundations of Britain's postwar immigration policy, and its legacy in terms of the citizenship rights of black people in Britain: this was most strikingly demonstrated in the words of Enoch Powell in November 1968: 'The West Indian or Asian does not, by being born in England, become an Englishman. In law he becomes a United Kingdom citizen; in fact he is a West Indian or Asian still' (quoted in Dummett and Dummett, 1987: 137). Here we see that black Britons are constituted as both *within and without citizenship*: while legal citizenship may be formally guaranteed, the subjectivity of British citizenship, as revealed in Powell's notion of 'Englishness', will be forever denied. In this way, even those who *possess* citizenship may be *dispossessed*. The 1990s version of Powell's polemic, the notion of the 'cricket test', will be examined below.

At this point it is important to contextualise the phenomenon of *Powellism*. It has been argued that, in the eyes of the political right, the 1950s and early 1960s were characterised by a deep-seated political and social malaise and signalled fears about 'the loss of British Imperial prestige' and 'disparagement of the state of England' (Rich, 1989: 46). Right-wing political discourse sought to link these perceptions of British decline with New Commonwealth immigration. Lord Salisbury (Under Secretary at the Commonwealth Relations Office) argued that most immigrants were drawn to Britain by the 'honeypot' of the welfare state, but warned that the implications of black immigration were a 'fundamental problem for us all' (Rich, 1989: 47). Such concerns were incorporated into Enoch Powell's populist appeal to English patriotism, most infamously articulated in his 1968 'Rivers of Blood' speech, after which 'Powell was transformed overnight by the media to become its leading expert on immigration and race, which enabled the theme of the *numbers* of "immigrants" and their "threat" to British "culture" to continue to dominate the agenda for subsequent discussion' (Ben-Tovim and Gabriel, 1987: 148). The final solution to the 'problem' (as defined by Powell) involved the total *exclusion* of black people through repatriation. Twenty-five years on, these conceptions of race and immigration have not disappeared, but have been transformed both into the language of racial abuse and into the expression of racial violence. As will be argued below, such discourses of exclusion and nationalism are, in the 1990s, again surfacing, with the rise of fascism in many European states, and with refugees and migrant workers as the primary targets.

Following on from the 1962 Act, instructions to immigration officers (issued in 1966) introduced the concept of *recourse to public funds*, which remains a vital theme in immigration control policy. Instructions ordered officers to refuse admission to husbands if 'there appears to be no reasonable prospect of maintenance for the man himself, or his family without recourse to public funds' (quoted in Gordon and Newnham, 1985: 7). This policy effectively marks the fusion of several of the themes discussed so far: the racialisation of the immigration issue, the 'numbers game', the fears of the political right and 'Little Englanders', the politics of exclusion and the allegedly damaging incentives to immigration offered by the 'honeypot' of the welfare state.

Although space does not allow for discussion of the provisions of subsequent immigration Acts, it is worth noting that immigration Acts of 1971 and 1988 (and the Immigration Rules which have put them into effect), have progressively extended the test of 'recourse to public funds' to the dependants of Commonwealth citizens. For the purposes of the 1988 Act, 'public funds' are defined as housing benefit, the provision of housing (under the 1985 Housing Act, to homeless persons), Family Credit and Income Support (CRE, 1989a). Crucially, since 1980, the recourse to public funds test has been linked directly to the social security regulations governing the right to means-tested benefits: this means that 'sponsors' are legally liable to support their dependants, and not the British welfare state. This effectively gives rise to a problematic status of *conditional* (and *thus partial*) *citizenship*. Moreover, it makes a formal connection between immigration status and entitlement to benefit. As I will argue later, this connection has worrying implications for black people in general, and black social security claimants in particular, whose status and citizenship is rendered *questionable* simply because of the colour of their skin: for instance, the (mis)use of passport checks by government departments – from the Home Office, the DSS and even in hospital waiting rooms – is testimony to the assumption made by many officials that the legal status of black people is invariably questionable (Arnott, 1987; Gordon and Newnham, 1985; NACAB, 1991).

To summarise, through a discussion of the principal themes underpinning British postwar immigration policy, I have argued that the legal and subjective citizenship of black people in Britain has always been regarded as questionable and problematic. Although the very word 'immigrant' may now appear dated and inappropriate, the racialised use of the term persists and has an impact upon the everyday experience of black people in Britain. Regardless of their legal rights and place of birth, black British citizens often find themselves regarded as 'alien', formally within, but informally without, citizenship. In addition, other vocabularies are developing which serve this same function of exclusion: the terms 'refugee' and 'asylum seeker' are no longer positive epithets and, as I will argue below, are now increasingly being connected within an essentially punitive discourse around 'dubious claims' to welfare and abode.

Within such a historical and socio-political context it is hardly surprising that agencies of regulation, whether Home Office and immigration officials or criminal justice agencies (particularly the police), continue to regard black people as problematic by definition. *Both their status and their actions are regarded as suspect* and this has profound consequences for criminal (as well as social) justice.

Citizenship in Practice: the Civil Element

Discussions on the theory of citizenship often focus on its positive rights, which confer freedoms and entitlements: to enjoy the rights of abode, justice and political rights, such as standing for and voting in parliamentary elections. But when connected with the issue of race, it is also important to broaden any discussion of the civil element of citizenship to stress 'negative' rights. These include the right of redress and complaint which is an essential element of the 'Charter' philosophy, and, crucially, include 'a black person's right to walk the streets unmolested' (David Donnison, in *The Guardian*, July 29, 1992. Police and politicians alike have been slow to respond to the threat that racist attacks pose to this most basic of freedoms: 'by the mid-1970's the voice of black Britain was showing signs of weariness, *impatience*, and anxiety at the lack of fit between policy and practice, talk and action' (Pearson et al., 1989: 136).

Research in areas as diverse as Leeds, Glasgow and Newham has demonstrated gross under-reporting of racial incidents (CRE, 1991b; Husbands, 1989). Despite the recent broadening of the official definition of a 'racial incident' to include incidents in which 'any allegation of racial motivation is made by any person', this problem remains (CRE, 1991b). Home Office figures show that there were 7,780 racial attacks in 1991, but research by the Anti-Racist Alliance monitoring group indicates that only one in ten incidents is reported, and thus they claim that a more accurate figure for racial attacks in 1991 would be around 70,000 (*The Guardian*, February 20, 1993).

There is still an official reluctance to acknowledge the seriousness of the problem, despite an escalation of racial violence in the 1990s, with eight deaths attributed to racial attacks in 1992, and despite racist motives becoming increasingly explicit. For instance, Joseph Conroy, who shot 15-year-old Navid Sadiq and his uncle in the course of an attempted robbery, gave a Nazi salute after his arrest; Wayne Lambert who murdered two Pakistanis in separate attacks in Manchester said at his court appearance, 'I hate Pakis, I will only be 43 when I get out . . . and I will kill another' (*The Guardian*, January 23, 1993). Although these are extremely disturbing individual cases, a more general and systematic form of racist violence is also becoming more evident: a recently opened further education college in (predominantly white) Bermondsey has been described as 'under siege'. High-level security measures have had to be taken following several racial attacks on black students (involving baseball bats and air rifles) (*The Guardian*, November 9, 1992). Although the British National Party may be involved in this instance, it would be a mistake to write off all racist attacks as the work of fascist organizations, though they may play a part in creating a climate which encourages racial violence (Kushner and Lunn, 1989).

The 1988 British Crime Survey confirmed that black people are more likely to be victims of both household crime (involving burglary, vandalism and vehicles) and personal crime (including assaults, threats and robbery) than their white counterparts. Moreover, many of the black victims surveyed believed the crimes against them to be racially motivated (Mayhew et al., 1989). Against this background, it seems that for many black people in contemporary Britain, even the negative rights of citizenship – the right of redress, the right to live in the community without fear – appear illusory. Donnison argues that such negative rights will not be achieved 'unless the victims of these attacks gain positive rights to equal status with the rest of the community in education, jobs, housing and so on'. The civil element of citizenship cannot, to this extent, be separated from the political and social.

The Political Element

> Political Rights in a representative democracy can function at full strength only at one point, and through one institution, the national sovereign parliament. It is true that they function also, in a subordinate way, at the level of the local community . . . But the ultimate power resides at the centre. (Marshall, 1981: 141)

According to the 1991 census, ethnic minorities account for 5.5 per cent of the British population (Owens, 1992). But just as women (who account for just over half the population) are grossly under-represented with only 59 women in a parliament of 651 seats, so are black people: there are currently six members of parliament from 'ethnic minority groups'. Moreover, the furore surrounding the 1992 election campaign in the constituency of Cheltenham demonstrated the strength of racist feeling in middle-class middle-England: here, a respected black lawyer was selected as the Conservative prospective parliamentary candidate for this 'safe' Tory constituency, much to the consternation of many local conservatives. The campaign was dogged by racist slurs often emanating from the candidate's own party. Clearly, many Conservative voters switched to the Liberal Democrat (white) candidate, who won the seat.

However, counting the numbers of black MPs is by no means an adequate measurement of political participation. As regards the primary right of political citizenship – the right to vote – there is evidence that the poll tax, in linking local taxation to electoral registration, has effectively disenfranchised individuals and groups who chose to lose the right to vote 'in exchange for an escape from an intrusive and unfair tax' (Esam and Oppenheim, 1989). Among the key groups so affected were members of black households who were:

1 More likely to be living in metropolitan areas where poll tax levels were highest, (According to the 1991 Census, Greater London alone contains 44.8 per cent of Britain's ethnic minority population: Owens, 1992).
2 More likely to include three or more (often young) adults, all of whom were liable to pay. This factor adversely affects ethnic minority communities with traditionally extended families.

In common with other poor groups, many black people have, in avoiding the poll tax, become excluded from the democratic political process. It remains to be seen if the demise of the poll tax (and advent of council tax), will reverse this process.

More generally, Lea and Young (1984) have argued (from a left-realist perspective), that black (and particularly young) people are marginalised both economically and politically. In relation to the latter, they argue that political marginality is not merely about possession of the vote but 'is above all the exclusion from the ability to form co-ordinated, stable interest groups able to function in a process of pressure group politics' (Lea and Young, 1984: 215). But Gilroy (1987b) offers an alternative perspective:

> It is not that blacks lack the means to organize themselves politically but that they do so in ways which are so incongruent with Britishness that they are incapable of sustaining life! Their distance from the required standards of political viability is established by their criminal character. Thus black crime and politics are interlinked. They become aspects of the same fundamental problem – a dissident black population. (Gilroy, 1987b: 117)

The issues at stake here not only concern alternative conceptions of 'politics', but also the notion of 'Britishness', a theme echoed by Solomos (1988) in his discussion of responses to the urban disorders of 1981 and 1985: 'By rioting . . . young blacks were seen as not only breaking the rules of conventional politics, but as engaging in activities which were somehow "alien" and outside the culturally sanctioned norms of British society' (Solomos, 1988: 218).

I do not wish to retrace here the 'race and crime debate' between the so-called left-realists and 'left-idealist' positions (for a fuller discussion see Chapters 1 and 7). But suffice it to say, for the purposes of this discussion of political participation, that whereas the former see crime as being politicised, the latter see politics as being criminalised; where realists see black people as essentially *reactive* to (and marginalised by) the conditions of poverty and deprivation in which they live, critics argue that black people are *active* citizens capable of choice and, moreover, that black cultures 'affirm while they protest' (Gilroy, 1987a). But when black people do protest, their active citizenship is denied and they are perceived as reacting (and often presented as over-reacting) in an irresponsible manner.

Clearly, the boundaries between what is perceived as crime and what is perceived as political protest may become blurred and, under certain historical and economic conditions, political struggles (such as the 1984 Miners' Strike) may be overtly criminalised. Just as one person's 'terrorist' is another's 'freedom fighter', so the events in Brixton, Toxteth, Moss Side, Handsworth and Broadwater Farm in 1981 and 1985 may be perceived as 'crime' or 'uprisings' and 'a cry for loot' or 'a cry for help', depending on the attribution of either criminal or political motivations to the actors involved. Avoiding the dangers of complete relativism, it is possible to argue in the light of the foregoing discussion of racism, immigration and citizenship, that the struggles of black people are more likely to be constituted as criminal than political: this is possible not only because of the powerful 'myth of black criminality' (Gilroy, 1987b), but also because those involved in such struggles are ideologically constructed as always already excluded from full and active citizenship, which by definition includes political participation.

Given the transformation of racial discourse (already outlined) from the issue of immigration and associated concerns about the 'enemy without', to the issue of law and order and concerns around the 'enemy within', it is difficult to disagree with Solomos' proposition that in contemporary Britain 'every black person is regarded as *a priori* a suspect, a potential criminal, a potential agitator' (Solomos, 1988: 218). For black people, the political element of citizenship is contingent upon the legal element: thus, the experience of political participation is similarly limited by (and constructed within) the racialised discourse of exclusion and questionable, that is to say 'un-British', citizenship. Consequently, both their status and their actions are seen as *suspect*.

The Social Element

Poverty and the stigma associated with the claiming of welfare benefits has long been associated with exclusion: the nineteenth-century workhouses of the New Poor Law (1834) were institutions of physical exclusion. Conditions in the workhouse (involving separation of the sexes, dietary and physical deprivation), rendered the lot of the pauper 'less eligible' than that of the lowest paid worker outside so as to deter all but the very poorest from entering (Cook,

1989). Within the poor, certain groups were distinguished as 'deserving' of relief from the ratepayer: the elderly, the infirm, the sick and children. But the able-bodied unemployed were regarded as essentially idle and 'undeserving'. Such divisions can be seen to persist in the 1990s, with lone mothers added to the list of the 'undeserving', together with New Age travellers and asylum seekers. It is significant that the Social Security Secretary, Peter Lilley, highlighted these groups in his call, at the 1992 Conservative Party Conference, for a clampdown on benefit fraud: the 'undeserving poor' are thus more likely to be targeted as fraud-prone and are therefore most readily criminalised.

Distinctions between the deserving and undeserving poor clearly fly in the face of notions of 'rights' and equal citizenship. But, according to Marshall (1981: 11), 'The pauper was a person deprived of rights, not invested with them.' Over two and half centuries on from the Poor Law, it appears that little has changed. This section will examine how the mechanisms of the welfare state and ideologies of welfare continue to exclude the poor from membership of 'productive' society, and how this experience of exclusion is compounded for black claimants.

For welfare benefit claimants in general, social exclusion operates at two levels: first, in the practicalities of life, through everyday experience: the ignominy of the post office queue on benefit pay days; the embarrassment of shabby clothing; the inability to provide for children's needs and wants. Secondly, at the level of ideology, particularly through New Right discourse, the poor are stigmatised as responsible for their own failure. This was most clearly articulated in the 1980s through the polarisation between the Thatcherite vision of the 'enterprise culture' and the parallel denunciation of the morally sapping dependency of the 'benefit culture'. An ideological divide was created which 'excluded' the poor, though this division was not without purpose: 'For success to glisten seductively at the winners, the failure of poverty must display its burden of guilt and shame' (Golding and Middleton, 1982: 244). Guilt and shame remain essential components of the claiming process, both in theory and in practice, and have been emphasised through the New Right's re-working of citizenship theory: as Ruth Lister has persuasively argued, the New Right focuses upon the duties and responsibilities which citizenship demands rather than the positive rights with which it is endowed. They thereby seek citizens who are independent (that is, working!), active (giving to charity, doing voluntary work in their spare time), but 'lurking behind the active citizen is the successful, self-reliant, enterprising citizen, alias the consuming, property-owning citizen. The unsuccessful and unenterprising are thereby excluded from the ranks of citizens' (Lister, 1990: 15).

In practical terms the vision of independent, active citizenship is promoted by deterring dependence on state benefits. The obstacle course of the claiming process effectively ensures a rationing of welfare, and there is much evidence that black people are presented with more obstacles (and their benefits thereby more rationed), than their white counterparts. The first obstacle may be the attitude of DSS staff, as the following comments from Asian claimants indicate:

> 'If you are black, you feel it, perhaps more . . . some officials are okay. Some pull their faces now and then. It hurts but you accept it and ignore it.'
> 'There is no doubt that they don't look well on us people and that is why it takes longer to get an answer from them.' (Cohen et al., 1992: 62)

Empirical studies of social security provision have shown a measure of overt racism on the part of some DSS staff (Beltram, 1984; Cooper, 1985; NACAB, 1991), and racist assumptions appeared to underlie the (informal) targeting of ethnic minorities for fraud investigations in the 1980s (Cook, 1989). Concern currently arises in instances where DSS officials have an element of discretion: for example, reports by the National Association of Citizens Advice Bureaux (NACAB) indicate a higher refusal rate of community care grants for refugee families; an analysis of social fund applications in one DSS office 'which had a long-established reputation for racist practice . . . has borne out fears that the exercise of discretion would bring this thread of practice more to the surface' (Amin and Oppenheim 1992: 56).

Some ethnic minority claimants may also be disadvantaged by routine bureaucracy: since the Social Security Act 1986 came into force in 1988, claimants applying for means-tested benefits face a 17-page claim form for Income Support and an 11-page claim form for Family Credit and Social Fund loans. As NACAB has pointed out, for claimants who write or speak little English, long and complex forms written only in English 'are likely to act as a significant barrier to take-up of benefits they are entitled to' (NACAB, 1991: 15). No recent figures are available from the DSS on unclaimed benefits, but for 1985–6 unclaimed means-tested benefits totalled £1,150 million. Surveys in Leicester, Halifax and Sandwell all indicated considerable underclaiming of benefits, particularly in the Asian community and among non-English speaking people (NACAB, 1991: 49). In another study (published by the Child Poverty Action Group), the Chaudry family described the problems involved in claiming: 'lots and lots of forms to fill in and lots of questions. They ask the same question in so many ways, it gets very confusing . . . so what about those who can't read or write?' (Cohen et al., 1992: 21). Also of concern are cases of black claimants who are wrongfully refused benefits: not only do such cases involve financial hardship, they may deter future claiming and foster the mistaken belief that 'they are not entitled as of right to benefits' (NACAB, 1991: 41).

As discussed earlier, current immigration rules have been linked to the social security system through the concept of 'no recourse to public funds': under these rules, most people are admitted to Britain on the condition that they make no claim on Income Support, Family Credit or local authority housing. This legislation has three consequences: the first is that many ethnic minority families are 'divided across continents' until it is demonstrated that the 'sponsor' can support them in Britain without recourse to state funds (Amin and Oppenheim, 1992); secondly, families may be subjected to financial hardship because of the requirement that sponsors meet the costs of supporting relatives rather than the welfare state; thirdly, the nature of the legislation itself involves the establishment of close contacts between the DSS and the Home Office, as immigration status is explicitly linked to welfare rights.

One important consequence of such links is the use of passport checks by DSS officials if they consider that a claimant may have 'recently come from abroad'. Although DSS guidelines tell staff to 'make every effort to deal with cases without asking to see passports', the practice of passport checking continues. For example, a 22-year-old student (born in the UK) was asked to produce his passport four times in one year when claiming benefit in Manchester and Huddersfield (Gordon and Newnham, 1985); a single parent who had been living in the UK since 1976 'with settled status' was asked to show her passport when she claimed Income Support (NACAB, 1991). Obviously some DSS officials consider skin colour as indicative of having 'recently come from abroad' and thus racism often determines whether a claimant is subjected to a passport check or not.

Not surprisingly, NACAB found that many black claimants 'gave up' trying to claim social security benefits, and those who persisted were likely to experience considerable delays (1991: 36). The implicit use of excessive bureaucracy and delay as techniques for deterring claims is not only evident in the DSS. The Home Affairs Select Committee Report of 1990 on the administrative delays in the Immigration and Nationality Department 'found evidence of exceptionally poor quality of service which, they concluded, "gives rise to understandable suspicion that bureaucratic delay is an instrument of control"' (NACAB, 1992: 12). But the effects of such delays, leading to queues at ports like Heathrow and at Lunar House

(Britain's central immigration office) at Croydon, have other worrying implications

> By maintaining the queues it gives the impression of the constant clamour to come to the UK and this in turn serves to reinforce the perception of the need for increasingly strict immigration control. Furthermore, since the queue is predominantly made up of black people, it can only serve to increase the actual and perceived racism of the system. (NACAB, 1992: 13)

Passport checking has long been a means of questioning citizenship and is used to query people who appear 'to be foreigners', and its use has not been restricted to the Home Office and DSS. As early as 1974 education authorities were found to be asking the parents of black children to produce their passports; in 1979 a DHSS circular entitled 'Gatecrashers' advised health authorities to check for abuse of the NHS by people from abroad, who were not entitled to free treatment (Gordon and Newnham, 1985). Understandably, therefore, Asian and Afro-Caribbean participants in a survey in Bristol commented that their contacts with the National Health Service made them feel 'like trespassers in someone else's land' (Fenton, quoted in Amin and Oppenheim, 1992). Fenton goes on to argue that racism 'poisons the atmosphere of the crowded surgery waiting room, the ante-natal clinic, the housing waiting list, the dole queue and visiting time at hospital. Its strength lies in its pervasiveness, in its fundamental character, and in the legitimacy with which it is accorded' (1992: 24).

If social citizenship is defined in terms of equal access to health, education and social welfare, it can be argued that welfare rationing and institutional racism serve to deny many black people their full citizenship rights. Immigration policy has profoundly influenced social policy: physical exclusion, by means of tough immigration controls, has been accompanied by, and given rise to, social exclusions, often effected through the mechanisms of the welfare state. Even when black people formally possess citizenship, they are dispossessed of it through the institutional racism of bureaucracies which deter, suspect, stigmatise, check and interrogate them. It is precisely these institutional tendencies which are the greatest cause of black people coming into contact with the criminal justice agencies, whether as victims, suspects or defendants.

'Citizen Cheaters'

As argued above, the exclusion of many of the poor from full social citizenship needs to be located within the context of ideologies of welfare which distinguish between the deserving and undeserving poor, the active and the dependent citizen. Within such discourses black people have often been constituted as 'cheats' and have, therefore, been more readily stigmatised and criminalised than many of their white counterparts. This section will examine ideological representations of black people which dispossess them of citizenship on the grounds that they are neither law-abiding nor truly 'British' citizens.

In 1982 Lord Denning, former Master of the Rolls, made the following comments about law-breaking within Britain's black community: 'They came from countries where bribery and graft are accepted . . . and where stealing is a virtue as long as you are not found out. They no longer share the same code of morals or religious beliefs' (quoted in the *The Guardian*, November 10, 1992). More than a decade on, crude racist stereotypes of black crime and dishonesty persist. In a *News of the World* article (January 19, 1992) entitled 'Citizens' Cheaters' Norman Tebbit MP described the activities of 'money-grabbing illegal immigrants' and their alleged involvement in a variety of welfare swindles, including multiple claiming from false addresses, obtaining housing as homeless persons and then 'bringing in other illegal immigrants, political asylum applicants or overstayers', and working while claiming benefit. Not satisfied with portraying black people as welfare scroungers, Tebbit went on to suggest that 'other and even more serious crime flourishes in this underworld', thereby closing the rhetorical circle which links black people with illegal citizenship, dishonesty and serious crime.

Racism has long been an important ingredient of 'scroungermania' (Golding and Middleton, 1982). For example, the infamous Operation Major fraud swoop against social security claimants in Oxford in 1982 led to 283 arrests and *The Sun* featured a cartoon depicting a conveyor belt of the accused fraudsters passing before the magistrates: five out of the 12 fraudsters in the cartoon were visibly black or Asian, whereas in reality only four of the 283 claimants arrested in Operation Major were black (and only one black person was convicted) (Franey, 1983: 48). Some time later, specialist social security fraud investigators were directed to investigate claimants with the surname Singh as 'this was a fertile area' (Cook, 1989: 140). The contradictions within the justification for this targeting embody the essential paradox of much racist rhetoric: Asian people were, on the one hand idle (hence claiming benefit) yet at the same time entrepreneurial (hence working too!).

Media-fuelled beliefs about black people's idleness and dishonesty tap into a rich vein of well-established racist thought: historically, 'negroes' had been caricatured as 'naturally' idle and inferior (Walvin, 1987). Such stereotypes of idleness clearly underlie the postwar fears about black immigrants flooding into Britain, drawn by the 'honeypot' of welfare state support though, ironically, popular racism simultaneously played upon fears that immigrants would 'take our jobs'.

Negative images of black people as 'citizen cheaters' thus become more potent when coupled with the racialisation of immigration, as the current panic over 'bogus' asylum seekers and refugees testifies. But the alarmist fears engendered by politicians such as Tebbit are not justified, as Britain maintains an ever-tightening grip on immigration. For example, Home Office statistics indicate that, although there were over 44,000 applications for asylum in 1991, only 1,260 cases decided in that year resulted in acceptances (Home Office Statistical Bulletin, 1992). None the less, the 'race card' was briefly played in the 1992 General Election campaign as the then Home Secretary Kenneth Baker warned that one dire consequence of electing a Labour government would be a flood of applications from 'bogus' asylum seekers.

The essentially racialised nature of the panic surrounding refugees and asylum seekers is highlighted by the contrasting political responses to (predominantly white) refugees caught up in the civil war in the former Yugoslavia. The Director of the Joint Council for the Welfare of Immigrants suggested that 'Britain's policies were devised to deny entry to Turkish, Tamils, Ugandans and Zaireans fleeing torture and suffering. We never heard a public outcry about them. But now we're talking about Europeans, the government has found it's caught in a trap of its own making' (quoted in the *The Guardian*, January 6, 1993.

Social Exclusion and the 'Cricket Test'

The social element of citizenship includes the right actively to participate in the social life of the community. But, for many black people, social inclusion is directly or indirectly denied on racial grounds. For example, the Commission for Racial Equality (CRE) conducted a formal investigation into Handsworth Horticultural Institute. Around 60 per cent of the local population of Handsworth comprise people 'of Asian and Afro-Caribbean origin . . . yet there is no evidence that a single person from those communities has ever been proposed for membership' (CRE, 1992c). The CRE successfully argued that the rule specifying that new members be sponsored by two existing members of the club, and thereafter be approved by a selection committee, was indirectly discriminatory and unlawful under the Race Relations Act. The club had argued that their selection committee served to 'weed out undesirables'. Judging by the ethnic composition of the club, black people do not appear to be considered 'desirable' members. The General Secretary of the club was even less equivocal: 'If any Tom, Dick or Harry, were to walk in off the street it wouldn't be a club. Would you want to join an Asian club? I wouldn't' (*The Observer*, February 2, 1992). Paradoxically, some elements of the media covered the Handsworth Horticultural Institute story in terms of the threat that the legal judgement posed for 'freedom' in general and for the exclusive membership of 'gentlemen's clubs' in particular.

As argued above, the social element of citizenship is conditional upon the legal element, yet black Britons may still be denied social citizenship if they fail to embody and display essential 'Britishness'. One example of such denial concerns an activity which itself epitomises Britishness – cricket. In the spring of 1990 the English cricket team were thoroughly beaten (at home). Norman Tebbit suggested that a proportion of the Asian community failed to support England and had failed the 'cricket test – which side do they cheer for?' He elaborated,

> If all the time somebody is looking over their shoulder to the country from which their family came instead of the country where they live and are making their home, you scratch your head if you are an integrationist and ask: 'Are they really integrated or just living here?' (*The Times*, April 21, 1990)

Ex-patriot Britons cheer for England in Australia without censure, and anyone suggesting that Scots and Welsh people cheer for English rugby teams would receive short shrift. But the racialisation of this seemingly trivial issue has important consequences as it reinforces ideologies of black people as un-British and consequently serves to deny their citizenship.

To continue the cricket theme, England's similarly resounding defeat in the summer of 1992 gave rise to allegations of the Pakistan team 'cheating' as bowler Wasim Akram was accused of ball-tampering. Akram himself commented that, 'They taught us cricket but now that we are winning, England are bad losers' (Serle, 1993: 50). None the less, many commentators associated un-sportsman-like behaviour not with the English tendency to be 'bad losers' at their national game, but with the national character of the victors: 'All summer long the Pakistanis have been wilful, capricious and hot-headed' (John Arlott quoted in Serle, 1993: 49). Similarly, the summer of 1992 saw the *Daily Mail* refer to their 'volatile nature' and the gutter tabloids went further in telling the visitors to 'Pak [*sic*] your bags'. Serle contextualises such racist media coverage:

> At the very same time that the ball-tampering controversy was being stoked up in the *Daily Mirror* . . . another Asian youth was shot at point-blank range and blinded in one eye by a racist gang in Harrow,

North London, and a mosque, a Sikh temple and a Hindu gurdwara were fire-bombed and attacked in South London. (Serle, 1993: 49)

It is difficult to disagree with Serle's contention that the jingoistic handling of the cheating allegations created the ideological conditions under which some individuals were 'goaded' into acts of violence and malice against the black community, and that 'such journalism is a mirror of daggers' (1993: 49).

The exclusive imagery of the 'cricket test' and negative images of deceit and 'graft' combined to create the contradictory ideological conditions within which black people were more readily constructed as criminal and dishonest in popular discourse, yet more likely to be victimised. Discussion will now turn to the material conditions in which these contradictions are realised.

Poverty and the Corrosion of Citizenship

The definition and measurement of poverty involves political as well as economic judgements. Absolute poverty is defined in terms of minimum standards of subsistence, whereas relative poverty is defined in relation to the standard of living experienced (and expected) in the wider society. This relative or 'consensual' approach to the measurement of poverty was adopted by the 'Breadline Britain – 1990s' survey, which estimated that one in five (or 11 million) people in Britain were living in poverty (Oppenheim, 1993). In 1978 the independent Supplementary Benefits Commission, chaired by David Donnison, had utilised a broadly consensual approach, but one which emphasised that to experience poverty was to be excluded from the community; their definition has a direct bearing not only upon our discussion of social citizenship, but also upon the impact of racism on patterns of exclusion, and so it is worth quoting in full:

> To keep out of poverty, people must have an income which enables them to participate in the life of the community. They must be able, for example, to keep themselves reasonably well fed, and well enough dressed to maintain their self-respect and to attend interviews for jobs with confidence. Their homes must be reasonably warm; their children should not be shamed by the quality of their clothing; the family must be able to visit relatives, and give them something on their birthdays and at Christmas time; they must be able to read newspapers, and retain their membership of trades unions and churches. And they must be able to live in a way which ensures, so far as possible, that public officials, doctors, teachers, landlords and others treat them with the courtesy due to every member of the community. (Donnison, 1982: 8)

As we have already seen, the treatment of black people by public officials, doctors etc. is far from courteous and is attributed to institutional racism compounding the already-excluding effects of welfare and the denial of legal and subjective citizenship. Analysis will now turn to the extent to which poverty itself corrodes the social citizenship rights of black people.

Britain's black population is concentrated in Greater London, the West Midlands and former heartlands of manufacturing industry (Owens, 1992). These are precisely the areas hardest hit by the recessions of the early 1980s, and now the 1990s, and so black people have been particularly affected. The 1989–91 Labour Force Surveys indicate that the unemployment rate for 'ethnic minority' men was 13 per cent compared with 7 per cent among white men; and for ethnic minority women the unemployment rate of 12 per cent compared with 7 per cent for their white counterparts. Unemployment rates are still higher for young people, with 22 per cent of ethnic minority young men between the ages of 16 and 24 unemployed, compared with 12 per cent of young whites. (Young people from ethnic minorities are also more likely to be unemployed following youth training.) In addition, the surveys showed that even with higher qualifications than white counterparts, people from ethnic minorities suffered higher unemployment, and were also more likely to be long-term unemployed (Amin and Oppenheim, 1992: 2).

However, these national figures conceal stark regional inequalities, and differences between genders and ethnic minority groups: for example, CRE figures indicate that in Cardiff the unemployment rate is around 42 per cent among Africans and Afro-Caribbean men, and is around 20 per cent for Asian men. Moreover, a Training Agency study of clients at a Cardiff Job Centre in 1986 showed that whites had to submit 21 applications, Asians 28, and Afro-Caribbeans 71 before receiving a placement (*The Guardian*, January 6, 1993). Such inequalities are attributable to structural and institutional racism as well as fundamental changes in the British economy (Amin and Oppenheim, 1992).

Low pay is also a major cause of poverty: evidence suggests that black people are concentrated in the industrial sectors with the lowest weekly wages, such as distribution; hotels and catering; clothing and leather goods manufacture; and the medical and health sectors. Moreover, they are over-represented at the unskilled level within these sectors, and under-represented at managerial levels (Amin and Oppenheim, 1992). In addition, ethnic minority women suffer most from the poorest pay and working conditions associated with home-working. One knock-on effect of unemployment and low wages is a difficulty in qualifying for contributory benefits (such as retirement pensions), and thus a greater likelihood of having to depend on means-tested benefits which, as the earlier discussion of social security provision illustrated, are characterised by rationing, deterrence and decreased eligibility.

In summary, it can be argued that 'Poverty among ethnic minorities is intimately connected with unemployment, low pay, industrial structure and racism' (Amin and Oppenheim, 1992: 20). But, to return to Donnison's definition, poverty not only entails lack of income, it entails the inability to participate in the life of the community and a lack of respect and dignity accorded by other members of society.

I have argued that the legal and ideological construction of black people as excluded from formal and subjective citizenship, conditions the social and official responses to them: therefore DSS, immigration and health officials operationalise legal definitions of citizenship which effectively render all black people *questionable citizens*. Concomitantly, black people are represented as unwelcome, unwanted and dishonest in popular and political discourses focusing on the 'numbers game' (now applied to refugees and asylum seekers rather than 'immigrants'), the 'cricket test' and 'citizen cheaters'. Under such economic, political and ideological conditions, we should not be surprised that black people are not merely represented as suspect, but as potential law-breakers.

Conclusion

To possess citizenship is to be a full member of the community and to enjoy the civil, political and social rights which constitute membership. In this chapter I have examined the promise and the actuality of citizenship for black people in contemporary Britain. The effective exclusion of black people – from legal and respectable citizenship, from full participation in social and political life – makes it more likely that both their legal status and their actions will be questioned and regarded as suspicious. Invariably, this leaves them open to excessive criminalisation. Criminalisation itself is an important feature of the discourse of exclusion. As Paul Gilroy has argued, 'Black lawbreaking supplies the historic proof that blacks are incompatible with the standards of decency and civilization which the nation requires of its citizenry' (1987a: 13).

When black people break the law, they are seen to close a rhetorical circle which links race and non-citizenship with criminal activity: I have focused on and critically addressed the first two links in that circle, arguing that racism and exclusion are generated and reinforced by postwar immigration and social policies and the ideologies which sustain them. For many black people in contemporary Britain the promise of full citizenship has not materialised, but the experience of racism and exclusion is all too real.

Note

1 In this chapter I use the term 'black' to describe all those minority ethnic groups who suffer from discrimination. But there are differences in the experiences of those groups, and when referring to such differences and to literature which uses alternative categories, distinctions will be made.

References

Adamson, C.R. (1984) 'Toward a Marxian penology: captive criminal populations as economic threats and resources', *Social Problems*, 31 (April): 435–8.

AFFOR (1978) *Talking Blues*. Birmingham: AFFOR.

Allen, H. (1987) *Justice Unbalanced: Gender, Psychiatry and Judicial Decisions*. Milton Keynes: Open University Press.

Amin, K. and Oppenheim, C. (1992) *Poverty in Black and White*. London: CPAG/Runnymede Trust.

Arnott, H. (1987) 'Second class citizens', in A. Walker and C. Walker (eds), *The Growing Divide: a Social Audit 1979–1987*. London: CPAG.

Ashworth, A. (1988) 'Criminal justice and criminal process', *British Journal of Criminology*, 28 (2): 241–53.

Auletta, K. (1982) *The Underclass*. New York: Random House.

Avi-Ram, A-F. (1989) 'Phallic reflections and other ways of thinking', in L. Kauffman (ed.), *Feminism and Institutions: Dialogues on Feminist Theory*. Oxford: Blackwell.

Bagley, C. (1975) 'Sequels of alienation: a social psychological view of the adoption of West Indian migrants in Britain', in K. Glaser (ed.), *Case Studies in Human Rights on Fundamental Problems*, vol. 2. The Hague: Nijhoff.

Banton, M. (1987) *Racial Theories*. Cambridge: Cambridge University Press.

Barbalet, J.M. (1988) *Citizenship*. Milton Keynes: Open University Press.

Bar Council (1989) *Race Relations Survey*. London: Bar Council.

Bar Council (1991) *Race Equality Policy*. London: Bar Council.

Batta, I.D., McCulloch, J.W. and Smith, N.J. (1975) 'A study of juvenile delinquency among Asians and half Asians', *British Journal of Criminology*, 15: 32–42.

Becker, H. (1967) 'Whose side are we on?', *Social Problems*, 14 (3): 239–47.

Beltram, G. (1984) *Testing the Safety Net*. London: Bedford Square Press/NCVO.

Ben-Tovim, G. and Gabriel, J. (1987) 'The politics of race in Britain, 1962–79: a review of the major trends', in C. Husband (ed.), *Race in Britain: Continuity and Change*, 2nd edn. London: Hutchinson.

Benyon, J. and Solomos, J. (eds) (1987) *The Roots of Urban Unrest*. Oxford: Pergamon.

Bottomley, A.K. and Pease, K. (1986) *Crime and Punishment: Interpreting the Data*. Milton Keynes: Open University Press.

Bottoms, A. and Stelman, A. (1988) *Social Enquiry Reports*. Aldershot: Wildwood House Ltd. in conjunction with Community Care.

Bowling, B. (1990) 'Conceptual and methodological problems in measuring "race" differences in delinquency: a reply to Marianne Junger', *British Journal of Criminology*, 30 (4): 483–92.

Bowling, B. and Saulsbury, W. (1992) 'A multi-agency approach to racial harassment', *Home Office Research Bulletin*, 32: 34–9. London: Home Office Research and Planning Unit.

Box, S. (1983) *Power, Crime and Mystification*. London: Tavistock.

Box, S. (1987) *Recession, Crime and Punishment*. Basingstoke: Macmillan.

Box, S. and Hale, C. (1982) 'Economic crisis and the rising prisoner population', *Crime and Social Justice*, 17: 20–35.

Brake, M. (1985) *Comparative Youth Culture: The Sociology of Youth Culture and Youth Subcultures in America, Britain and Canada*. London: Routledge and Kegan Paul.

Brittan, A. and Maynard, M. (1984) *Sexism, Racism and Oppression*. Oxford: Blackwell.

Brod, H. (1990) 'Pornography and the alienation of male sexuality', in J. Hearn and D. Morgan (eds), *Men, Masculinities and Social Theory*. London: Unwin Hyman.

Brown, C. (1984) *Black and White Britain*. London: Policy Studies Institute.

Brown, I. and Hullin, R. (1992) 'A study of sentencing in the Leeds magistrates courts', *British Journal of Criminology*, 32 (1): 41–53.

Brown, J. (1977) *Shades of Grey*. Cranfield: Cranfield Institute of Technology.

Brown, L. and Willis, A. (1985) 'Authoritarianism in British police recruits: importation, socialisation or myth?', *Journal of Occupational Psychology*, 58: 97–108.

Browne, D. (1990) *Black People, Mental Health and the Courts*. London: NACRO.

Brownmiller, S. (1975) *Against our Will: Men, Women and Rape*. London: Secker and Warburg.

Bryan, A. (1992) 'Working with black single mothers: myths and reality', in M. Langham and L. Day (eds), *Oppression and Social Work*. London: Routledge.

Bulmer, M. (1984) 'Introduction', in M. Bulmer (ed.), *Social Research Methods*, 2nd edn. Basingstoke: Macmillan.

Burney, E. (1990) *Putting Street Crime in its Place*. London: Goldsmiths' College Centre for Inner City Studies.

Cain, M. (1986a) 'Realism, feminism, methodology and law', *International Journal of the Sociology of Law*, 14 (3–4): 255–67.

Cain, M. (1986b) 'Socio-legal studies and social justice for women: some working notes on a method'. Paper presented at the Australian Law and Society Association conference, Brisbane, December.

Cain, M. (ed.) (1989) *Growing up Good*. London: Sage.

Cain, M. and Sadigh, S. (1982) 'Racism, the police and community policing', *Journal of Law and Society*, 9 (1): 87–102.

Carlen, P. (1983) *Women's Imprisonment: a Study in Social Control*. London: Routledge and Kegan Paul.

Carlen, P. (ed.) (1985) *Criminal Women*. Cambridge: Polity Press.

Carlen, P. (1988) *Women, Crime and Poverty*. Milton Keynes: Open University Press.

Carlen, P. (1989) 'Crime, inequality and sentencing', in P. Carlen and D. Cook (eds), *Paying for Crime*. Milton Keynes: Open University Press.

Carlen, P. (1990) *Alternatives to Women's Imprisonment*. Milton Keynes: Open University Press.

Carlen, P. (1992) 'Criminal women and criminal justice: the limits to, and potential of, feminist and left realist perspectives', in R. Matthews and J. Young (eds), *Issues in Realist Criminology*. London: Sage.

Carothers, J.C. (1953) *The African Mind in Health and Disease: A Study in Ethnopsychiatry*. WHO Monograph Series No. 17. Geneva: World Health Organization.

Carr-Hill, R. and Drew, D. (1988) 'Blacks, Police and Crime' in A. Bhat, R. Carr-Hill and S. Ohri (eds), *Britain's Black Population: A New Perspective*, 2nd edn. Aldershot: Gower.

Cashmore, E. and McLaughlin, E. (eds) (1991) *Out of Order? Policing Black People*. London: Routledge.

Cashmore, E. and Troyna, B. (eds) (1982) *Black Youth in Crisis*. London: Allen and Unwin.

Centre for Contemporary Cultural Studies (1982) *The Empire Strikes Back*. London: Hutchinson.

Chesney-Lind, M. (1973) 'Judicial enforcement of the female sex role: the family court and the delinquent', *Issues in Criminology*, 8: 51–69.

Chesney-Lind, M. (1977) 'Judicial paternalism and the female status offender: training women to know their place', *Crime and Delinquency*, 23: 121–30.

Chigwada, R. (1989) 'The criminalization and imprisonment of black women', *Probation Journal*, September: 101–105.

Chigwada, R. (1991) 'The policing of black women', in E. Cashmore and E. McLaughlin (eds), *Out of Order? Policing Black People*. London: Routledge.

Citizens' Charter (1991) *Citizens' Charter: Raising the Standard*. Cmnd. 1599. London: HMSO.

Clarke, C.F.O. (1970) *Police/Community Relations*. Report of a Conference at Ditchley Park, 29 May–1 June, Ditchley Foundation.

Clegg, S. (1975) 'Feminist methodology – fact or fiction?', *Quality and Quantity*, 19: 83–97.

Cloward, R. and Ohlin, L. (1960) *Delinquency and Opportunity*. New York: The Free Press; London: Routledge and Kegan Paul.

Cohen, R., Coxall, J., Craig, G. and Sadiq-Sangster, A. (1992) *Hardship Britain*. London: CPAG.

Cohen, S. (1972) *Folk Devils and Moral Panics*. London: Paladin.

Cohen, S. (1981) 'Footprints on the sand: a further report on criminology and the sociology of deviance in Britain', in M. Fitzgerald, G. McLennan and J. Pawson (eds), *Crime and Society: Readings in History and Theory*. London: Routledge and Kegan Paul.

Colman, A. and Gorman, P. (1982) 'Conservatism, dogmatism and authoritarianism in police officers', *Sociology*, 16: 1.

Commission for Racial Equality (1989a) *Race, Housing and Immigration*. London: CRE.

Commission for Racial Equality (1989b) *Racial Discrimination in Liverpool City Council*. London: CRE.

Commission for Racial Equality (1990) *Racial Discrimination in an Oldham Estate Agency*. London: CRE.

Commission for Racial Equality (1991a) *Lost in the System: Evidence to the Royal Commission on Criminal Justice*. London: CRE.

Commission for Racial Equality (1991b) *Racial Attacks and Policing: a Blueprint for Action*. London: CRE.

Commission for Racial Equality (1992a) *Cautions v. Prosecutions: Ethnic Monitoring of Juveniles by Seven Police Forces*. London: CRE.

Commission for Racial Equality (1992b) *A Question of Judgement: Race and Sentencing*. London: CRE.

Commission for Racial Equality (1992c) *Commission for Racial Equality Annual Report 1991*. London: CRE.

Commission for Racial Equality (1992d) *Code of Practice in Non-rented (Owner-occupied) Housing*. London: CRE.

Commission for Racial Equality (1992e) *Ruled Out: Report of a Formal Investigation into Handsworth Horticultural Institute*. London: CRE.

Cook, D. (1989) *Rich Law, Poor Law: Different Responses to Tax and Supplementary Benefit Fraud*. Milton Keynes: Open University Press.

Cooper, S. (1985) *Observations in Supplementary Benefit Offices: the Reform of Social Security*, Working Paper C. London: Policy Studies Institute.

Cope, R. (1989) 'The compulsory detention of Afro-Caribbeans under the Mental Health Act', *New Community*, April: 343–56.

Cope, R. and Ndegwa, D. (1990) 'Ethnic differences in admissions to regional secure units', *Journal of Forensic Psychiatry*, 1(3): 365–78.

Craib, I. (1987) 'The psychodynamics of theory', *Free Association*, 10: 32–56.

Critcher, C. (1976) 'Structures, cultures and biographies', in S. Hall and T. Jefferson (eds), *Resistance through Rituals*. London: Hutchinson.

Crow, I. and Cove, J. (1984) 'Ethnic minorities in the courts', *Criminal Law Review*, 413–17.

Daly, K. (1989) 'Neither conflict nor labelling nor paternalism will suffice: intersections of race, ethnicity, gender and family in criminal court decisions', *Crime and Delinquency*, 35: 136–68.

Dean, G. (1981) 'First admissions of native born and immigrant people to psychiatric hospitals in South East England', *British Journal of Psychiatry*, 139: 506–12.

Dear, G. (1985) *Handsworth/Lozells, September 1985*. Report of the Chief Constable, West Midlands Police. Birmingham: West Midlands Police.

De Haan, W. (1990) *The Politics of Redress: Crime, Punishment and Penal Abolition*. London: Unwin Hyman.

Demuth, C. (1978) *'Sus': A Report on the Vagrancy Act*. London: Runnymede Trust.

Department of the Environment (1989) *Tackling Racial Violence and Harassment in Local Authority Housing: A Guide to Good Practice*. London: HMSO.

Donnison, D. (1982) *The Politics of Poverty*. Oxford: Martin Robertson.

Downes, D. (1966) *The Delinquent Solution*. London: Routledge and Kegan Paul.

Dummett, A. and Dummett, M. (1987) 'The role of government' in C. Husband (ed.) *Race in Britain: Continuity and Change*, 2nd edn. London: Hutchinson.

Dunn, J. and Fahy, T.A. (1990) 'Police admissions to a psychiatric hospital: demographic and clinical differences between ethnic groups', *British Journal of Psychiatry*, 156: 373–8.

Eaton, M. (1986) *Justice for Women? Family, Court and Social Control*. Milton Keynes: Open University Press.

Eaton, M. (1993) *Women after Prison*. Buckingham: Open University Press.

Edelman, M. (1971) *Politics as Symbolic Action: Mass Arousal and Quiescence*. Chicago: Markham.

Edwards, S. (1984) *Women on Trial*. Manchester: Manchester University Press.

Eichler, M. (1988) *Nonsexist Research Methods*. Winchester, MA: Allen and Unwin.

Emms, T.W., Povey, R.M. and Clift, S.M. (1986) 'The self-concept of black and white delinquents', *British Journal of Criminology*, 26 (4): 385–93.

Esam, P. and Oppenheim, C. (1989) *A Charge on the Community: the Poll Tax, Benefits and the Poor*. London: CPAG/Local Government Information Unit.

Farran, D. (1990) '"Seeking Susan": producing statistical information on young people's leisure', in L. Stanley (ed.), *Feminist Praxis*. London: Routledge.

Fielding, N. (1988) *Joining Forces*. London: Routledge.

FitzGerald, M. (1989) 'Legal approaches to racial harassment in council housing: the case for re-assessment', *New Community*, 16 (1): 93–106.

FitzGerald, M. (1991) 'Ethnic minorities and the criminal justice system in the UK: research issues'. Paper presented to the British Criminology Conference, July, University of York.

FitzGerald, M. and Ellis, T. (1991) 'Racial harassment: the evidence', in C. Kemp (ed.), *Current Issues in Criminological Research*, vol. 2. Bristol and Bath Centre for Criminal Justice.

FitzGerald, M. and May, C. (forthcoming) *Ethnic Minorities and the 1988 British Crime Survey*. London: Home Office.

Fitzpatrick, P. (1987) 'Racism and the innocence of law', in P. Fitzpatrick and A. Hunt (eds), *Critical Legal Studies*. Oxford: Blackwell.

Foot, P. (1965) *Immigration and Race in British Politics*. Harmondsworth: Penguin.

Franey, R. (1983) *Poor Law*. London: CHAR/CPAG/CDC/NAPO/NCCL.

Gelsthorpe, L. (1986) 'Towards a sceptical look at sexism', *International Journal of the Sociology of Law*, 14 (2): 125–52.

Gelsthorpe, L. (1989) *Sexism and the Female Offender*. Aldershot: Gower.

Gelsthorpe, L. (1990) 'Feminist methodologies in criminology: a new approach or old wine in new bottles?', in L. Gelsthorpe and A. Morris (eds), *Feminist Perspectives in Criminology*. Buckingham: Open University Press.

Gelsthorpe, L. (1992) 'Response to Martyn Hammersley's paper "On Feminist Methodology"', *Sociology*, 26 (2): 213–18.

Gelsthorpe, L. and Morris, A. (eds) (1990) *Feminist Perspectives in Criminology*. Buckingham: Open University Press.

Genders, E. and Player, E. (1989) *Race Relations in Prison*. Oxford: Clarendon Press.

Gilligan, G. (1982) *In a Different Voice*. London: Harvard University Press.

Gilroy, P. (1982) 'Police and thieves', in Centre for Contemporary Cultural Studies (ed.), *The Empire Strikes Back*. London: Hutchinson.

Gilroy, P. (1987a) *There Ain't No Black in the Union Jack*. London: Hutchinson.

Gilroy, P. (1987b) 'The myth of black criminality', in P. Scraton (ed.) *Law, Order and the Authoritarian State*. Milton Keynes: Open University Press.

Gilroy, P. and Sim, J. (1985) 'Law, order and the state of the left', *Capital and Class*, 25: 15–55.

Glazer, N. (1975) *Affirmative Discrimination: Ethnic Inequality and Public Policy*. New York: Basic Books.

Godson, D. and McConnell, C. (1989) 'Social enquiry reports: a study of policy, practice and process'. Paper presented to the British Criminology Conference, Bristol.

Golding, P. and Middleton, S. (1982) *Images of Welfare*. Oxford: Martin Robertson.

Gordon, P. (1986) *Racial Violence and Racial Harassment*. London: Runnymede Trust.

Gordon, P. (1988) 'Black people and the criminal law: rhetoric and reality', *International Journal of Sociology of Law*, 16: 295–313.

Gordon, P. (1991) 'Forms of exclusion: citizenship, race and poverty', in S. Becker (ed.), *Windows of Opportunity*. London: CPAG.

Gordon, P. and Newnham, A. (1985) *Passport to Benefits? Racism in Social Security*. London: CPAG.

Gottfreidson, D. (1987) 'An evaluation of an organisation development approach to reducing school disorder', *Evaluation Review*, 11 (6): 739–63.

Graef, R. (1990) *Talking Blues; the Police in their own Words*. London: Fontana.

Guest, C.L. (1984) 'A comparative analysis of the career patterns of black and white young offenders' Unpublished manuscript, Cranfield Institute of Technology.

Habermas, J. (1976) *Legitimation Crisis*. London: Heinemann.

Hall, S. (1980) *Drifting into a Law and Order Society*. London: Cobden Trust.

Hall, S., Critcher, C., Clarke, J., Jefferson, T. and Roberts, B. (1978) *Policing the Crisis*. London: Macmillan.

Hardiker, P. (1975) 'Ideologies in social enquiry reports'. Final progress report to the Social Science Research Council, University of Leicester.

Harding, S. (ed.) (1987) *Feminism and Methodology*. Milton Keynes: Open University Press.

Harris, R. (1992) *Criminal Justice and the Probation Service*. London: Routledge.

Harrison, G., Ineichen, B. and Smith, J. (1984a) 'Psychiatric hospital admissions in Bristol: social and clinical aspects of compulsory admission', *British Journal of Psychiatry*, 145: 605–11.

Harrison, G., Owens, D., Holton, A., Neilson, D. and Boot, D. (1984b) 'Psychiatric hospital admission in Bristol: geographical and ethnic factors', *British Journal of Psychiatry*, 145: 600–11.

Harrison, G., Owens, D., Holton, A., Neilson, D. and Boot, D. (1988) 'A prospective study of severe mental disorder in Afro-Caribbean patients', *Psychological Medicine*, 18 August (3): 643–57.

Hartsock, N. (1987) 'The feminist standpoint: developing the ground for a specifically feminist historical materialism', in S. Harding (ed.), *Feminism and Methodology*. Milton Keynes: Open University Press.

Hawkins, D.F. (1986) 'Trends in black–white imprisonment: changing conceptions of race or changing patterns of social control', *Crime and Social Justice*, 24: 187–209.

Hawkins, D.F. and Hardy, K.A. (1989) 'Black–white imprisonment rates: a state-by-state analysis', *Social Justice*, 16 (4): 75–93.

Hawkins, D.F. and Thomas, R. (1991) 'White policing of black populations: a history of race and social control in America', in E. Cashmore and E. McLaughlin (eds), *Out of Order? Policing Black People*. London: Routledge.

Headley, B.D. (1989) 'Introduction: crime, justice and powerless racial groups', *Social Justice*, 16 (4): 1–9.

Hine, J., McWilliams, W. and Pease, K. (1978) 'Recommendations, social information and sentencing', *Howard Journal of Penology and Crime Prevention*, 17 (3): 131–54.

Hitch, P.J. and Clegg, P. (1980) 'Modes of referral: overseas immigrants and native born first admissions to psychiatric hospital', *Social Science and Medicine*. 14C: 369–74.

Hobbs, D. (1989) *Doing the Business*. Oxford: Oxford University Press.

Holdaway, S. (1983) *Inside the British Police*. Oxford: Blackwell.

Holdaway, S. (1991) *Recruiting a Multi-Racial Police Force*. London: Home Office.

Holdaway, S. and Allaker, J. (1990) 'Race issues in the probation service'. Report for ACOP, Sheffield University, Department of Sociological Studies.

Home Affairs Committee (1986) *Racial Attacks and Harassment*. Third Report of the Home Affairs Committee, Session 1985–6, HC 409. London: HMSO.

Home Affairs Select Committee (1981) *Racial Disadvantage*. Fifth Report, Session 1980–1. London: HMSO.

Home Office (1981) *Racial Attacks: a Report of a Home Office Study*. London: Home Office.

Home Office (1991) *Statistical Monitor Issue*, No. 1, November. London: Home Office Research and Statistics Department, S3 Division.

Home Office (1992a) *Race and the Criminal Justice System*. London: HMSO.

Home Office (1992b) 'Circular: race and ethnic monitoring, CPO 39/92'. London: Home Office.

Home Office Statistical Bulletin (1986) *The Ethnic Origin of Prisoners: The Prison Population on 30 June 1985 and Persons Received July 1984–March 1985* (HOSB 17/86). Croydon: Home Office Statistical Department.

Home Office Statistical Bulletin (1989a) *Crime Statistics for the Metropolitan Police District by Ethnic Group 1987: Victims, Suspects and Those Arrested*. Croydon: Home Office Statistical Department.

Home Office Statistical Bulletin (1989b) *The Ethnic Group of Those Proceeded Against or Sentenced by the Courts*. Croydon: Home Office Statistical Department.

Home Office Statistical Bulletin (1992) *Control of Immigration: Statistics – Third and Fourth Quarters and Year 1991*, Croydon: Home Office Statistical Department.

Hood, R. (1992) *Race and Sentencing: A Study in the Crown Court*. Oxford: Clarendon Press.

Horsley, G. (1984) *The Language of Social Enquiry Reports*. Social Work Monograph.

Hudson, B. (1988) 'Content analysis of social enquiry reports written in the Borough of Middlesex'. Unpublished manuscript, Middlesex Area Probation Service.

Hudson, B. (1989a) 'Discrimination and disparity: the influence of race on sentencing', *New Community*, 16 (1): 23–34.

Hudson, B. (1989b) 'Race issues in social enquiry reports'. Research report for the boroughs of Brent and Haringey. Unpublished manuscript, Middlesex Area Probation Service.

Hudson, B. (1992) 'Penal policy and racial justice'. Paper given to the Cropwood Conference on Minority Ethnic Groups in the Criminal Justice System, Cambridge: 30 March–1 April.

Hudson, B. (1993) *Penal Policy and Social Justice*. Basingstoke: Macmillan.

Humphry, D. (1972) *Police Power and Black People*. London: Panther.

Hunt, G. and Mellor, J. (1980) 'Afro-Caribbean youth: racism and unemployment', in M. Cole et al. (eds), *Blind Alley*. Ormskirk: G.W. and A. Hesketh.

Hunte, J. (1966) *Nigger Hunting in England*. London: West Indian Standing Conference.

Husband, C. (ed.) (1987) *Race in Britain: Continuity and Change*, 2nd edn. London: Hutchinson.

Husbands, C.T. (1983) *Racial Exclusionism and the City: the Urban Support of the National Front*. London: George Allen and Unwin.

Husbands, C.T. (1989) 'Racial attacks: the persistence of racial harassment in British cities', in T. Kushner and T. Lunn (eds), *Traditions of Intolerance*. Manchester University Press.

Inniss, L. and Feagin, J.R. (1989) 'The black "underclass" ideology in race relations analysis', *Social Justice*, 16 (4): 13–34.

Jackson, H. and Smith, L. (1987) 'Female offenders in analysis of social enquiry reports', *Home Office Research Bulletin*, 23: 8–11.

Jaggar, A. (1983) *Feminist Politics and Human Nature*. Sussex: Rowman and Allanheld.

Jankovic, I. (1977) 'Labour market and imprisonment', *Crime and Social Justice*, 8: 17–31.

Jefferson, T. (1988) 'Race, crime and policing: empirical, theoretical and methodological issues', *International Journal of Sociology of Law*, 16 (4): 521–41.

Jefferson, T. (1990) *The Case against Paramilitary Policing*. Milton Keynes: Open University Press.

Jefferson, T. (1991) 'Discrimination, disadvantage and police work', in E. Cashmore and E. McLaughlin (eds), *Out of Order? Policing Black People*. London: Routledge.

Jefferson, T. (1992) 'The racism of criminalization: policing and the reproduction of the criminal other'. Paper presented to the Cropwood Conference on Minority Ethnic Groups in the Criminal Justice System, Cambridge: 30 March – 1 April.

Jefferson, T., Walker, M.A. and Senevirate, M. (1990) 'Ethnic minorities, crime and criminal justice', in D. Downes (ed.), *Unravelling Criminal Justice*. Basingstoke: Macmillan.

John, G. (1970) *Race in the Inner City: a Report from Handsworth*. London: Runnymede Trust.

Jones, T., MacLean, B. and Young J. (1986) *The Islington Crime Survey*. Aldershot: Gower.

Jowell, R. and Witherspoon, S. (1985) *British Social Attitudes: the 1985 Report*. Aldershot: Gower.

Judicial Studies Board (1992) *First Annual Report of the Ethnic Minorities Advisory Committee*. London: Judicial Studies Board.

Junger, M. (1988) 'Racial discrimination in The Netherlands', *Sociology and Social Research*, 72: 211–16.

Junger, M. (1989) 'Ethnic minorities, crime and public policy', in R. Hood (ed.), *Crime and Criminal Policy in Europe*. Oxford: Centre for Criminological Research.

Junger, M. (1990) 'Studying ethnic minorities in relation to crime and police discrimination: answer to Bowling', *British Journal of Criminology*, 30 (4): 493–502.

Keith, M. (1991) 'Policing a perplexed society?' in E. Cashmore and E. McLaughlin (eds), *Out of Order? Policing Black People*. London: Routledge.

Keith, M. (1993) *Race, Riots and Policing: Lore and Disorder in a Multiracist Society*. London: UCL Press.

Kelly, L. (1988) *Surviving Sexual Violence*. Cambridge: Polity Press.

Kelly, L. (1990) 'Journeying in reverse: possibilities and problems in feminist research on sexual violence', in L. Gelsthorpe and A. Morris (eds), *Feminist Perspectives in Criminology*. Buckingham: Open University Press.

Kerruish, V. (1991) *Jurisprudence as Ideology*. London: Routledge.

King, M. (1991) *Making Social Crime Prevention Work: the French Experience*. London: NACRO.

Kleck, G. (1985) 'Life support for ailing hypotheses: modes of summarizing the evidence for racial discrimination in sentencing', *Law and Human Behaviour*, 9 (3): 271–85.

Klein, S., Petersilia, J. and Turner, S. (1990) 'Race and imprisonment decisions in California', *Science*, 247 (16 February): 812–16.

Kushner, T. and Lunn, T. (eds) (1989) *Traditions of Intolerance*. Manchester: Manchester University Press.

Laffargue, B. and Godefroy, T. (1989) 'Economic cycles and punishment: unemployment and imprisonment', *Contemporary Crises*, 13: 371–404.

Lambert, J.R. (1970) *Crime, Police and Race Relations: A Study in Birmingham*. London: Oxford University Press.

Landau, S.F. and Nathan, G. (1983) 'Selecting delinquents for cautioning in the London Metropolitan Area', *British Journal of Criminology*, 23: 128–49.

Lea, J. (1986) 'Police racism: some theories and their policy implications', in R. Matthews and J. Young (eds), *Confronting Crime*. London: Sage.

Lea, J. and Young, J. (1984) *What is to be Done about Law and Order?* Harmondsworth: Penguin.

Lipsky, M. and Olson, D. (1977) *Commission Politics: the Processing of Racial Crisis in America*. New Brunswick, NJ: Transaction Books.

Lister, R. (1990) *The Exclusive Society: Citizenship and the Poor*. London: CPAG.

Littlewood, R. and Lipsedge, M. (1979) *Transcultural Psychiatry*. London: Churchill-Livingstone.

McConville, M. and Baldwin, J. (1982) 'The influence of race on sentencing in England', *Criminal Law Review*, 652–8.

McCrudden, C., Smith, D. and Brown, C. (1990) *Racial Justice at Work*. London: Policy Studies Institute.

McDermott, K. (1990) 'We have no problem: the experience of race relations in prison', *New Community*, 16 (2): 213–28.

McGovern, D. and Cope, R. (1991) 'Second generation Afro-Caribbeans and young whites with a first admission diagnosis of schizophrenia', *Social Psychiatry*, 26 March (2): 95–9.

McWilliams, W. (1986) 'The English social enquiry report'. PhD dissertation, University of Sheffield.

Maden, A., Swinton, M. and Gunn, J. (1992) 'The ethnic origin of women serving a prison sentence', *British Journal of Criminology*, 32 (2): 218–21.

Mair, G. (1986) 'Ethnic minorities, probation and the magistrates' courts' *British Journal of Criminology*, 26 (2): 147–55.

Mair, G. and Brockington, M. (1988) 'Female offenders and the probation service', *Howard Journal of Criminal Justice*, 27 (2): 117–26.

Marshall, T.H. (1950) *Citizenship and Social Class and Other Essays*. Cambridge: Cambridge University Press.

Marshall, T.H. (1981) *The Right to Welfare and other Essays*. London: Heinemann.

Mathiesen, T. (1974) *The Politics of Abolition*. Oxford: Martin Robertson.

Mathiesen, T. (1990) *Prison on Trial: a Critical Assessment*. London: Sage.

Matthews, R. (1989) 'Alternatives to and in prisons: a realist approach', in P. Carlen and D. Cook (eds), *Paying for Crime*. Milton Keynes: Open University Press.

Mayhew, P., Elliott, D. and Dowds, L. (1989) *The British Crime Survey*. Home Office Research Study no. 111. London: HMSO.

Melossi, D. and Pavarini, M. (1981) *The Prison and the Factory: Origins of the Penitentiary System*. London: Macmillan.

Merton, R. (1964) 'Anomie, anomia and social interaction', in M. Clinard (ed.), *Anomie and Deviant Behaviour*. New York: The Free Press.

Miles, R. and Solomos, J. (1987) 'Migration and the state in Britain: a historical overview', in C. Husband (ed.), *Race in Britain: Continuity and Change*, 2nd edn. London: Hutchinson.

Mills, C. Wright (1959) *The Sociological Imagination*. Hardmondsworth: Pelican.

Milner, D. (1971) 'Prejudice and the immigrant child', *New Society*, 23 September.

Modood, T. (1988) ' "Black" racial equality and Asian identity', *New Community*, 14 (3): 397–404.

Moodley, P. and Perkins, R. (1991) 'Routes to psychiatric in-patient care in an inner London borough', *Social Psychiatry and Psychiatric Epidemiology*, 26: 47–51.

Morgan, D. (1981) 'Men, masculinity and the process of sociological enquiry', in H. Roberts (ed.), *Doing Feminist Research*. London: Routledge and Kegan Paul.

Moxon, D. (1988) *Sentencing Practice in the Crown Courts*. Home Office Research Study no. 103. London: HMSO.

Mullard, C. (1991) 'Towards a model of anti-racist social work', in CCETSW (ed.), *One Small Step towards Racial Justice*. London: CCETSW.

Murray, C. (1984) *Losing Ground*. New York: Basic Books.

Nanton, P. (1989) 'The new orthodoxy: racial categories and equal opportunity policy', *New Community*, 15 (4): 549–64.

Nanton, P. and FitzGerald, M. (1990) 'Race policies in local government: boundaries or thresholds?' in W. Ball and J. Solomos (eds), *Race and Local Politics*. Basingstoke: Macmillan.

National Association of Citizens Advice Bureaux (1991) *Barriers to Benefit: Black Claimants and Social Security*. London: NACAB.

National Association of Citizens Advice Bureaux (1992) *A Charter for All? CAB Evidence on Immigration and Nationality*. London: NACAB.

National Association for the Care and Resettlement of Offenders (1989) *Race and Criminal Justice: a Way Forward*. Second report of the NACRO Race Issues Advisory Committee. London: NACRO.

National Association for the Care and Resettlement of Offenders (1991) *Black People's Experience of Criminal Justice*. London: NACRO.

National Association for the Care and Resettlement of Offenders (1992a) *Black People Working in the Criminal Justice System*. London: NACRO.

National Association for the Care and Resettlement of Offenders (1992b) *Race Policies into Action*. London: NACRO.

National Association for the Care and Resettlement of Offenders (1993) *Race and Criminal Justice: Training*. London: NACRO.

Newman, K. (1983) 'Fighting the fear of crime', *Police*, September: 26–30, October: 30–32.

Newman, K. (1986a) 'Police–public relations: the pace of change', Police Federation Annual Lecture, 28 July.

Newman, K. (1986b) *Public Order Review: Civil Disturbances 1981–85*. London: Metropolitan Police.

Neyroud, P. (1992) 'Multi-agency approaches to racial harassment: the lessons of implementing the Racial Attacks Group report', *New Community*, 18 (4): 567–78.

Oakley, A. (1980) *Women Confined: towards a Sociology of Childbirth*. Oxford: Martin Robertson.

Oppenheim, C. (1993) *Poverty: the Facts*. London: CPAG.

Owens, D. (1992) *Ethnic Minorities in Britain: Settlement Patterns*. (1991 Census Statistical Paper no. 1). University of Warwick Centre for Ethnic Relations.

Parker, H. (1974) *A View from the Boys*. Newton Abbott: David and Charles.

Parmar, P. (1982) 'Gender, race and class: Asian women in resistance', in Centre for Contemporary Cultural Studies (ed.), *The Empire Strikes Back*. London: Hutchinson.

Pateman, C. (1986) 'The theoretical subversiveness of feminism', in C. Pateman and E. Gross (eds), *Feminist Challenges: Social and Political Theory*. Sydney: Allen and Unwin.

Pearson, G. (1983) *Hooligan: a History of Respectable Fears*. London: Macmillan.

Pearson, G. (1987) *The New Heroin Users*. London: Batsford.

Pearson, G., Sampson, A., Blagg, H., Stubbs, P. and Smith, D. (1989) 'Policing racism', in R. Morgan and D. Smith (eds), *Coming to Terms with Policing*. London: Routledge.

Perry, F. (1974) *Information for the Court: a New Look at Social Enquiry Reports*. Institute of Criminology Occasional Series, 1. Cambridge: Institute of Criminology.

Petersilia, J. (1985) 'Racial disparities in the criminal justice system: a summary', *Crime and Delinquency*, 31: 15–34.

Piliavin, I. and Briar, S. (1964) 'Police encounters with juveniles', *American Journal of Sociology*, 70: 206–14.

Pinder, R. (1984a) 'Probation and ethnic diversity'. MSc thesis. University of Leeds.

Pinder, R. (1984b) 'Probation work in a multi-racial society', research report. Leeds: University of Leeds Applied Anthropology Group.

Pipe, R., Bhat, A., Matthews, B. and Hampstead, J. (1991) 'Section 136 and

African/Afro-Caribbean minorities', *International Journal of Social Psychiatry*, 37 (1): 14–23.

Pitts, J. (1986) 'Black young people and juvenile crime: some unanswered questions', in R. Matthews and J. Young (eds), *Confronting Crime*. London: Sage.

Pitts, J. (1988) *The Politics of Juvenile Crime*. London: Sage.

Pitts, J. (1990) *Working with Young Offenders*. Basingstoke: Macmillan.

Pitts, J. (1991) 'Less harm or more good? Politics research and practice with young people in crisis', in J. Dennington and J. Pitts (eds), *Developing Services for Young People in Crisis*. London: Longman.

Pitts, J. (1992) 'Juvenile justice policy in England and Wales', in J.C. Coleman and C. Warren-Adamson (eds), *Youth Policy in the 1990s: The Way Forward*. London: Routledge.

Pitts, J. (1993) 'Bullying and racism: a whole school approach', in D. Tattum (ed.), *Understanding and Managing Bullying*. London: Heinemann.

Policy Studies Institute (1983) *Police and People in London*, vols I–IV. London: Policy Studies Institute.

Pratt, M. (1980) *Mugging as a Social Problem*. London: Routledge and Kegan Paul.

Pryce, K. (1979) *Endless Pressure*. Harmondsworth: Penguin.

Quinney, R. (1977) *Class, State and Crime: on the Theory and Practice of Criminal Justice*. New York: David McKay.

Racial Attacks Group (1989) *The Responses to Racial Attacks and Harassment: Guidance for Statutory Agencies*. London: HMSO.

Radcliffe Richards, J. (1982) *The Sceptical Feminist: a Philosophical Enquiry*. Harmondsworth: Penguin.

Radelet, M.C. and Pierce, G.L. (1985) 'Race and prosecution discretion in homicide cases', *Law and Society Review*, 19 (4): 587–621.

Ramsay, M. (1982) 'Mugging: fears and facts', *New Society*, 26 March: 467–9.

Reeves, F. (1983) *British Racial Discourse*. Cambridge: Cambridge University Press.

Reiner, R. (1985) 'The police and race relations', in J. Baxter and L. Koffman (eds), *Police: the Constitution and the Community*. Abingdon: Professional Books.

Reiner, R. (1988) 'British criminology and the state', *British Journal of Criminology*, 28 (2): 268–88.

Reiner, R. (1989) 'Race and criminal justice', *New Community*, 16 (1): 5–22.

Reiner, R. (1991) *Chief Constables: Bobbies, Bosses or Bureaucrats*. Oxford: Oxford University Press.

Reiner, R. (1992) 'Race, crime and justice: models of interpretation'. Paper given to the Cropwood Conference on Minority Ethnic Groups in the Criminal Justice System, Cambridge, 30 March–1 April.

Reinharz, S. (1992) *Feminist Methods in Social Research*. New York: Oxford University Press.

Rex, J. (1988) *The Ghetto and the Underclass: Essays on Race and Social Policy*. Aldershot: Gower.

Rice, M. (1990) 'Challenging orthodoxies in feminist theory: a black feminist critique', in L. Gelsthorpe and A. Morris (eds), *Feminist Perspectives in Criminology*. Milton Keynes: Open University Press.

Rich, P. (1989) 'Imperial decline and the resurgence of English national identity 1918–79', in T. Kushner and T. Lunn (eds), *Traditions of Intolerance*. Manchester: Manchester University Press.

Richey Mann, C. (1989) 'Minority and female: a criminal justice double bind', *Social Justice*, 16 (4): 95–112.

Riley, D. and Vennard, J. (1988) *Triable-either-way Cases: Crown Court or Magistrates Court*. Home Office Research Study no. 98. London: HMSO.

Rock, P. (1988) 'The present state of criminology in Britain', *British Journal of Criminology*, 28 (2): 188–99.

Rushdie, S. (1982) 'The new empire within Britain', *New Society*, 9 December.

Rutherford, A. (1986) *Growing out of Crime*. Harmondsworth: Penguin.

Rutter, M., Yule, W., Berger, M., Yule, B., Morton, J. and Bagley, C. (1974) 'Children of West Indian immigration: rates of behavioural deviance and psychiatric disorder', *Journal of Child Psychology and Psychiatry*, 15: 241–62.

Rwegellera, G. (1980) 'Differential use of psychiatric services by West Indians, West Africans and English in London', *British Journal of Psychiatry*, 137: 428–32.

Sabol, W.J. (1989) 'Racially disaggregated prison populations in the United States: an overview of historical patterns, and review of contemporary issues', *Contemporary Crises*, 13: 405–32.

Sampson, A., Stubbs, P., Smith, D., Pearson, G. and Blagg, H. (1988) 'Crime, localities and the multi-agency approach', *British Journal of Criminology*, 28: 478–93.

Scarman, Lord (1981) *The Brixton Disorders*. Cmnd 8427. London: HMSO.

Scraton, P. and Sim, J. (eds) (1987) *Law, Order and the Authoritarian State*. Milton Keynes: Open University Press.

Serle, C. (1993) 'Cricket and the mirror of racism', *Race and Class*, 34 (3): 45–54.

Select Committee on Race Relations and Immigration (1969) *The Problems of Coloured School Leavers*. London: HMSO.

Select Committee on Race Relations and Immigration (1972) *Police/Immigrant Relations*. London: HMSO.

Select Committee on Race Relations and Immigration (1977) *The West Indian Community*. London: HMSO.

Shah, R. and Pease, K. (1992) 'Crime, race and reporting to the police', *Howard Journal*, 31 (3): 192–9.

Shallice, A. and Gordon, P. (1990) *Black People, White Justice? Race and the Criminal Justice System*. London: Runnymede Trust.

Shaw, C. (1986) 'Latest estimates of ethnic minority populations', *Population Trends*, 51, Spring. London: HMSO.

Shaw, C. and McKay, H. (1942) *Juvenile Delinquency and Urban Areas*. Chicago: Chicago University Press.

Shaw, R. (1982) *Who Uses Social Enquiry Reports?* Institute of Criminology Occasional Series 7. Cambridge: Institute of Criminology.

Sillitoe, K. (1987) 'Questions on race ethnicity and related topics for the census', *Population Trends*, 49, Autumn. London: HMSO.

Skogan, W. (1990) *The Police and Public in England and Wales*. Home Office Research Study no. 117. London: HMSO.

Smart, C. (1976) *Women, Crime and Criminology*. London: Routledge and Kegan Paul.

Smart, C. (1984) *The Ties that Bind*. London: Routledge and Kegan Paul.

Smart, C. (1989) *Feminism and the Power of Law*. London: Routledge.

Smith, C., Farrant, M. and Marchant, H. (1972) *The Wincroft Youth Project*. London: Tavistock.

Smith, D. (1988) *The Everyday World as Problematic. A Feminist Sociology*. Milton Keynes: Open University Press.

Smith, D.J. (1983) *A Survey of Londoners: Police and People in London*, vol. 1. London: Policy Studies Institute.

Smith, S. (1989) *The Politics of 'Race' and Residence*. Cambridge: Polity Press.

Social Justice (1992) 'Ideology and penal reform in the 1990s (Editorial)' *Social Justice*, 17 (4): 1–6.

Solomos, J. (1988) *Black Youth, Racism and the State*. Cambridge: Cambridge University Press.

Solomos, J. and Rackett, T. (1991) 'Policing and urban unrest: problem constitution and policy response', in E. Cashmore and E. McLaughlin (eds), *Out of Order? Policing Black People*. London: Routledge.

Solomos, J., Findlay, B., Jones, S. and Gilroy, P. (1982) 'The organic crisis of British capitalism and race: the experience of the seventies', in Centre for Contemporary Cultural Studies (ed.), *The Empire Strikes Back*. London: Hutchinson.

Stanley, L. and Wise, S. (1983) *Breaking Out: Feminist Consciousness and Feminist Research*. London: Routledge and Kegan Paul.

Stanley, L. and Wise, S. (1990) 'Method, methodology and epistemology in the feminist research process', in L. Stanley (ed.), *Feminist Praxis*. London: Routledge.

Stevens, P. and Willis, C. (1979) *Race, Crime and Arrests*. Home Office Research Study no. 58. London: HMSO.

Sumner, C. (ed.) (1990) *Censure, Politics and Criminal Justice*. Buckingham: Open University Press.

Taylor, I., Walton, P. and Young, J. (eds) (1977) *The New Criminology*. London: Routledge and Kegan Paul.

Tuck, M. and Southgate, P. (1981) *Ethnic Minorities, Crime and Policing*. London: HMSO.

Unger, R. (1983) *The Critical Legal Studies Movement*. Cambridge, MA.: Harvard University Press.

Van den Berghe, P.L. (1984) 'Race: perspective two', in E. Ellis Cashmore (ed.), *Dictionary of Race and Ethnic Relations*. London: Routledge and Kegan Paul.

Vass, A.A. (1990) *Alternatives to Prison: Punishment, Custody and the Community*. London: Sage.

Voakes, R. and Fowler, Q. (1989) *Sentencing, Race and Social Enquiry Reports*. Wakefield: West Yorkshire Probation Service.

Waddington, D. (1992) *Contemporary Issues in Public Disorder*. London: Routledge.

Walker, A. (1992) *Possessing the Secret of Joy*. London: The Women's Press Bookclub.

Walker, M. (1988) 'The court disposal of young males in London in 1983', *British Journal of Criminology*, 28 (4): 441–60.

Walker, M. (1989) 'The court disposals and remand of white, Afro-Caribbean and Asian men (London, 1983)', *British Journal of Criminology*, 29 (4): 353–67.

Walker, M., Jefferson, T. and Senevirate, M. (1990) *Ethnic Minorities, Young People and the Criminal Justice System*. ESRC Project No. E06250023 (unpublished).

Wallman, S. (1986) 'Ethnicity and the boundary process', in D. Mason and J. Rex (eds), *Theories of Race and Ethnic Relations*. Cambridge: Cambridge University Press.

Walvin, J. (1987) 'Black caricature: the roots of racialism in C. Hubsand (ed.), *Race in Britain*. London: Hutchinson.

Waters, R. (1988) 'Race and the criminal justice process', *British Journal of Criminology*, 28: 82–94.

Waters, R. (1990) *Ethnic Minorities and the Criminal Justice System*. Aldershot: Avebury.

White, S. (1978) 'The nineteenth century origins of the pre-sentence report', *Australia and New Zealand Journal of Criminology*, 11: 157–78.

Whitehouse, P. (1983) 'Race, bias and social enquiry reports', *Probation Journal*, 30: 43–9.

Whyte, W.F. (1943) *Street Corner Society*. Chicago: Chicago University Press.

Williams, F. (1991) 'The welfare state as part of a racially structured and patriarchal capitalism', in M. Loney et al. (eds), *The State or the Market*. London: Sage.

Willis, C.F. (1983) *The Use, Effectiveness and Impact of Police Stop and Search Powers*. Home Office Research and Planning Unit. London: HMSO.

Wilson, J.Q. (1975) *Thinking About Crime*. New York: Vintage.

Wilson, J.Q. and Herrnstein, R. (1985) *Crime and Human Nature*. New York: Simon and Shuster.

Woodward, D. and Chisholm, L. (1981) 'The expert's view? The sociological analysis of graduates' occupational and domestic roles', in H. Roberts (ed.), *Doing Feminist Research*. London: Routledge and Kegan Paul.

Worrall, A. (1990) *Offending Women. Female Lawbreakers and the Criminal Justice System*. London: Routledge.

Yinger, M. (1986) 'Intersecting strands', in D. Mason and J. Rex (eds), *Theories of Race and Ethnic Relations*. Cambridge: Cambridge University Press.

Young, J. (1987) 'The tasks facing realist criminology', *Contemporary Crises*, 11: 337–50.

Young, J. (1988) 'Radical criminology in Britain: the emergence of a competing paradigm', *British Journal of Criminology*, 28 (2): 289–313.

Young, K. and Connelly, N. (1981) *Policy and Practice in the Multi-Racial City*. London: Policy Studies Institute.

Young, M. (1991) *Inside Job: Policing and Black Culture in London*. Oxford: Clarendon Press.

Zizeck, S. (1989) *The Sublime Object of Ideology*. London: Verso.

Index

Abbott, Diane, MP 140
anti-racism 11, 12, 96, 103–6, 116
Anti-Racist Alliance 143
Association of Black Probation Officers 80
asylum seekers 142, 147, 152

Bar Council 31
Birmingham Six ix
Blackbird Leys, Oxford xiv, 134
British Crime Survey 4, 31, 33, 35, 48, 144
British National Party 143
British Nationality Act (1948) 138
Brixton, London 23, 97–8, 107, 115, 125, 128, 146
see also 'riots', urban
Broadmoor Special Hospital 65
Broadwater Farm, London 24, 131, 146

cautioning 6, 8, 9, 34, 41, 53
Census (1991) 50, 58, 144
Central Council for Education and Training in Social Work (CCETSW) 103
Chicago School 5
citizenship xiii–xiv, 136–8
    civil 143–4
    legal 138–42
    political 144–6
    social 146–50
Commission for Racial Equality 36, 38, 76, 79, 152
Commonwealth Immigrants Act (1962) 140, 141
Community Relations Commission 122, 126
'cricket test' 22, 152–4
Criminal Justice Act (1991) ix, xiv, 4, 40, 42, 86

criminal justice system, black workers in 28–31
criminal statistics, official 3, 4, 50–3
criminology
    administrative xi, xiii, 2, 5–12, 105, 108
    critical 19–26
    feminist 2, 87–93
    mainstream 2–5, 6, 105
    radical 12–19, 98–9, 145
    realist xi, 14, 19–20, 26, 100, 145
Crown Prosecution Service 8, 30, 33
culture 5, 22, 111–13, 116, 123

Dear, Geoffrey 130–1
Denning, Lord 151
Department of Employment 46, 47
Department of Social Security 142, 148–50, 156
discretion 6, 11, 40, 53, 148
discount principle 8, 40, 41
    see also sentencing
discrimination
    direct xi, 6, 9, 11, 29, 43, 83–4
    indirect xi, 7–8, 11, 30, 31, 39–43, 46, 83–4
drapetomania 65
drugs 9, 11, 28, 29, 51, 68, 107, 130–1

Europe 4, 5, 24, 110, 140, 141

family, patterns of 10, 15, 41, 108, 112, 123, 145
fear of crime 20
feminism xii, 2, 87–93

Grant, Bernie, MP 109, 131

Handsworth, Birmingham 119–21, 122, 128, 130, 146, 152

harassment, racial 28, 33, 47–8, 57
   see also racist attacks; victimisation
Home Office 6, 19, 32, 75, 79, 103
Home Office Research and Planning
   Unit 2
Hurd, Douglas 130, 131

immigration xiii, 15, 24, 66, 114, 132,
   136, 138–42, 149–50, 152
Immigration Acts (1971 and 1988) 141
imprisonment 4, 16–17, 26, 28, 29, 34, 39
Institute of Race Relations 119
institutional racism 104–5, 154, 155
   see also discrimination

Labour Force Surveys 52, 155
Lord Chancellor's Department 38, 80
Los Angeles riots 109

Major, John xiv, 104, 137
managerialism 101–3, 106
marginalisation 13–16, 108, 145
Mark, Robert 127
Marxism 20, 91, 99–101
Meadow Well, Tyneside xiv, 16, 134
Mental Health Act (1959) 65
Mental Health Act (1983) 65, 76
Mental Health Foundation 75
Metropolitan Police 4, 50, 119, 125–7,
   129
monitoring 6, 12, 42–3, 80–1, 83, 86, 93
Miners' Strike (1984–5) 101, 146
Moss Side, Manchester 128, 146
'mugging' xiv, 20, 25, 123–4, 129, 134

NACRO 6, 75, 76
National Association of Probation
   Officers 80, 81
National Opinion Polls 35
'New Age' travellers 21, 147
Newman, Sir Kenneth 23, 133
Notting Hill 120, 125, 127, 128, 139–40
   Carnival 23, 126

Office of Population Censuses and
   Surveys 58, 79

Poor Law (Amendment) Act (1834) 146
police 6, 9, 15, 16, 18–19, 21, 28, 33–5,
   41, 98, 107, 118–23, 133–5
policing, paramilitary xiv, 23–4, 27

Policy Studies Institute 9, 19, 32
poverty xiv, 13, 17, 101, 116, 124, 138,
   146, 154–6
   see also marginalisation;
      unemployment
Powell, Enoch 119, 125, 126, 129,
   139–41
pre-sentence reports 9, 40
Prevention of Terrorism Act 14
prison, statistics 4, 34, 50
   see also imprisonment
probation service 9–10, 73, 79, 84–6, 103
Proctor, Harvey, MP 129
psychiatry xii, 18, 64–76

'race'
   classifications of xii, 51–2, 58–9, 73–4,
      79–80, 81–3, 110–11
   definitions of 54–7, 82–3
Race Relations Act (1976) 6, 30
racist attacks xi, 25, 31–3, 141, 143–4,
   154
   see also harassment, racial;
      victimisation
rape 25, 31
reserve army of labour thesis 114, 139
refugees 24, 142
'riots', urban (1981, 1985) xiii, 16, 23,
   97–8, 107, 118, 124, 128–32, 145
Royal Ulster Constabulary 23
Runnymede Trust 35

Scarman, Lord 9
schizophrenia 65, 68
'scroungers' 21, 151–2
Select Committee on Race Relations
   and Immigration 121–3, 126, 127
sentencing 6–11, 25, 34, 36–41
Sentencing Project 11
slavery 65, 112
social inquiry reports 77–9, 83, 85
   see also probation service; pre-
      sentence reports
Social Security Act (1986) 148
Socialist Workers Party 97
Special Branch 14
Special Patrol Group (SPG) 23, 127
'sus' laws 14, 98, 127
SWAMP 81 exercise 23

Tebbit, Norman, MP 22, 151, 152, 153

Thatcher administration 21, 101, 110, 137, 147

underclass 4, 5
'undeserving poor' 112, 147, 150
unemployment xiv, 13, 14, 15, 41, 43, 107, 123, 135, 155
USA 5, 9, 13, 21, 99, 109–10

victimisation 7, 25, 31–3, 47–50, 109, 116, 144

see also harassment, racial; racist attacks

West Midlands Serious Crimes Squad ix
women, black xiii–xiv, 17–18, 27, 29, 51, 85, 87, 138, 155

youth, black xiv, 14–15, 20, 96–8, 99, 107–8, 114–16, 120–2, 126–7, 129–31, 134.